HERE

The Kingdom Of Heaven Is

By Paul Tubach, Jr.

HERE

"HERE" by Paul B. Tubach, Jr. is licensed under a Creative Commons Attribution-NonCommercial-NoDerivatives 4.0 International License

You are free to copy, share and redistribute the material in any medium, format or language as long as the text and content is not altered or misconstrued. Freely it was received… freely it is given. The licensor cannot revoke these freedoms as long as you follow these license terms:

- **Attribution** — You must give appropriate credit, provide a link to the website, and indicate if any changes were made. You may do so in any reasonable manner, but not in any way that suggests the author endorses you or your use. "Attribute this work" as: Paul Tubach, Jr., www.newearthministries.org.
- **NonCommercial** — You may not use the material for commercial purposes, i.e. not for any private, corporate, nonprofit or otherwise financial gain.
- **NoDerivatives** — If you remix, transform or build upon the material, you may not distribute the modified material. The creation or development of any derivatives, secondary workbooks or manuals from this book is reserved solely by the author.
- **No additional restrictions** — You may not apply legal terms or technological measures that legally restrict others from doing anything the license permits.

Paperback ISBN 978-1-949892-35-2
Library of Congress Number - pending
Produced in the United States of America
New Earth Ministries

Scriptures taken from the New King James Version. Copyright © 1982 by Thomas Nelson. Used by permission. All rights reserved.

Books and other materials are available online through www.newearthministries.org.

March 2018

Table of Contents

A)	Introduction	xiii
1)	Understanding Spiritual Things	1
2)	New Earth Introduction	5
3)	Do Men Go To Heaven	13
	• Heaven Is God's Throne	16
	• An Earthly Misunderstanding	21
	• Men Are Spiritual Beings	26
	• Men Are Houses and Habitations	28
	• Carry Me Home	42
	• "What" Matters Most	45
	• Man's Purpose On Earth	57
	• Home – Is Where Your Heart Is	64
	• Oneness With The Father	79
4)	Nigh, At Hand	93
5)	The Five Keys	105
	• The True Bride Awakens	106
	• 2 Corinthians 5:1-10	106
	• False Heaven Doctrine	114
	• Literal Greek (2 Cor. 5:1-10)	118
6)	Where Do We Go From Here?	129
	• Hades and Death	129
	• Places With Purpose	132
	• Death	135
	• What Happens In Hades	138
	• What Is Torment	143
	• Gates, Doors and The Entrance	160
	• Clothed In Christ	165
	• Carried By Angels	172
7)	Judgment and Resurrection	177
8)	The Earthly (Kingdom of) Heaven	199

9) Paradigm Shift 213
   - Transition 219
   - The Tree of Liberty 222
   - Why Earth, Lord? 228
   - The Oneness Condition 242
   - Co-manifest Upon The Earth 243
   - The Co-manifest Kingdom 249
   - The Kingdoms In Conflict 260
   - Learning From Job 264
   - The End of Earth? 266
   - Removing The Elements 267
   - Why Not Here, Why Not Now 368
   - Temple Type and Shadow 372
   - Restoring The Kingdom 276
   - A New Culture For Living 278
   - Passed Away 280
   - The Earth Abides Forever! 285
   - Miracle Man 287
   - Be Like Angels 292
   - Worldly Kingdoms On Earth 298
   - The Promise 303
   - The Essence of A New Day 304

10) New Earth Residents 305
    - Changed By Truth 309

11) America, The New World 313
    - The Land of We 317
    - Leader of The Free World 324
    - A New Day Begins 324
    - A New Word 326
    - Closure 328

12) Walking In Dominion Obedience 331
    - Governance and Dominion 331
    - Personal Guidance 331
    - Grace and Glory 332
    - Christ In Us 333
    - Idols In Our Hearts 334

13) The Eternal Paradigm 337
    - Two Scenario Finale 343

The Image Bearer Series

2. Listen – How To Hear God's Voice – better
3. Image – The Revelation Of God Himself
4. Dominion – Our Heavenly Mandate To Occupy Earth
5. Understand – What Jesus Wants You To Know – and Why
6. Commission – Created On Purpose For A Purpose
7. Gateways – Manifesting Heaven In The Midst Of Chaos
8. Here – The Kingdom Of Heaven Is

The Image Bearer Series is based upon Genesis 1:26-28: "Let us make man in Our image, according to Our likeness… and grant them dominion."

"Image" explains 'who' the Lord of Heaven and Earth is, "Understand" explains 'why' we are here, "Commission" explains 'what' man is and 'how' we were created by the Lord, "Dominion" explains 'what' we are supposed to be doing, "Gateways" explains 'how' we are to accomplish our earthly mission, and "Here" explains our eternal destination is actually – Earth.

Many tools were given to mankind that enables us to accomplish our mission objective to have dominion over the kingdom of darkness – and we need to comprehend this truth: earth is our 'Here' – and our 'when' is now! How God created us – and why – is directly related to our sanctification and accomplishing our multifaceted mission for being on earth.

Why are you here – and what's your purpose in life? These books will answer those questions.

When I began writing in August 2012, four drafts were completed within a year, then on Sept. 27, 2013, the Lord spoke to me and said: "You are My writer. Now write!" and then the Spirit directed me to finish draft #4 which became the initial book, *"Regenesis: A Sojourn To Remember Who We Are,"* released in August 2014. Next, the Spirit directed me to work on draft #3 (in reverse order) and then, on October 24, the Spirit told me, "That is not one book with seven chapters – those are seven books." Thus, I have been writing the Image Bearer series under His anointing by hearing His voice and writing what I am directed to write.

Regenesis helped us discover man's true identity, as spiritual beings that are having a human experience, who were created good and upright by God "in His Own image according to His likeness" (Gen. 1:26-27), whereby we have been blessed with many wonderful grace attributes by the Lord to accomplish all that He purposed for man… since the beginning.

Yet for most of us, we've forgotten who we are… and we've forgotten what we are supposed to be doing. Regenesis reminds us who we are, and now, the Image Bearer series is reminding us what we are supposed to do, how we should do it – and more importantly "why" we are doing it.

The Image Bearer series builds upon that knowledge of truth that mankind was created good so as to become what we were created for: to bear His image and imitate Jesus in every respect according to His earthly example – and operate as His heavenly ambassadors for earth.

The heavenly pattern for mankind is: imitate Jesus.
The earthly pattern for this world is: become like heaven.

Who you are is not based upon what you do; "what you do" is based upon "who you are." We get our identity from Jesus. This realigned perspective regarding "who" we are … is to reorient the applecart of faith pointing in the right direction, to focus on Jesus, and to accomplish our primary mission: have dominion on earth – in the name of Jesus.

The numeric order in which the Spirit directed these books: 1,2,8,3,5,4,6,7 was not linear in the least. Let the Spirit guide you in the order He wants you to read them; however, learning how to "Hear God's Voice" is always mission critical to get started on His path for anyone.

On October 24, 2015, the Lord told me to put these books on the internet for free. This was unexpected, and then the Lord whispered to me, "Can you make money on My words? Freely you have received… freely give."

When the Lord tells you what to do, He will also give you His authority, with power and provision, to do all that He commands. We need to embrace this perspective regarding our life on earth in order to understand and comprehend who we are and what we are supposed to be doing. There is much joy and peace living in this manner, and yet… we all make this choice daily to live according to His purpose for His glory – or to live according to our best laid plans. If I can do it – so can you.

Jesus did it, and therefore – "As He is, so are we in this world" (1 John 4:17). I hope you enjoy the Image Bearer series. Grace and peace be yours in abundance.

It's all about Jesus – and God gets the glory!

Glossary of Terms and Definitions

These are some keys to help navigate and understand the scriptures.

Heaven – God's throne, God's home and the permanent place where God's glory dwells
heaven – the spiritual reality of God's kingdom and Christ's presence upon earth
Glory – the fullness of God's presence; the fullness of all God is
Shekinah Glory – the manifest presence of God's Spirit
Christ – the manifest expression of God in Jesus, and regenerate (born anew) men
Jesus – the manifested Living God; Lord of heaven and earth; Lord of Glory; Lord of Hosts
Host – army (a very important term omitted in the NIV and some other versions)
Host of heaven – angels; sons of God and our heavenly brethren (Rev. 19:10)
Host of earth – sons of men, becoming sons of God in the regeneration
Man – the generic term for male and female to connote mankind, humanity, etc.
Earth – the planet; one of three permanent places within the kingdom of God
Hell – the absence of God; one of three permanent places within the kingdom of God; the pit
World – temporary realm on earth under the dominion and operational control of Satan
Satan – Prince of "this world" (formerly known as Lucifer before he rebelled and fell to earth)
Sin – the operating system of this world in opposition to God's sovereignty; separation from God; things done that cause separation
Spirit – the operating system on earth under the Lord's dominion; the Holy Spirit; God's Spirit
Grace – attributes of God's character that are freely given to man

Light – a metaphor implying God's truth
Darkness – a metaphor implying evil – and sinful lies of "this world"
Wickedness – taking credit for what God has done
Evil – using God's glory and power to accomplish your personal agenda
Paradigm – the operating systems of sin or "by the Spirit" on earth
Paradise – the earthly realm in oneness with God apart from sin
Dwelling – a temporary place to live
Abode – a permanent place to live (of existence)
Rest – the permanent state of being where God's presence abides (in your heart and in heaven)
Kingdom of God – all places under the authority of Jesus
Kingdom of heaven – a term used exclusively in the gospel of Matthew to describe the kingdom of God as it pertains to earth under the Lordship of Jesus Christ

- Life – the source from which all creation exists, and is made alive, as coming from God through Christ Jesus, who is "the Life" and the "author and finisher" of faith (John 14:6; Heb. 12:2)
- Living – those persons spiritually alive with life, who no longer operate in the shadow of Death while sojourning in earthen vessels that will eventually perish for lack of life
- Alive – the spiritual state of being in existence from God's perspective, even apart from the body, and abiding eternally in communion with God's Presence and Spirit
- Dead – the spiritual state of being in existence from God's perspective, but temporarily separated from Him; the eventual disposition of the earthen body without life
- Death – the spiritual state of being permanently and eternally separated from God; the temporary holding place of unregenerate dead that wait there until the judgment

Introduction

For the past 2,000 years, Christian doctrines have taught us many things about life, faith in Jesus Christ, and hope for eternal life in heaven. However, Jesus never promised us heaven, the apostles never preached it, our creeds don't teach it – and there is an astounding reason why!

When was the last time you read a book that…

1. Fundamentally altered your perception about eternal life and the kingdom of heaven
2. Radically changed your view about man's reason for life on earth – and earth itself
3. Outlined the three-fold mission of Jesus on earth that created within you a deeper hunger to know Him, love Him and serve Him

Read this scripture-based book with an open mind and listen to the Holy Spirit as we prepare for the greatest revival movement in human history. This book encourages the reader to embrace a spiritual paradigm shift that seems contrary to the way we've been thinking about heaven, man's reason for being on earth, and what God wants us to do as we stand at the intersect between two places in the kingdom of God: Heaven and Earth.

> *"It seems we have been waiting for something to happen that has already happened, yet hoping to inherit something we were never promised."*

Let me ask you this question: if you were not promised Heaven… would you still love God?

Deeply ponder that question… because it will create a shift in your thought process regarding faith, ideas about eternity, and affect your motivation and desire to manifest God's plan – on Earth – as it is in Heaven.

Jesus promised us life eternal, not heaven. This book presents a new reality of thought regarding heaven, eternity, the resurrection and our eternal destination. You will soon discover that Heaven, the kingdom of heaven and heavenly places represent three of fourteen distinct places mentioned in scripture (purgatory is not one of them) and you will definitively know where you go after your body dies.

> *"The kingdom of heaven is neither up nor down – but in. And now it's time to let heaven out!"*

> **"It must be considered that there is nothing more difficult to carry out, nor more doubtful of success, nor more dangerous to handle, than to initiate a new order of things. For the reformer has enemies in all those who profit by the old order, and only lukewarm defenders in all those who would profit by the new order, this lukewarmness arising partly from fear of their adversaries, who have the laws in their favour; and partly from the incredulity of mankind, who do not truly believe in anything new until they have had the actual experience of it."** [1]
>
> *Machiavelli (1513)*

---

[1] The Prince and the Discourses; The Modern Library, Random House, Inc., 1950, Page 21, Chapter VI.

1. Understanding Spiritual Things

Before we get started, it is imperative that all readers begin with the same point of reference.

This book, like all others that I write, is about the spiritual reality that surrounds us. This reality can be naturally discerned just by looking at creation itself to see that a Greater Power has orchestrated such marvelous wonder, beauty and majesty; however, understanding this reality does not come naturally – it can only be revealed in the new birth by the Holy Spirit. For example, we can see by observation how 'the power of three' and the simplicity of the seed's physical design is replicated, not only in other aspects of creation, but also in the design of the Jewish Temple – and also in the earthly temple known as man; it is not by accident or coincidence in the universe whereby these same spiritual patterns have been replicated to help guide us to the truth that already resides within us for one reason: newness again.

Everyone living upon this planet has been born once, through water, in the hope of being born anew – a second time, through the Spirit. The reason we need to be born anew is for one reason: to understand and perceive the spiritual reality and the kingdom of God that surrounds us. This understanding does not come by way of observation with natural eyes, because it can only be spiritually discerned as a person experiencing it as a new spiritual person (John 3:3-8).

There are two spiritual kingdoms on this planet; there is the worldly kingdom that stands in rebellion against Jesus Christ and His kingdom, and there is the spiritual kingdom that is yielded to and aligned with the Lordship of Jesus that operates according to the Spirit. Choose to live in one or the other, because trying to live in between is a lukewarm choice and vain endeavor.

Likewise, there are two types of people on this planet. Either you are a human being that is hopelessly trapped in a physical worldly reality, or you are a spiritual being having a human experience that has been set free from the snare of hopelessness and, therefore, are now living life in liberty within the spiritual reality of "Christ in you."

These two types of "what are you" people living on the planet today represent the redeemed and unregenerate. Until a conversion happens within your consciousness that affects your sense of identity and future destiny, then you are merely a fleshly human being wandering around this planet without understanding, but when you come to the knowledge of the truth in Christ whereby you are born anew and yield to His spiritual reality that surrounds you, then you have been regenerated as a "new creation" to live according to that reality "in the Spirit."

It is not enough to say that you are born anew; it must be lived by faith daily. You can profess to have a born again theology and talk the talk, but if you are unable to understand and comprehend the spiritual reality that surrounds you, or you continue to live in hostility to the truth of the gospel in opposition to righteousness, peace and joy, then you are merely walking in the spirit of religion and not the spiritual illumination resulting in conversion. The truth of Jesus is a light that must radiate His spiritual newness and truth into every dimension of your life – whereby Jesus is the focus of your life, and therefore – you give all glory to Jesus in everything you think, say and do.

Jesus taught us about two types of "what" people that live within these two realities:

> "That which is born of the flesh, is flesh; and that
> which is born of the Spirit, is spirit" (John 3:6)

Firstly, until you understand 'what you are' which spiritually determines 'whose' you are, then life on this planet is lived in futility. Our sense of doing is inextricably related to our being.

Secondly, we were not born anew so we may go to Heaven, but so we may understand the spiritual kingdom of God that surrounds us.

Faith determines where we go; understanding determines how we get there. Jesus made it very clear that we must be born anew in order to perceive '*oida*' this kingdom of God (John 3:3). The word '*oida*' translated as "see" and also "tell" in verse 8 seems to have been translated with perhaps the weakest possible meaning. Jesus is telling us this divine truth: you cannot '*oida*' *perceive and understandably comprehend* the kingdom of God apart from the Spirit because it is a spiritual reality that you must enter in *and* receive by way of the Spirit. This spiritual reality cannot be '*ginosko*' known through intellectual ascent, nor can you tell where it comes from, nor can it be completely understood by comprehending all aspects of the spiritual reality apart from the Spirit – it can only be *perceived* and experienced once you have been born anew as a new creation, according to Gal. 2:20, that operates as a new person in spiritual newness – with the Holy Spirit guiding you.

If you have *not* been born anew, then this book will probably make little if any sense to you, as I write to a born anew community who faithfully follow Christ – and Jesus Christ only – who are getting ready for global revival. If you desire to be born anew, then read *Regenesis* or ask someone in whom the Spirit of God is clearly manifest and professes Jesus Christ as Lord, Master, Savior and Sovereign King. Hearing His voice is step one; being born anew is step two.

Understanding the spiritual kingdom of God is our only key to comprehending what we are, who we are, whose we are, why we are on this planet and what we are supposed to be doing. We live in a culture that is obsessed with knowing who we are; however, the spiritual journey to understand all things can begin only after we realize our existence is based upon "what" we are and "Whose" we are. The salvation of our soul through sanctification is just one aspect of this exciting faith journey as we sojourn on the earth for one season of eternity. Once you have been redeemed and saved unto salvation from "what" you were, only then will you learn and completely comprehend "who you are" and the three reasons why all people are on planet earth, which is, another working of the Spirit to be revealed in you – and through you.

Through faith in Christ, you are a spiritual being having a human experience, so enjoy the journey as you live for Jesus.

Don't go where the path leads. Rather, go where there is no path and leave a trail…

The kingdom of heaven is at hand – and – is nearer then when we first believed.

        It's all about Jesus – and God gets the glory!

2) New Earth Introduction

Not long ago, I heard a message about dietary changes during the past century. There were periods of time past when milk was good until it became bad and then good again, whereby mother's milk was insufficiently healthy for newborn babies so pediatric nutritionists promoted "formula" until breast-milk was exonerated.

Eggs are incredibly healthy, but cholesterol warnings deemed them bad, so, in order to get our cholesterol into the healthy range, we were prescribed medications with potentially harmful side effects to reduce health risks that are often easily managed by lifestyle adjustments of diet, exercise and stress management. Pork was dangerous because of trichinosis, fish was bad because of mercury, mad cow affected beef, and salmonella in chicken and poultry is still a valid concern; the fear of E. coli caused apprehension from improper food handling and cooking, and ptomaine poisoning was used as a general term to describe an often misconstrued, ambiguous and inaccurate term for various causes of food poisoning before the actual causes were known.

Today, we know what causes "ptomaine poisoning" because science has demystified it.

Likewise, the church has often served as the benchmark to understand and comprehend religious and spiritual matters, but much like bad dietary advice that has changed as a result of scientific truth, religious doctrines continue to change when confronted by scriptural truth to the contrary. Many Christian leaders like Martin Luther, John Wesley, Moody, Edwards, Spurgeon, Chambers and so forth have altered our religious perceptions because they simply told us one thing: the truth. Change for the sake of change is never a good idea, but change for the sake of living truthfully according to the truth has always been a safe harbor for anyone on a spiritual journey to discover divine truth – and thus discover the true meaning of life.

The theological and spiritual impacts by these great leaders inspired within us a spiritual hunger and deeper yearning to live life according to the manner in which we were created, to live in divine communion with God, whereby we forsake the cares of this world to embrace the deeper reality of "Christ is us – our hope of glory."

Such a journey began with me on January 14, 2015, when, during morning prayer and devotions, the Holy Spirit asked me a question: "Do men go to heaven?" The answer I found will surprise many and perhaps shock institutional religious leaders with cries of contempt, not because this truth is shocking or heretical or inconsistent with God's truth found in hundreds of scriptures, but because it will open our eyes to understand the real reason why man is living upon the earth. Regardless of what your traditions have taught you, this truth will help you to see your mission upon earth within a much larger context – and God's tangible, purposeful, marvelous and loving plan for you as something truly worth living for! You will never see yourself – or life on earth – the same way again.

This teaching is not meant to, nor could it ever, dissolve or minimize any teachings of Jesus Christ; but, to the contrary, it will actually sharpen our focus and strengthen our resolve to know Him, love Him and serve Him in the manner He so desires whereby we enter into a deeper love and trust personal relationship with Him. Not our will, but "Thy will be done, on earth as it is in heaven" was Jesus' prayer for His disciples – and it is His timeless prayer for you and me today.

When we understand our true reason for "being" on this planet, it will dramatically revolutionize our way of thinking – away from "man-centric doctrines" toward a New Earth doctrine focused upon following Jesus Christ, serving God and being obedient to the command He gave us from the beginning: have dominion over the earth – as we host His presence while we show brotherly love toward one another.

However, before we can focus the fullness of our attention to accomplish the things we are commanded to accomplish upon the earth, we need to take a serious look at the question, "Do men go to heaven?" We have been taught this doctrine for nearly 2,000 years, but can we find this doctrinal message in the Bible? Did Jesus ever tell us we will go to or ascend into heaven? Faithful followers will inherit life eternal in the resurrection, to be certain, but do the scriptures actually tell us where we will go? What do our creeds teach us? Keep reading and find out!

Jesus told us the truth, but our predetermined "heaven-only" destiny for man's eternal soul has clouded this lens of truth whereby we may have translated and perhaps misinterpreted some Greek and Hebrew texts with this idea that "heaven is our eternal home." *If* we have built a great many principles and doctrines upon heaven-only, then this may even contradict God's heavenly truth in other areas as well – because by looking through that lens – we saw what we wanted to see as if looking to interpret scripture and perceive truth "with an idol in our heart" (Ezek. 14:3-4) by desiring "heaven" more than fixing our gaze upon Jesus Only (Heb. 12:2).

I am not suggesting we start over; rather, start looking over what we believe and focus on truth. We need to stop promising Heaven – and start focusing on Jesus only.

The purpose of bringing this fresh revelation to the Christian community is not to tip the applecart of faith, but *to turn it around so it faces the right direction.* It does not affect your salvation – it merely helps everyone get on the same page to initiate global revival the likes of which this planet has never seen before. We have just one more chance to get this right before the great tribulation begins; just look around and consider the signs around us… does your spirit confirm this truth? Does it appear that the end time is getting closer?

In one respect, as you will soon discover, our eternal destination will be as grand and glorious as Heaven itself because we will know and understand why we do… what we do… from now on.

Life on earth is not a fatalistic lesson in futility; we really have something totally awesome and incredible to live for, but we need to awaken from our slumber and complacency to perceive this truth.

Believing in Jesus is something worth dying for; inheriting our birthplace is something worth fighting for.

When we grasp and correctly internalize the truth of "where do men go after death?" then and only then are we able to focus the fullness of our spiritual attention, power and understanding to live according to the first commandment: have dominion over the earth – in Jesus' name. We were given delegated authority with power over the earth by Jesus to use, for better or worse, yet the reason we were given this authority with power was not to subjugate the elements of earth or its inhabitants, but to overthrow the kingdom of darkness that has spiritually stolen and taken captive this planet and mankind through fear, chaos, destruction, terror, lies, doubt and unbelief for one reason: to rob God of His glory. It was never about us – life on earth has always been a show-forth and demonstration of God's goodness, faithfulness, longsuffering, lovingkindness and tender-hearted mercies toward His free-will ambassadors of truth who stand in opposition to Satan and his rebellious worldly kingdom that he established on earth that is against (anti) Christ.

If you want to make a difference in the world and change it for the better, including attaining your idealistic and elusive understanding of "world peace" and "brotherly love toward one another," then this spark of truth will light a campfire in your mind to pursue God like never before… because you will soon discover that there really *is* something incredibly awesome worth living for as you sojourn upon the earth. Living with this divine truth will ultimately change our global dynamics according to how we were intended to live – ever since our beginning in the Garden.

It seems global revival as an awakening by the Holy Spirit is waiting for two things: an obstruction to be removed and a spark to ignite dramatic, radical change. The change resulting from comprehending this revelatory truth is nothing short of astonishing that will help ignite global awakening and spiritual revival to arouse a sleeping church to fulfill its divine mission to establish the kingdom of heaven – on earth – right now.

What is Heaven? What is the kingdom of heaven? Can you describe it? How can you describe an ocean to someone who has lived upon a mountaintop their whole life? How do you begin to describe a snowflake to someone who has only known a hot barren desert? How can you describe a rainbow in the sky or a sunrise to someone born blind? Or how can you describe living under water in a submarine to a primitive tribal person with ancient customs? So, how can anyone describe Heaven if they've never been there? Simply stated – I haven't – so I don't.

There are always going to be some things that will be difficult to explain without having some context to help other persons comprehend what you are communicating, such as, describing the God's spiritual reality to someone who only comprehends the physical reality, or communicating "the kingdom of heaven is at hand" without some basis for knowing what heaven and eternity are? Such was the case when Jesus taught about the kingdom of heaven; He used many examples to communicate divine truth in a way that we might hopefully understand today.

Unfortunately, the people who heard Jesus' message had preconceived ideas about faith, heaven, the messianic King, dominion, the restored kingdom, grace and eternity – and likewise so do we. Only one Person is able to describe the kingdom of heaven authoritatively because Jesus is the only one who has ascended and descended from heaven (John 3:13). Now, with fresh eyes, let us consider the truth of heaven from the perspective Jesus taught us, not as theologians looking through the predetermined "heaven-only" lens as regenerate man's eternal destination, but to discover the spiritual home Jesus went to prepare for those who love God with all their heart and soul.

We are all sojourners upon the earth. Once we remember what we are and whose we are – and what we are supposed to be doing – this planet will then become an extraordinarily awesome place to live and move and have our being... as we focus on our high calling *in* Christ Jesus.

This teaching to understand what the kingdom of heaven is – will not make sense unless you understand what you are, what you are supposed to do, Who is helping you do it – and why:

1. Unless you have been born anew according to the Spirit (John 3:3-8), you cannot understand any of this.
2. You are a spiritual being having a human experience; you are not a human being in search of a spiritual experience. You are a gateway through which heavenly things are supposed to flow through.
3. You are a sojourner and citizen of heaven who is here as the "host of earth" and given a command: have dominion.
4. Jesus promised and sent the Holy Spirit to come alongside you and then, through faith, dwell within you as your constant companion to guide you into all truth and empower you to live according to the manner you were called.
5. You are here to fulfill your commission mandate to: A) *have* dominion: B) *host* God's presence, C) *hear* His voice and *obey* Him, D) *understand* and *know* Him, E) *occupy* the land, F) *hallow* Him and *follow* His leading and G) disregard the enemy.
6. We have been living under a thoroughly open '*dianoigo-1272*' heaven for 2,000 years and even now the resources of heaven are being released in these last days to change human history with a simple choice: do you want spiritual revival or do you prefer tribulation?

Jesus came proclaiming, "The kingdom of heaven is at hand," and it is just as true today as it was 2,000 years ago. All it takes is conversion according to divine truth for us to operate in spirit and in truth with a spiritually transformed and renewed mind. Newness is happening all around us!

Now, let's get started, to live as we were intended to – and let's start living like we mean it!

Grace and peace,

Paul

3) **Do Men Go To Heaven?**

> Jesus said: "No one has ascended to heaven but He who came down from heaven, that is, the Son of Man who is in heaven" (John 3:13).

Do not read this unless you – and "your" world – are willing to be changed by the truth of God.

If I were to gather together 100 or even 100 million faith believing, Spirit filled, born again Christians to ask them if they were going to Heaven or Hell when they die, we would all answer the same way: to Heaven. And if I asked why, their response would be similar to this: I am saved by the grace of God through faith in Jesus Christ and, therefore, I am going to Heaven, not because of what I've done, but because of what Jesus did for me on the cross.

Up until a couple days ago, I would have responded the same way – and I would have been wrong (in regards to the premise of Heaven, not the declaration of faith).

On January 14, 2015, while I was in prayer and meditation, the Holy Spirit asked me a question: "Do men go to heaven?" So I replied, yes, absolutely, and then He replied, "Go look it up." I have been taught my whole Christian life that, when I die, I will go to Heaven and be with Jesus for all eternity because that is where Jesus will be – in Heaven. So, I searched the scriptures and this is what I found regarding heaven – as it relates to man:[2]

- "Go to heaven" – no occurrences
- "Go into heaven" – only two times, and both apply to Jesus (Acts 1:11; 1 Pet. 3:22) with angels and authorities and powers having been made subject to Him

---

[2] The author uses the same meaning with respect to the term "man" as both the Lord and the Bible, implying all people and persons, both male and female, living upon the earth. No gender partiality, distinction or sexism is to be construed in any manner.

- "Gone… into heaven" – once, said of angels (Luke 2:15)
- "Go up to heaven – none
- "Go up into heaven" – none

Well, that was unexpected, so I began searching other verb combinations with similar meaning.

- "Raise(d) into heaven" – none
- "Raise(d) up into heaven" – none
- "Take(n) into heaven" – none
- "Take(n) up into heaven" – once, referring to "the sheet" in Peter's vision (Acts 10:16)
- "Take up" and "went up" into heaven – both times referring to Elijah (2 Kings 2:1, 11)
- "Enter in(to)" – 36 occurrences of entering into covenants, gates, judgment, peace, life, joy, temptation, and Christ entering His glory – but it never says men enter into heaven
- Arise or attain heaven – none
- "Come to" heaven – none
- "Come in(to)" heaven – none
- "Come up" to heaven – once, referring to the two faithful witnesses (Rev. 11:12)
- "Ascend(ed) up into heaven" – none
- And oppositely "descend(ed) into" (as in hell) – none
- "Ascend into heaven" – five times, including once said by Satan, and they are:

1. "For you have said in your heart: 'I will ascend into heaven, I will exalt my throne above the stars of God; I will also sit on the mount of the congregation on the farthest sides of the north" (Isa. 14:13; an utterance by Satan told to Isaiah by the Spirit)
2. "It is not in heaven, that you should say, 'Who will ascend into heaven for us and bring it to us, that we may hear it and do it?'(Deut. 30:12)
3. "Who has ascended into heaven, or descended? Who has gathered the wind in His fists? Who has bound the waters in a garment? Who has established all the ends of the earth?

> What is His name, and what is His Son's name, if you know?" (Prov. 30:4; A: Jesus)
> 4. "*If* I ascend into heaven, You are there; *If* I make my bed in hell, behold, You are there" (Psa. 139:8; these are rhetorical "if" statements)
> 5. And most importantly…
>
>> "But the righteousness of faith speaks in this way, "Do not say in your heart, 'Who will ascend into heaven?'" (that is, to bring Christ down *from above*)" (Rom. 10:6).

Well, to be sure, this was not what I expected. "Go to heaven" as it relates to man is not found in the scriptures. When Christians begin their conversation with unsaved individuals, three questions are typically asked: 1) Are you saved? 2) Do you know Jesus as your personal Lord and Savior? and 3) If you were to die today, would you go to Heaven? We have been inculcated to believe we are going to Heaven, and we earnestly desire to spend eternity anywhere except upon the earth, but what did Jesus teach us?

> "Not everyone who says to Me, 'Lord, Lord,' shall enter the kingdom of heaven, but he who does the will of My Father in heaven" (John 7:21).

Jesus told us that "some" may enter into the kingdom of heaven, but you will soon learn this for yourself: Jesus never promised us we will enter into Heaven. You will also learn that "Heaven" and "the kingdom of heaven" and "heavenly places" are three distinct places within the kingdom of God – and that the kingdom of heaven is already being manifested upon the earth by saints – even now – according to faith in Christ Jesus.

It seems we have been waiting for something to happen that has already happened, yet hoping to attain something that we were never promised.

If you were to ask a congregation of believers in the Christian faith to tell you whether they are going to heaven or not, their response might surprise you.[3] If you were to ask this same group if there are only two places to go after you die, what do you think their response would be? And if it was proven to a substantial number of Christians that there is no such after-death place called purgatory or limbo before the after-life begins, would this then result in only two places where we are raised in the resurrection? So, what would you say if I told you there was a third place?

Heaven Is God's Throne

> "Heaven is My throne, and earth is My footstool. Where is the house that you will build for Me? says the Lord, or what is the place of My rest?" (Isa. 66:1; Acts 7:49).

Heaven exists and Jesus is in Heaven with the Father, as the scriptures teach, "Heaven is My throne." Some extraordinary men are in Heaven, but there is no direct evidence of *ordinary* earthly men going into Heaven. We will carefully examine all the inconclusive scriptures that man's religion has used to create the heaven-only doctrine for man's eternal destination, and we will also allow the scriptures to speak truth to us so we may understand what happens when we die – and where we actually go. All these answers are found in the scriptures!

Heaven is a real place with physical characteristics that exists in the spiritual realm, which is also the home of angels, who are "our" brethren and host of Heaven. We have been taught there are three heavens, yet only four *extraordinary* people groups from earth

---

[3] Baylor University; 2008 Baylor Religion Survey of 1,648 randomly selected adults nationwide regarding religious views of Americans found the following: 67% believe in heaven (89% among conservative Protestants), but only 73% believe hell absolutely or probably exists, which may explain why only 46% are "quite certain" they will go to heaven. The 2005 Baylor Survey found 61% of Evangelical Protestants and 46.4% of black Protestants believe that only Christians will get into heaven. By contrast, 66.9% of Catholics say all or most non-Christians will.

(other than Jesus) are recorded in the scriptures as "being" in heaven:

1. By invitation only: Enoch, Elijah (and Moses since he appears with Elijah on the Mount of Transfiguration) and two faithful witnesses in Revelation (which hasn't happened yet)
2. Those saints who have been martyred on account of Christ[4] and will participate in the first resurrection of the dead (Rev. 20:4)
3. 144,000 virgins (Rev. 14:1-5)
4. And those who come out of the great tribulation (Rev. 7:8, 14, 15 which hasn't happened yet).

Other than that, it is my understanding the "up" into Heaven is a cultural – and perhaps theological – misunderstanding born out of centuries of religious tradition rooted in the dark age of indulgences.

You would think there would be at least ONE biblical verse that speaks directly to "men go to heaven" since it is the benchmark for most of our gospel messages – but it's not there.

The scriptures are very clear that "those saved for salvation unto eternal life" will be resurrected *at* the last day into newness of life, but *none* of the Apostles taught that we will go to – or ascend into – Heaven. Why is that? While this may be heretically shocking to most of us (and believe you me, I was just as shocked), the Spirit began to teach me truth and to put the concepts of "have dominion" and "delegated authority given" and "men are houses for the Divine" into a unified thought, and to consider the merit of this theological premise: do men go to Heaven when we die?

This is an open challenge for everyone to read all 692 scripture references for "Heaven" which includes 168 references for

---

[4] Rev. 6:9. This may explain the extreme willingness of resolute Christians to surrender their lives during the early Christian era – and since.

"heavens." Do not just believe what I am going to teach you… search the scriptures and believe it for yourself.

The cosmos is His sanctuary (Isa. 40:22; Psa. 103:19). "The Most High does not dwell in houses made with hands" (Acts 7:49), *but Jesus abides in "houses" that have human hands* (i.e. our hearts; Eph. 3:17). The sons of men are houses for the Divine, as Jesus said, "I will make My home in you" (John 15:5-7) and "We (Father and Son) will make Our home *with* you" (John 14:23), thereby giving us some indication where our eternal destination will be.

The reason They make Their home in us is because we cannot go home to Them.

Nonetheless, men are houses for the Divine, so where is the house that *you* are building for Jesus to inhabit – and what kingdom are you building within your heart and upon the earth that is bringing glory to the Father and the Son?

> "You are God's fellow workers; you are God's field, *you are God's building*" (1 Cor. 3:9).

We were saved by grace through faith to become living tabernacles for Jesus, our Immanuel (God with us), to abide *in* us so that we may abide *with* God Most High as He abides *with* us, as sons of God, to operate as prophets and priests and kings in the kingdom of our God. Many of us have been taught that God only dwells in buildings and we routinely attend church or synagogue to visit with God as an alternative to building a relationship with Him in our hearts, but what does the scripture teach:

> "But will God indeed dwell with men on the earth? Behold, heaven and the heaven of heavens cannot contain You. How much less this temple which I have built!" (1 Kings 8:27; 2 Chron. 6:18; refers to the temple Solomon built for God).

> "For Christ has not entered the holy places made with hands, which are copies of the true, but into heaven itself, now to appear in the presence of God for us" (Heb. 9:24).

Well, it seems Jesus does not dwell in houses of worship or churches or cathedrals or synagogues or houses made with human hands. Jesus Christ entered Heaven and is seated at the right hand of the Father, and thus, "The mystery of faith is: Christ in us – the hope of glory" (Col. 1:27). The mystery of faith is: Christ dwells in us and, thus, we manifest His presence whenever we worship the Lord in spirit and in truth. The Lord is made manifest when "you" bring Him into any room or sanctuary. Therefore, you are a holy tabernacle for Jesus – and Christ is revealed through you as you enter the room of any building.

We enter into His presence; then His presence enters into us – and we reflect His glory.

The presence we enter into is the realm of the Spirit Himself. On earth, the Lord is made manifest in you and through you as He abides in your heart, according to faith, but He has not entered holy buildings. The Spirit of the Lord is everywhere, so inviting Him to enter into a building where He already exists seems kind of silly.

That may be a very foreign concept to you, but if you adopt this spiritual truth, then you will be able to unlock many mysteries hidden within the scriptures. Jesus is in Heaven, but if we are not raised up into Heaven, then can you prove this to me? And where do we go? Yes I can!

> "*No one* has ascended to heaven but He who came down from heaven, *that is,* the Son of Man who is in heaven" (John 3:13).

Read it again. No one has ascended into Heaven – except Jesus. Read it again! [5]

Ponder this verse in regard to Heaven – and some other place (13:36). This may not be enough proof for some, so what does Jesus Himself say about any man's ability to ascend into heaven?

> Jesus said, "Where I am you cannot come" (John 7:34).
>
> Then He said, "Where I am going you cannot come" (John 13:33).
>
> And then again, "Where I am going you cannot follow Me now, but you shall follow Me afterward" (John 13:36; pertaining to the resurrection).

Well, you say, are there any other scriptures than this word spoken by Jesus? (I am horrified to think that anyone would diminish the authority of Christ's words, but yes, there are.)

> "Who has ascended into heaven, or descended? Who has gathered the wind in His fists? Who has bound the waters in a garment? Who has established all the ends of the earth? What *is* His name, and what is His Son's name, if you know?" (Prov. 30:4; His name is Jesus, and Jesus confirmed this truth).

Under the inspiration of the Holy Spirit, the Apostle Peter confirmed what Jesus said, "No one has ascended into heaven." Not even King David!

> "For David did not ascend into the heavens, but he says himself: 'The Lord said to my Lord, "Sit at My right hand" (Acts 2:34).

---

[5] Jesus is able to make this proclamation in regard to eternity past, present and future – as Lord and King of Heaven.

An Earthly Misunderstanding

It seems our pious, religious misunderstanding of what heaven is, as something high and lifted up that we have been taught to attain, as a exalted place of ascension far beyond the touch of earthly man, and where it is, has sufficiently clouded our understanding to the point whereby we live life seeking "to go up into" a place that scripture records only two people have ascended into, namely, Jesus and Elijah.

> "Then it happened, as they continued on and talked, that suddenly a chariot of fire appeared with horses of fire, and separated the two of them; and Elijah *went up* by a whirlwind into heaven" (2 Kings 2:11).

> "And while they (the Apostles) looked steadfastly toward heaven as He *went up*, behold, two men stood by them in white apparel, [11] who also said, "Men of Galilee, *why do you stand gazing up* into heaven? This same Jesus, who was *taken up* from you into heaven, will so come in like manner as you saw Him go into heaven" (Acts 1:10, 11).

Peter had an interesting vision of a sheet filled with unclean animals, and after three times, this vision was "taken up" into heaven (Acts 10:16), but other than that, only angels are recorded as having ascended or gone "a little father" into heaven. Of angels, they appear to us and disappear without actually coming down or being taken up (see Acts 1:10). "So it was, when the angels had *gone away* from them into heaven, that the shepherds said to one another..." (Luke 2:15).

To understand this reality that heaven is "just a little farther," do a word study on '*anabaino*' (Strong's 305) to perceive the kingdom of heaven is not that far away – and is near at hand.

We do not come up to Heaven – heaven comes into us at the spiritual new birth by the Spirit.

> "So then, after the Lord had spoken to them, He was **received up** [*analambano*] into heaven, and sat down at the right hand of God" (Mark 16:19).

'*Analambano*' (353) traditionally means "taken up" – of Jesus, Acts 1:2, 11, 22; the vision of the sheet, Acts 10:16; and can also be translated "take in, take into, take" – under sail, Acts 20:13; Christ received up in glory, 1 Tim. 3:16; get (pick up) Mark, 2 Tim. 4:11; "take up" the whole armor of God, Eph. 6:13; "taking up" the shield of faith, Eph. 6:16).[6]

Jesus Himself did not tell anyone that they would ascend into Heaven. He only said that we may enter into "the kingdom of heaven" as a citizen of the kingdom, by grace through faith. But if we do not become permanent residents of Heaven, then where do we go? It seems we will arise in the resurrection into the third option and become residents of "the kingdom of heaven," which remains upon the Earth:

> "From that time Jesus began to preach and to say, "Repent, for the kingdom of heaven is at hand" (Matt. 4:17).

> "Now after John was put in prison, Jesus came to Galilee, preaching the gospel of the kingdom of God, [15] and saying, "The time is fulfilled, and the kingdom of God is at hand. Repent, and believe in the gospel" (Mark 1:14, 15).

Jesus came teaching about and proclaiming… the kingdom of heaven:[7]

---

[6] Strong's Concordance.
[7] The term "kingdom of heaven" is found only in the gospel of Matthew. Matthew was writing to Jewish people who regard the name of God with such religious zeal that they sometimes substitute the word "heaven" for God. This

- "For I say to you, that unless your righteousness exceeds the righteousness of the scribes and Pharisees, you will by no means enter the kingdom of heaven" (Matt. 5:20)
- "Not everyone who says to Me, 'Lord, Lord,' shall enter the kingdom of heaven, but he who does the will of My Father in heaven" (Matt. 7:21)
- "Assuredly, I say to you, unless you are converted and become as little children, you will by no means enter the kingdom of heaven" (Matt. 18:3)
- "Then Jesus said to His disciples, "Assuredly, I say to you that it is hard for a rich man to enter the kingdom of heaven" (Matt. 19:23)
- "But woe to you, scribes and Pharisees, hypocrites! For you shut up the kingdom of heaven against men; for you neither go in yourselves, nor do you *allow those who are entering to go in*" (Matt. 23:13; *this last phrase bears further consideration*)

We often focus our attention on Christ's ability to have authority over demons, but look closely at a statement Jesus made regarding "who" the kingdom of God has come upon, both then and now...

> "But if I cast out demons by the Spirit of God, surely the kingdom of God has **come upon** you" (Matt. 12:28)

Jesus didn't simply bring the kingdom of heaven to earth with Him and then ascend into Heaven at His resurrection with the kingdom in His back pocket... He came, He established it and His kingdom *came upon* those who believed in Him.

If you are living your life without any expectation of remaining upon the Earth after the resurrection of the dead, it is because you have been taught that you will supernaturally ascend into Heaven to be with Jesus. It has already been concluded that heaven is

---

subtle difference allows us to understand the kingdom of God better, especially in light of who Jesus is: Lord of heaven and earth!

neither up nor down – but in[8] – and now it will be shown that we are not raised up into Heaven as previously supposed.

> "Then the King will say to those on His right hand, 'Come, you blessed of My Father, inherit the kingdom prepared for you from the foundation of the world'" (Matt. 25:34)

Jesus (the King) did not tell us that we will inherit paradisiacal bliss as a place in Heaven; He told us we will "inherit *the kingdom* prepared for you" by a foundation of philanthropic angels (sorry, I couldn't stop myself)… "from the foundation of the world." Earth is *the kingdom of heaven* and the Lord's dominion (in transition) that we need to turn our attention toward as we keep our eyes focused upon Jesus our Savior. Now, let's jump back quickly to the beginning of creation to consider what God said regarding the foundation of the world:

- The Lord God created everything, the earth and the fullness thereof, including the host of heaven and the host of earth (Genesis 2:1; mankind is the host of earth, and we are also called the sons of men)
- And God said, "Let them [mankind] have dominion over the earth" (Gen. 1:26)

Dominion over the earth was granted to the host of earth (men) – and this represents the first command by God to mankind – to operate this planet under His delegated authority. The foundation of the earth remains glorious in its original form, but when Satan was cast here, he took dominion over the earth and established the foundation of "this world" as his demonic domain with chaos and darkness (Gen. 1:2). This is the dominion of sin that all men were born into. That's the bad news; however, here's good news… through faith in Jesus Christ, we can live in the dominion of grace governed by Christ – right now.

---

[8] Word study on ascend - '*anabaino*' (305), from "Kingdoms" section titled: "Onward, Inward then Upward" (to our high calling in Christ Jesus).

If Jesus is in your heart through faith, and you are in Christ, then it stands to reason that in the resurrection, your soul will be raised up with Christ by the power of the Spirit and you will be seated with Him in heavenly places, but the word "Heaven" is never mentioned. Never! The term "raise you up at the last day" is mentioned four times in John's gospel (John 6:39, 40, 44, 54) indicating these scriptures describe the resurrection, but Heaven is never mentioned.

Jesus said, "I have come down from heaven" (John 6:38), and just as Jesus was sent to Earth from the Father, so also Jesus sent us into the world (John 17:18), but never does Jesus say *we* will go up into Heaven. Jesus does tell us we will be raised, and this, by Jesus Himself:

- "And God both raised up the Lord and will also raise us up by His power" (1 Cor. 6:14)
- "Knowing that He who raised up the Lord Jesus will also raise us up with Jesus, and will present *us* with you" (2 Cor. 4:14)
- "I have power to lay it (My life) down, and I have power to take it up again. This command I received from My Father" (John 10:18).
- "And this is the will of Him who sent Me, that everyone who sees the Son and believes in Him may have everlasting life; and ***I will raise him up*** at the last day" (John 6:40).

Ponder this: Jesus was sent to earth – and so were you. You were inserted into the timeline of this world by the overshadowing of the Most High whereby you were conceived in your mother's womb – by the Holy Spirit – by the union of two parents. You were predestined – at just the right time – and sent into this world by Jesus, and Jesus will raise you up – by the power of the Spirit – on the last day. What you are and how you got here… requires a paradigm shift!

Men Are Spiritual Beings

There is one scripture that comes close to saying men "go to heaven." Jesus said:

> "For in the resurrection they neither marry nor are given in marriage, but *are like angels* of God in heaven" (Matt. 22:30).

"Like angels" – yes, but "in Heaven" – no! In the resurrection, since we are not going to Heaven, then consider this verse on its own merit – and what type of glorified bodies we will be resurrected into (1 Cor. 15:35-45). We will be raised up into heavenly places, having already been blessed with every spiritual blessing in heavenly places in Christ (Eph. 1:3) and seated together with Christ in heavenly places according to grace (Eph. 2:6). Yes, we will we be in "heavenly places," but in "Heaven," no! Is there a difference? Yes, in many regards, which will be explained a little later.

The scripture that comes closest to justifying our traditions that we will be in heaven is this: [9]

> "For we know that if our earthly house, this tent[10], is destroyed, we have a building *from* [*ek*] God, a house not made with hands, eternal in the *heavens*" (2 Cor. 5:1).

If this last scripture had said "heaven" rather than "heavens," then I would have no reason to write, but because it says "heavens"

---

[9] Vine's Expository, in which he describes '*ouranos*-3772' heaven as "the eternal dwelling place of saints in resurrection glory." As exhaustive as Vine and Strong are, this one lone scripture is hardly conclusive of our eternal destination for a word that is also translated "*heavenly*" Father (Luke 11:13) and "eunuchs for the kingdom of *heaven's* sake" (Matt. 19:12). Not even Willmington's Guide to the Bible on the Doctrine of Salvation mentions the word "heaven" once, as it pertains to man, except for the joy that is expressed "in heaven" over one repentant sinner (Luke 15:7)! See p.730.

[10] Tent (4636 - *skenos*) a hut or temporary residence; tabernacle; here and in v.4.

(*ouranos*-3772-heaven is plural) then we need to examine this scripture more closely. The scope of this message is not to present a comprehensive teaching about the three (or more) heavens that reside above the firmament of the earth or the nature of heavenly places, but rather… the purpose of this teaching is to show that we, as "ordinary" believers, do not go/ascend/arise into Heaven – for Heaven is God's throne.

"For our citizenship is in heaven, *from which* we also eagerly wait for the Savior, the Lord Jesus Christ" (Phil. 3:20) because we were sent from Heaven to this world; we have "an inheritance incorruptible and undefiled and that does not fade away, reserved in heaven for you" (1 Pet. 1:4) and we are "registered in heaven" (Heb. 12:23), – **_but_** – our residency as the host of earth (men) is forever upon the Earth, which is our present dominion and eternal estate. The reason this may not make sense at this point is because many of us are still thinking of Earth according to the physical dimension and not the spiritual paradigm that includes Paradise.

If we have an inheritance in heaven, then, what is it and when can we have access to it? Well, you can have access to it even now, for as the scripture says,

> "It shall be, in regard to their inheritance, that *I am* their inheritance. You shall give them no possession in Israel, for *I am* their possession" (Ezek. 44:28).

> "I will declare the decree: the LORD has said to Me, 'You are My *Son*, today I have begotten *You*. [8] Ask of Me, and I will give *You* the nations for Your inheritance, and the ends of the earth for Your possession" (Psa. 2:7, 8).

Jesus is our inheritance – and our very great reward. This Earth is the Lord's, the Earth is His dominion, the Earth is His footstool and it all belongs to Jesus – and everything that dwells upon the Earth is *His* inheritance, including you and me! We are partners and partakers of this inheritance, so as to "have a share in" the glorious riches of His inheritance (Eph. 1:18), and through faith (Rom. 8:32; 2 Pet. 1:3), Jesus will put all things under our feet (Psa. 8:6), including the dominion of this Earth.

> "And as we have borne the image of the man of dust, we shall also bear the image of the heavenly Man" (1 Cor. 15:49).

Men are Houses and Habitations

The sons of men are houses for the Divine, as Jesus said, "I will make My home in you" (John 15:5-7) and "We (Father and Son) will make Our home *with* you" (John 14:23), thereby giving us some indication where our eternal destination will be. We are going to spend several pages discussing the meaning and intent of many specific words the Apostle Paul used in 2 Corinthians 5:1-4 with the purpose of discerning this message: men are houses for the Divine.

> "For we know that if our earthly *house* [*oikia*-3614], this tent [4636; temporary hut or tabernacle], is destroyed, we have a *building* [*oikodome*-3619] *from* [*ek*] God, a *house* [3614] not made with hands, eternal in the *heavens*" (2 Cor. 5:1).

> "For in this we groan, earnestly desiring to be clothed with our *habitation* [3613] which is *from* [*ex - from out of*] heaven" (2 Cor. 5:2).

There are several Greek words translated "house" that represent very different things. Understanding these three words (all having the same root word – *oikos*-3624) within these two verses is the key to comprehending our future dwelling place in the heavens.

- *Oikia*-3614 – residence; a house, dwelling, abode; used figuratively for our body
- *Oikos*-3624 – a dwelling place; *oikos* denotes the entire estate while *oikia* represents the house or dwelling only (Attic Law)

- *Oikodome*-3619 – is a combination of *oikos* and *doma*-1430 (a rooftop); *oikodome* needs to be interpreted within the spiritual context in which it occurs, where *doma* (rooftop) represents a heavenly covering over the *oikos* (estate) that protects the house, dwelling, inhabitants – verily, everything. One meaning is: "we have a spiritual covering from God, a dwelling place not made with hands, eternal in the heavens" that conveys this principle: even if our temporary earthly body (house/tent) is destroyed, we have great confidence and assurance through faith that we are still under God's covering of grace and "dome" of protection. God Himself is our protection. "For over all the glory there will be a covering" (Isa. 4:5). *Oikodome* occurs 18 times to describe: A) "literal buildings;" Matt. 24:1; Mark 13:1; and ascribed once to Jesus (Mark. 13:2); and B) "edification – to build up another (Rom. 14:19; 15:2); a local church as a spiritual building (1 Cor. 3:9); the whole church as the body of Christ (Eph. 2:21); and the strengthening effect of teaching (1 Cor. 14: 3, 5, 12, 26; 2 Cor. 10:8; 12:10; 13:10)"... yet only once is it "used figuratively of the believer's resurrection body (2 Cor. 5:1)."[11] Translating *oikodome* as a building, and only perceiving it as such, diminishes the spiritual significance of this word used in context of Paul's message. Man's biggest problem to perceive spiritual matters is the physical house he temporarily resides within (i.e. his body)
- *Oiketerion*-3613– a *habitation, residence (*problematically translated *house* – in KJV)

However, the word we need to focus on '*oiketerion*-3613 – *habitation'* is a word that is highly significant yet occurs only twice in the scriptures, which refers to:

---

[11] Strong's Concordance. "The English word "dome" ultimately derives from the Latin *domus* ("house")—which, up through the Renaissance, labeled a revered house, such as a *Domus Dei*, or "House of God", regardless of the shape of its roof. Domes and tent-canopies were also associated with the heavens in Ancient Persia and the Hellenistic-Roman world." Source: Wikipedia.

A) The former home of angels that did not keep their "first estate, proper domain" residence which was in heaven, but had to leave their abode/*habitation* on account of unlawful deeds (Jude 6), and
B) As it refers to our new "habitation" residence (as coming to us '*ex*' "from out of" heaven) which we will receive after the resurrection as we abide upon our "first estate and proper domain" – Earth.

The first estate and proper domain (*oiketerion*) of angels is Heaven, but some angels, because of unlawful deeds, were condemned by God into everlasting chains and darkness to await judgment; and likewise, mankind also fell from his first estate and proper domain (Paradise in Eden) on account of sin, disobedience and unlawful deeds. Do you see the spiritual parallel between Heaven and Earth and what has been happening to all persons in the kingdom of God?

'*Oiketerion*' is a very interesting word; it is a combination of two words (*oiketer*- "an inhabitant" + *oikos*- "a dwelling") which means more than just a habitation, residence or house… it implies the inhabitant and the habitation are – one and the same. The person and the dwelling "co-habit" the same space and place… in oneness. (This truth represents another paradigm shift).

This principle is easier to understand when we consider our soul as having an earthly sojourn within an earthen body. The body you currently have is a temporary earthen vessel; it was given to you by God in order to accomplish His will while you are on Earth, yet when your body dies, that body must abandon your soul – and you must wait on Earth (either in Hades or Death) for the judgment and resurrection. When some angels in Heaven committed unlawful deeds, they left their '*oiketerion*' – whereby they had to leave Heaven <u>and</u> their heavenly body behind (their proper domain and first estate, respectively) to await judgment in darkness.

What is Paul telling us? Spiritual beings are given a body (house/tent/habitation) that is compatible with the place they are living in. When we violate God's law, we forfeit oiketerion.

"What house would you build for Me?" asks the Lord. Contemplate this question as one of your reasons for being on earth. "Where is the house you are building for Me?" These are spiritual questions about a spiritual house that God wants you to build in your heart – for Him to abide.

Now consider: "What type of true riches or unrighteous mammon are you storing up for eternity for your use when you get to the other side (Luke 16:9-16)... and where these resources are being stored?" Which *oiketerion* are you "building" in your heart? Where is your treasure?

> "For where your treasure is, there your heart will be also" (Matt. 6:21; 12:35).

The remainder of this book, along with all the others being written, will be much easier to comprehend if you can perceive this truth: **you are building your future "oiketerion – home" and kingdom in your heart – right now.** Is the Lord your covering? This is the cornerstone of much revelation and revival: your heart is your eternal '*oiketerion*' dwelling place.

> "A good man out of the good treasure of his heart brings forth good things, and an evil man out of the evil treasure brings forth evil things" (Matt. 12:35).

Perhaps the main reason some cannot comprehend this truth comes as a direct result from misunderstanding man's spiritual and physical construction. If you think you are a human being that was given a soul, then your understanding is completely backwards. You do not have a soul, per se... you ARE a soul (a spiritual being that is having a human experience) whereby a body was formed upon you and a spirit was formed within you (Gen. 2:7; Zech. 12:1) both of which belong to God (1 Cor. 6:19, 20). Your soul desires a house so as not to be found naked and ashamed, yet our current house (body) is just a temporary covering for a soul that is in transition – from death to life.

> "For as in Adam all die, even so in Christ all shall be made alive" (1 Cor. 15:22).

Our current body of flesh is compatible with "this world" which was passed down to all of us by Adam and Eve "after" they entered into sin, fell from grace, and had to leave their original *oiketerion* – Paradise in Eden.[12] And likewise, when you entered into sin, you also fell from grace and entered into sin leading to death; however, if you desire "to continue to live eternally" (Psa. 49:9), then you must repent, abandon the operating system of this world (which is sin), convert (turn around and declare your obedience to Jesus as Lord of your life) and now…live according to the operating system of grace according to the Spirit, whereby you shall receive new clothes in the resurrection to match the place that is being prepared for you… according to your deeds of righteousness through faith.

Beloved, we must leave "it" (the body of sin) behind, and, if we have done so, we will receive "it" (a body with glory) and life eternal on the "New Earth" after the resurrection.

Jesus said, "You must be born anew" (John 3:3-8). You were born into this worldly paradigm governed by sin – through water, but if you want to have life eternal, then you must be born again (anew from above) – through the Spirit. If you have been born anew, then you are in transition – from what you were… to becoming what you will be – in the resurrection.

---

[12] In the Garden of Eden, Adam and Eve were living in grace wherein they, being clothed with glory, were naked yet not ashamed. When they acted in an unlawful manner by taking and eating from the tree they were commanded not to, they entered into sin… whereby the forfeited their oiketerion (glory clothes and Eden) and they perceived their nakedness – in sin. The Lord created worldly oiketerion clothes for them, and these are the clothes that the Lord is using to proof us and sanctify us in preparation for eternity. By grace, through faith, we are able to exchange this worldly body for a resurrection body to live the New Earth that comes down to us 'ex' – from out of – Heaven.

Spiritual beings have need of (oiketerion) – a house (i.e. clothing) that is compatible within the place they reside. [13]

> "For in this we groan, earnestly desiring to be *clothed* (1902) with our habitation which is from (*ex-out of*) heaven, ³ if indeed, having been *clothed* (1746), we shall not be found naked. ⁴ For we who are in *this tent* (4636) [14] groan, being burdened, not because we want to be unclothed, but further *clothed* (1902), that mortality may be swallowed up by life" (2 Cor. 5:2-4).

Paul is very specific about his word choices. Our "*clothing*" (*ependuomai*-1902, occurs only twice) – refers to the body as something which is "clothed upon, caused to be put on over us,"[15] to imply our earthen tent (verse 5:1; body) and our future, eternal '*oiketerion*' habitation-body (v.2), which comes to us "*ex* – from out of" Heaven and is "put on over us." Let me say this clearly: both our future body and our future residence – comes to us "from out of" Heaven. And thus, having put on the new man (Eph. 4:24; Col. 3:10), "*if indeed, having been clothed*" in salvation (*enduo*-1746 – to enter into), our new house (resurrection body) will be "put on over" us as New-Earth men. We do not go into Heaven to get this house (body) – it comes to us "from out of" Heaven – and is superimposed onto us.[16] Is this starting to make sense now?

What are these transitional clothes that Paul mentions: "If indeed, having been clothed"? Let me ask you: have you been clothed [1746] "in Christ"? Have you put on [1746] Christ?

---

[13] Even demons and unclean spirits have need of a house. Consider the 6,000 demons that begged Jesus to enter 2,000 swine, and the unclean spirit that finds seven more spirits to retake its former house (Luke 8:26-33; 11:24-26).

[14] Tent: a hut or temporary residence; tabernacle. See footnote (previous page) for the only other occurrence.

[15] Strong's Concordance.

[16] Refer to footnote #52 regarding '*ependuoma*' meaning: to superimpose.

> "But put on [1746] the Lord Jesus Christ, and make no provision for the flesh, to *fulfill its* lusts" (Rom. 13:14).

> "For as many of you as were baptized into Christ have put on [1746] Christ" (Gal. 3:27).

Has Christ become your garment of salvation and your new spiritual '*oikodome*' covering so you will not be found naked without a body?

> "For He has clothed me with the garments of salvation,
> He has covered me with the robe of righteousness,
> As a bridegroom decks *himself* with ornaments,
> And as a bride adorns *herself* with her jewels" (Isa. 61:10).

If indeed, through repentance leading to faith, you have been clothed "with" the garment of salvation, which is Christ, you should have also been given His robe of righteousness which you must be wearing at the wedding feast of the Bride and Bridegroom (Jesus), that is, unless you took it off in order to operate according to the garment of sin – yet again. Jesus told us there will be some that enter this feast not wearing the wedding garment whereby they shall be cast into outer darkness.

> "But when the king came in to see the guests, he saw a man there who did not have on a wedding garment. [12] So he said to him, 'Friend, how did you come in here without a wedding garment?' And he was speechless. [13] Then the king said to the servants, 'Bind him hand and foot, take him away, and cast him into outer darkness[17]; there will be weeping and gnashing of teeth" (Matt. 22:11-13).

---

[17] Outer darkness is an eternal place reserved for hypocrites, wicked, lazy, unprofitable servants and unfaithful stewards where eternal torment following judgment occurs; to be explained in Chapter 8: "Places With Purpose."

Our "first estate and proper domain" as sons of men and the host of earth – is Earth. Earth was created for us – and we were created for the Earth; we are in the '*topos*' place prepared for us.

However, when we entered freely into sin, we forfeited our first estate (our body in grace) even though we remain in our proper domain – Earth. Through the first man, Adam, we forfeited our *oiketerion* in Paradise on account of disobedience, whereby the sons of men are being given a second chance – through sanctification – to return to our *oiketerion* in Paradise through faithful obedience to the last Adam, Jesus Christ (1 Cor. 15:45).

When we die, our soul does not go into Heaven as we are taught. Our body returns to the Earth where it came from and our spirit returns to God who gave it, but our soul waits (on Earth) for the judgment followed by the resurrection of life or resurrection of condemnation (John 5:29).

> "Then the dust will return to the earth as it was, and the spirit will return to God who gave it" (Eccl. 12:7).

> "His spirit departs, he returns to his earth; in that very day his plans perish" (Psa. 146:4).

In the beginning, we were sons of God with glory (in Eden), but we abandoned our first estate and exchanged glory clothes for garments of sin and became sons of men; however, through faith in Jesus, grace and mercy cleanses us from all sin and unrighteousness whereby we are in transition of becoming again – sons of God and sons of the resurrection – wherein we will be given new *oiketerion* spiritual clothes for the resurrection of life in the New Earth. Through sanctification, we are becoming – again – what we were in the beginning: sons of God.

This is very Good News, but somehow, we have been taught otherwise, as doctrines made by men without understanding, hoping to attain something the Lord never promised us – Heaven.

Paul is not too concerned about "where" this happens because he knows, by revelation, the Earth is our inheritance, and the New Earth is Paradise: our Promised Land. Paul is going into detail about the temporary body that we leave behind (which oftentimes gets in the way of our ability to perceive spiritual matters) to talk about the resurrection body (and future *oiketerion* residence) that is going to be superimposed upon our soul. People in Paul's day were very concerned about the disposition of their body (and we are even more so today), and though Paul is teaching us what will happen to the body, he is also teaching us not to be too concerned by what happens to the temporal body; ***you should be more concerned about where you will live for all eternity***.

Part of our problem results from translation errors wherein words were inserted to help produce clarity of meaning – or perhaps – the interpretation we think makes the most sense, yet at some expense to the original text. For example, the word "with" in verse 5:2 is not found in the Greek:[18]

> "καὶ (indeed) γὰρ (for) ἐν (in) τούτῳ (this) στενάζομεν (we groan), ³τὸ (the) ⁴οἰκητήριον (oiketerion-dwelling-place) ⁵ἡμῶν (of us) τὸ (-)⁶ἐξ (out of) ⁷οὐρανοῦ (heaven) ²ἐπενδύσασθαι (to put on) ¹ἐπιποθοῦντες (greatly desiring)" (2 Cor. 5:2).

"For in this we groan, greatly desiring to put on the dwelling place of us [from] out of heaven." Verse one talks about our current earthly oiketerion house which dissolves and verse two talks about our desire for our future heavenly oiketerion house which is eternal. Not once does Paul mention we are going in(to) Heaven to receive this new dwelling-place. We are exchanging the worn-out baggage of the old man for glorious new clothes for the man with better promises… and life eternal… in the New Earth! Now, play close attention to these words used in context with one another…

> "² καὶ γὰρ ἐν τούτῳ στενάζομεν, τὸ οἰκητήριον ἡμῶν τὸ ἐξ οὐρανοῦ ἐπενδύσασθαι ἐπιποθοῦντες, ³

---

[18] Greek text copied from the SBL Greek New Testament.

εἴ γε (if ye) καὶ (indeed) ἐνδυσάμενοι (being clothed) οὐ (not) γυμνοὶ (naked) εὑρεθησόμεθα (we shall be found). ⁴ καὶ γὰρ (for indeed) οἱ (the one's) ὄντες (being) ἐν (in) τῷ (the) σκήνει (tabernacle) στενάζομεν (we groan) βαρούμενοι (being burdened) ἐφ' ᾧ (inasmuch) οὐ θέλομεν (we do no not wish) ἐκδύσασθαι (to put off) ἀλλ' (but) ἐπενδύσασθαι (to put on), ἵνα (in order that) ³καταποθῇ (may be swallowed up) ¹τὸ (the) ²θνητὸν (mortal) ὑπὸ (by) τῆς (the) ζωῆς (life)" (2 Cor. 5:2-4).

Line by line, and verse by verse (in correct order)…

"Indeed for in this we groan, greatly desiring to put on the (*oiketerion*) dwelling-place of us (from) out of heaven, ³ if ye indeed being clothed not naked shall be found. ⁴ For indeed the one's being in the tabernacle we groan being burdened inasmuch we do not wish to put off but to put on (superimpose), in order that the mortal may be swallowed up by the life" (2 Cor. 5:2-4).

Beloved, pay careful attention to what is written! In our current estate, we are groaning as we wait while in this earthen tabernacle, and… if we are not found naked, having been clothed with salvation and righteousness – in Christ, a new *oiketerion* will be superimposed upon us so that mortality may be swallowed by the life.

What is meant by "the life"? Jesus told us, "I am the Life" (John 14:6) and Jesus also said…

"I am the resurrection and the life. He who believes in Me, though he may die, he shall live" (John 11:25).

John, the beloved disciple, and incredible theologian of the New Covenant, never implied that we will be raised up *or* taken up *or* go to *or* ascend into Heaven. Not once! So then, what does this mean for those who have accepted Jesus as Lord and Savior? Will we be raised up at the last day to fulfill the scriptures? Absolutely! Does any of this teaching affect our salvation? Absolutely not! And will we be raised up incorruptible in the resurrection? Most certainly; however, we will not go up to Heaven as our doctrines teach. Surely, we will be in the kingdom of heaven (that is at hand even now *within* those with saving faith) because **heaven is wherever Jesus is – and because Jesus abides within us – we are "already" in the midst of heaven.**

What, then, or perhaps what impact, then, does this teaching have to do with anything? It has everything to do with our original mandate from God – to have dominion over the earth!

Our first estate and proper domain is – Earth – and it's our responsibility to establish the kingdom of heaven here! The institutional church has been selling and promoting Heaven, but we must keep our focus and affections on Jesus only! Stop wishing for Heaven and start converting this planet from darkness to light – with Christ abiding in you – and with His covering upon you!

As we continue to sojourn upon the earth in earthen bodies or in resurrected glorified bodies –Christ will abide in us, through faith, and because Christ is in us, as a living deposit by the Spirit… the *kingdom of heaven and eternity are within us* as well.

"He has put eternity in your heart" (Eccl. 3:11).

The reason this does not make sense to most people is because we have never asked the Holy Spirit or Jesus why we were sent to Earth in the first place. To gain a fuller knowledge of "why" please read the books: "Dominion" and "Understand."

We were sent to Earth to have dominion – but the spirit of religion prefers to keep us in darkness rather than living in the truth of Christ! Beloved, our soul is in transition from that which is temporary to that which will be eternal; wherefore, we are being sanctified and proofed in this life before we are raised in the resurrection of life into life eternal and given new *oiketerion* clothing. Ponder this: do you want to continue living in that wretched body with death for all eternity – or the clothes of a pauper – or glory clothing? Do you desire to trade up? You shall "continue to live eternally" according to your measure of faith – even as you are living now, but I challenge you… do you want to dwell in Paradise as one passing through the flames just barely escaping condemnation, or do you desire to be granted places, regions, cities and nations as kings and queens of the King? Arise into your fullest measure – in Christ!

I was taught the Baltimore Catechism that our purpose on earth was "to know Him, love Him and serve Him," but this does not answer the reason *why* we were sent here to begin with. We were doing those things in His presence before we were sent here, so why were we sent to earth? Why is a function of "*what*" we are!

> "*What* is man that you are mindful of Him" (Psa. 8:4; 144:3; Heb. 2:6)

We are spiritual beings who were created to have dominion over the Earth as we sojourn in fleshly baggage (earth suits) having been sent to live upon the Earth in this manner during one season of eternity. In the resurrection, all fleshly baggage is removed and we become, once again, like our *spirit messenger* brethren in Heaven (*angelos*), as sons of God and mighty ones – to reside upon the New Earth in heavenly bodies. From out of the dust of the earth or from the depths of the sea, all souls will be raised in resurrection – in the judgment of both living and dead – either to receive a new body with glory, that is, *if* you have bowed the knee to Jesus *and* you hear His voice *and* you obediently follow Him, according to faith – or to receive condemnation resulting in eternal torment.

In the regeneration, all things will begin anew, and Earth will begin anew as it has once before, but before the regeneration of all things, the kingdom must be restored into the kingdom of God and His Christ. And we will be raised in resurrection newness for this reason: to finish our original mission to have dominion over the Earth. The Earth (as a kingdom of heaven) will be one step closer to being restored and united in oneness again, in the kingdom of God, before Satan was cast here wherein he took the glory of this earth captive – and many souls as well.

Jesus is coming back to restore the kingdom! What house (tabernacle) have you built in your heart for the Lord to dwell in?

> "Thus says the Lord: "Heaven is My throne, and earth is My footstool. Where is the house that you will build Me? And where is the place of My rest?" (Isa. 66:1).

Your heart is the place where the Lord wants "you" to build a house (abode) for Him to abide. This is the place where eternity resides... and is where you find rest for your soul. This is the place Jesus told us "We will come to him and make Our *home* (*mone*-abode) with him" (John 14:23). The heart of the unregenerate man is just a temporary staying place (*meno*) where God dwells, but the new heart of the regenerate man that has been born anew becomes a permanent abode (*mone*) where God abides and this, then, become His place of rest... and yours as well.

- *Mone* – (3438), occurs only 2 times (John 14:2, 24) said by Jesus, and implies a residence, "the place of staying," and corresponds to the English "manse" as a dwelling place for a minister.[19] This is the place where one abides (*meno*, 3306, to stay in a given place) in, at or within the *mone* (abode) of the Father's *oikia* (house) within the *oikos* (estate)[20]

"You had an original 'meno' (temporary staying place) in your heart, but what kind of house 'mone' (permanent abiding place)

---

[19] Strong's Concordance.
[20] Excerpt copied from "Dominion" section titled "Heavy and Wordy."

are you building in your new heart for God to abide?

"Beloved, I tell you the truth: whatever kingdom you are building now – in your heart – is the kingdom you will be living in for all eternity – because eternity is already in your heart!"[21]

This is why the Lord gives the regenerate new man… a new heart and a new spirit (Ezek. 36:26)… so that God can abide in us and work together with us as redemption partners to convert this planet from darkness to light. You soul isn't just saved through faith in Christ so you can avoid the pit – you are being activated to fight the good fight of faith and establish His kingdom in the midst of His enemies – in the place you dwell. You were sent here as a servant soldier… in which battles are won by obedient disciples on bended knees in prayer.

> "***God***, who made the world and everything in it, since He is Lord of heaven and earth, ***does not dwell in temples made with hands***" (Acts 17:24).
>
> ***God dwells in temples that have human hands***!

How, then, do we even begin to erase 2,000 years of false heaven doctrine? I guess, with just one resurrection of the living at a time, coupled with heavenly visitations that very many have already experienced in recent years.

Carry Me Home

So now, it seems true, that the resurrection of the dead to newness of life does not mention being raised into Heaven. There is, however, one parable account of angels being employed to "carry up" Lazarus (not Christ's friend) into the Bosom of Abraham, but as Biblical scholars can attest, Abraham's Bosom is not heaven

---

[21] Excerpt copied from "Gateways" section titled: "A Heavenly Perspective On Man."

(Luke 16:22). Well, has anyone ever been carried into Heaven? Yes, but…

> "Now it came to pass, while He blessed them, that He was parted from them *and carried up into heaven*" (Luke 24:51; italicized words appear in most, but not all, Greek manuscripts).[22],[23]

Jesus was '*anaphero*' taken up (not carried up) to a higher place where He is seated in majesty at the right hand of the Father in Heaven. Followers of Jesus Christ will also be "taken up" in the resurrection into newness of everlasting life to receive our new superimposed tent as something having come "from out of" Heaven, but to presume we are raised "into Heaven" as the higher place is something the scriptures never mention. Will we be "raised up higher" than this physical earthly dimension into a new spiritual reality? Absolutely yes… but into Heaven itself? Apparently not.

So I ask you… do you want the gospel that is – or the gospel you want? Do you want the God who is – or the God you want? I challenge everyone who wants to serve Jesus as the God who is, who is Lord of Heaven according to the Heaven that is, to do a word search to test and prove that what I am saying is the truth.

The Apostle Paul had an interesting experience that bears consideration.

> "I know a man in Christ who fourteen years ago—whether in the body I do not know, or whether out of the body I do not know, God knows—such a one was *caught up* to the third heaven" (2 Cor. 12:2).

---

[22] Strong's Concordance erringly lists the word as 339 – '*anakathizo*' which means "to sit up" but is actually 399 – '*anaphero*' meaning "to take up." '*Analambano*' (353) "to take up" is the word used in Mark's gospel, (v.16:19).

[23] Regarding the italicized words in v.51, there are "conjectures pertaining to the words and accents only or the division of words; the letters in the manuscripts are illegible and must be inferred;" Synopsis of the Four Gospels, Kurt Aland, German Bible Society, 14th Edition, 2009, p. xii.

Elijah "went up," Paul "was caught up," Ezekiel was lifted up by the Spirit (3:12-14; 11:24) and the Apostle John was "in the Spirit" on the Lord's Day, yet of these four, only Elijah remained (up) in Heaven. Saints of God, we can make an "example" out of one man, but we cannot make a doctrine of it.

Are there any other possible scriptures that might infer we go up in(to) Heaven? Only these:

- Went up – none
- Went into – none
- Went up into – once, regarding Jonah's prayer going up into God's temple (Jonah 2:7)
- Rose up – none
- Bring up – once, referring to Saul's séance request to consult the dead prophet, Samuel:

> "And the king said to her, "Do not be afraid. What did you see?" And the woman said to Saul, "I saw a spirit (*elohim*) <u>ascending out of the earth</u>." [14] So he said to her, "What is his form?" And she said, "An old man is coming up, and he is covered with a mantle." And Saul perceived that it was Samuel, and he stooped with his face to the ground and bowed down. [15] Now Samuel said to Saul, "Why have you disturbed me *by bringing me up*?" (1 Sam. 28:13-15).

Well, I was looking for just one person in the entirety of scripture that had been brought up or ascended up to Heaven, but this was not what I was expecting at all. The prophet Samuel was brought up, to be sure, but as a spirit (*elohim*) ascending "out of" the earth. There is only one scripture for this occurrence, so we should not consider making any doctrine of this either; however, it does give us an idea about where we "wait" for the resurrection, since Samuel came up out of the earth (1 Thess. 4:14; 1 Cor. 15:51, 52).

Thus far, I have researched 692 passages of scripture with the word heaven in it, as well as 2,974 various verb combinations that may be used as a means for us to get "up" or "into" heaven, and scrutinized every word spoken by Jesus on the subject, but the only person that "went up" is Elijah (Luke 1:17; Matt. 11:14; 17:12). What might this mean concerning Elijah? Perhaps a better question is: what was Elijah?[24]

So, I ask you, *how can we make a doctrine from something that is not found in the scriptures?*

Clearly, only Jesus has ascended into Heaven (Eph. 4:10) because Heaven is His throne, who Himself "has become *higher than the heavens*" (Heb. 7:26), but there is a first heaven that sits above the circle of the earth, and this heavenly place (earth) is His footstool – and this dominion of the earth has been placed under our feet in obedient service to Him who "sits upon the throne" (Psa. 8). OK, so, where does Jesus say "we may be"? Well, it's in the place you '*oida*' know very well (John 14:4). It's called: Earth!

> "Father, I desire that they also *whom You gave Me* **may** be with Me *where I am*, that they *may* behold My glory which You have given Me; for You loved Me before the foundation of the world" (John 17:24; NKJV).

> "Father, *what* You have given to me, I wish that *where I am* those also **may** be with Me, that they *may* behold My glory which You have given to Me because You did love Me before the foundation of the world" (John 17:24; literal Greek).

This scripture requires close attention. Begin by doing a comparison/contrast between these two translations and what do you see? There is a significant difference between the modern translation "whom" and the literal Greek "what." Indeed, there is

---

[24] The answer to this question may astonish you, so read "The Final Chapter" in "Gateways."

perhaps an eternal difference. "What" is the answer, not whom or where. Let me explain…

"What" Matters Most

John Chapter 17 constitutes the Lord's prayer (in contrast to the familiar prayer that He taught the disciples to pray, Luke 11:2-4) in which Jesus offers the following petitions: A) He prays for Himself (v. 1-5); B) general petitions for His disciples (v. 6-10); C) particular petitions He puts up for them (v. 11-16); D) that they may be sanctified (v.17-19); E) that they may be united (v. 20-23); and F) that they may be glorified (v.24-26).[25]

Jesus cannot contradict His own word – "Where I am you cannot come" (John 7:34) and "Where I am going you cannot come" (John 8:21; 13:33), so what is Jesus really telling us?

The "what" in this regard is the future glorification of believers, not *in* an eternal destination, but *with* our heavenly King wherever He chooses to lead us, as an eternal determination, from glory to glory, so as "to be with Him to share in His glory." [26]

Beloved, we struggle greatly with knowing where we go, yet we should be more focused on "what" the Father gave Jesus (John 17:24) because… the Father has also given this "what" to you and me. What we were given – is the Father's glory!

And yet, there are many old school fundamentalists and pentecostals who must remind us: God does not give His glory to another; to which I respond: He has already given it. Whether we choose to accept it and act on it – or not – is entirely up to you.

---

[25] Matthew Henry's Commentary, Volume 5, p.1149. Henry comments further: "Three things make heaven. It is where Christ is: 1) in paradise where Christ's soul went at death; 2) in the third heaven where His soul and body went at the ascension; and 3) where He is to be shortly and eternally;" p. 1166-1167.
[26] IBID; p. 1167, 4.2.

How dare we allow the doctrine of sin to triumph over the doctrine of grace!

> "And the glory which You gave Me I have given them, that they may be one just as We are one" (John 17:22).

As sons of men, *where* do we expect to have a share in this glory, prepared for us before the foundation of the world? In Heaven, on the Earth, or in Paradise, or wherever Christ is during the millennium, or wherever He resides after the regeneration of all things in the New Heaven and New Earth – or in Christ? *Regardless* of wherever He leads us, we will be with Him and in Him – in glory – in the kingdom of heaven! The heart-house of your soul makes this possible.

Men are sojourners in transition from glory to glory. We always have been – and always will be.

Now consider who wrote this, and when. The Apostle John heard these words and soon after Christ was received into glory, then approximately 50 years later the Holy Spirit inspired John to write it down; and then, about ten years after that, John was "in the Spirit" to experience Jesus in Heaven (Rev. 1:10) – while he remained upon the Earth as a man.

You really need to focus on this next statement: we can experience Jesus through dreams, visions and supernatural (spirit-normal) events, so that "where we are" is irrelevant to "going to" or "being" wherever Jesus is when you host His presence. Jesus is IN you! And heaven is wherever the presence of Jesus is made manifest!

"What" as it pertains to glory in eternity – is what really matters! Besides, remember this: Jesus is God and God is everywhere. What we really need is a paradigm shift to understand the spiritual realities of Who Jesus is, "what" glory is, and "what" the kingdom of heaven is, rather than narrow-minded theologies of where Heaven is, how it looks and who gets to live there.

Beloved brethren of Jesus, don't you remember why we were created? Was it not to give Him all the glory? And likewise, all creation in Heaven and on the Earth reflects the glory of the Lord, so then, it is not an issue of where – but rather – "what" and "Whom." So, why were we saved? Was it not to enter into the Lord's salvation! So now, hear His voice, follow Him and try to keep it simple. The Lord wants to release His glory in you to establish His dominion and the kingdom of heaven upon the earth in the manner He so intended – *through gateways of grace called men.*

Men are open gateways through which heavenly things pass through, A) to transform the earth and redeem it, B) to have dominion over all the earth, C) to take back from the enemy what was stolen from the Lord and D) then deliver it back into the authority of Christ so that His kingdom can be fully restored at the regeneration of all things.

Whatever spiritual seeds you have planted, including deeds of righteousness – will come back to you as an eternal inheritance along with any abundant increase credited to you in the hereafter as you continue to live out your fullness of days *upon the earth* in glorified bodies after the resurrection – because we are the host of earth. Earth is our eternal mission field!

The Earth itself is waiting to rejoice in this day (Psa. 97:1) and is waiting eagerly for the sons of God to be revealed (Rom. 8:18-21), so that mountains may sing and trees may clap their hands (Isa. 44:23; 49:13; 55:12). Creation itself will sing and burst into songs of rejoicing when the enemies of the Lord are utterly vanquished, when the Earth is redeemed and the kingdom has been restored, as it was in the beginning, before the great rebellion in Heaven spilled over onto the Earth. *And the sky, in that day, will be filled with rainbows of joy from the tears of the saints who suffered on Christ's behalf.*

> "Sing, O heavens, for the Lord has done it! Shout, you lower parts of the earth; Break forth into

singing, you mountains, O forest, and every tree in
it! For the Lord has redeemed Jacob, and glorified
Himself in Israel" (Isa. 44:23).

Rejoice and be glad! The time is coming when we will rule and reign as kings in the Lord's Dominion upon a glorified Earth that is alive with singing and rejoicing! So, ask yourself this: if you are raised up into Heaven after you die, then how in Heaven can you reign with Christ as kings upon earth after the millennium? Sadly, we cannot. You believe you are going somewhere, so just remember this: ***after the regeneration… we are coming back***! For indeed, the end of this age approaches quickly – and the kingdom of heaven has been at hand for the past 2,000 years, but the institutional church, beholden to the spirit of religion, has lulled us to sleep with a heaven-only doctrine to escape Earth.

"Rejoice and be exceedingly glad, for great is your
reward *in heaven*, for so they persecuted the
prophets who were before you" (Matt. 5:12)

Your reward is in Heaven, to be certain; however, this scripture has been used (as one of many) to justify the heaven-only doctrine, so allow me to use a common earthly practice to convey a spiritual principle. Most of us have retirement funds in an "off-site" account for your use when you get to the other side (i.e. retirement). Likewise, your savings and investments are not stored in your house or carried about your person; they are safely secured in banks or some off-site location. The same is true of your eternal "true riches" which are being stored "in Heaven" until the day of recompense when God rewards us for deeds of righteousness. We do not go up to get these riches.... they come back to us "ex- from out of" Heaven. When you retire, will you have to drive to Atlanta, Cincinnati or San Diego to get your monthly retirement checks? I hope not.

"Listen, my beloved brethren: has God not chosen
the poor of this world to be rich in faith and heirs of
the kingdom which He promised to those who love
Him?" (James 2:5).

Which kingdom does James write about? Is it not the kingdom that Jesus came preaching, "Blessed are the poor in spirit, for theirs is the kingdom of heaven" (Matt. 5:3).

Your citizenship is heavenly, to be certain, because you were originally made and created there (Gen. 1:26, 27), and then you were sent to earth from Heaven, and thus...you have a dual citizenship (spiritual and physical). Citizens of a specific country do not need to earn or purchase that citizenship if they were "born" there; it is their right to claim that citizenship, and since we "were in Christ before the foundation of this world" (Eph. 1:4) your true, rightful and original citizenship is in/of/from Heaven (yet we rarely act as if this is true). Regardless of whichever country you were born upon earth – you are a dual citizen – but your true and faithful allegiance is supposed to be to the God of Heaven! Here is the problem: we adopted the citizenship of "this world" that operates according to sin – which compromised our rightful citizenship (heavenly). This would be like living in America but choosing to denounce your citizenship by declaring your house and property is now an independent country. How absurd! Life on earth is a test to determine our true allegiance to the God of Heaven as we continue to live out our days – and sanctify our soul. When we entered into sin and rebellion, we severed our life from the Vine, but by grace through faith, we are adopted back into the Father's family through faith in Jesus and grafted back onto the Vine through faith in the Son (Gal. 3:26; Eph. 2:18; Rom. 8:14; 1 John 3:1).

On earth *is the kingdom of heaven that Jesus established "at hand"* within the hearts of those who, by grace through faith, believe Him and work the works of God – and therefore, we wait as sons of God to be revealed according to grace.

> "That in the dispensation of the fullness of the times He might gather together in one all things in Christ, both which are in heaven and which are on earth— ***in Him***. [11] *In Him also we have obtained an inheritance*, being predestined according to the

purpose of Him who works all things according to the counsel of His will" (Eph. 1:10, 11).

All things "which are in heaven and which are on the earth" – are being gathered together (summed up) *in Him*, Christ Jesus, even Heaven itself, "and *in Him* all things consist" (Col. 1:17). Our great reward is in Heaven and our inheritance is in Heaven, and His name is Jesus!!! And, since we know that *Heaven is wherever Jesus is*, then we should embrace His kingdom theology "on earth as it is in heaven."

Verily… we not only need a bigger boat, w*e need a paradigm shift of titanic proportions!*

It seems we have been waiting to ascend into a place that was never promised, yet enter into a place that has already been given to us.

We *are* the redeemed of the Lord. No longer self-ingratiated sinners, but by grace through faith, we *are* now mighty saints, servants and soldiers of the Most High God. So now, let's fulfill the commandments of our Victorious King! He commanded us to love one another and have dominion over the earth – *and dominion it will be*! But, you ask, how can we have dominion over the earth – *if* – we are going to be taken from earth and into Heaven in the rapture? Indeed, we cannot. Why? The rapture happens only once… on the every last day before the regeneration of all things… which is at least a millennium away… so let get this revival party stated! Stop praying for sweet by-and-by; start acting on: Thy kingdom come, Thy will be done!

> "I do not pray that you should take them out of the world, but that you should keep them from the evil one" (John 17:15).

We are here *upon the earth* for the duration! We are in this world, but we are not of it. Life on earth is going to get very difficult, but God always takes us to a place of grater grace to bear up under the trials and tribulations that will come our way. Pray... for greater grace!

"For in the resurrection they neither marry nor are given in marriage, but are like angels of God in heaven" (Matt. 22:30). We will not be in Heaven, but we will be like angels that are in Heaven. Think about this for a second... where will you be... and what manner of body will you have... and what greater works will you be doing (John 14:12)? Think about it! Comprehend this and '*suniemi*' assemble this truth in your mind with only the assistance of the Holy Spirit revealing this truth to you. That is what He (the Spirit of truth) is here for – to reveal the truth to anyone who will listen to Him!

Jesus did not pray for us to be taken out of this world, so then, what is the place He told us that He is preparing for us? We will get to that in just a moment.

What will you become? What you are becoming – even now! Are you being transformed into the image of Christ Himself? What will your mission parameters be? And if you are not being transformed by the sanctifying work of the Holy Spirit, then how can you be His beloved?

We struggle to find "God's will" for our lives when the reality of faith is this: be transformed through sanctification to become His representative upon the earth. Just get started, and yield to the Holy Spirit's guidance along this way. "Whose" you are *becoming* is all that really matters.

Jesus, our King, is Lord of Heaven and Earth. Jesus came preaching, "The kingdom of heaven is at hand." And again, I say to you, Jesus is King – and wherever the King is, so also is the kingdom. And if the King is in you, then the kingdom of God is within you (Luke 17:21) and, therefore, the kingdom of heaven is also at hand – with every step you take, and with every breath you breathe... heaven is being released through you. Jesus established the kingdom of heaven (Matt. 11:12) and He Himself is releasing heaven – and His glory – according to grace, through you, as His sanctified heavenly ones who "*host His presence*" upon the earth.

> "Do not be overcome by evil, but overcome evil with good" (Rom. 12:21).

Fear not! The Father is in you, also. And if the Father and Son are in you, heaven abides within you, and no weapon formed against you will prosper.

> "Do you now believe? [32] Indeed the hour is coming, yes, has now come, that you will be scattered, each to his own, and will leave Me alone. And yet I am not alone, because the Father is with Me. [33] These things I have spoken to you, that **in Me you may have peace.** In the world you will have tribulation; but be of good cheer, **I have overcome the world**" (John 16:31-33).

Jesus has already overcome the world and the prince of this world. Christ's kingdom will be on the earth – and we must fight to take it back. Behold, "I am training your mind for war."

> "The kingdom of heaven suffers violence and violent men *take it by force*" (Matt. 11:12; *violent men are pressing in forcefully and taking it for themselves*).

Saints of God, evil men have been forcefully and violently taking the kingdom of heaven (earth) for themselves and NOW it's time to start taking back this kingdom from the enemy who has forcefully pressed and advanced itself *against* the kingdom of heaven, but we must take it back, not with flesh and blood, or human will or determination... but by the Spirit of God (Zech. 4:7; 2 Cor. 10:4; John 1:13). We desperately need the baptism of the Holy Spirit to operate within us and release '*exousia*' delegated authority with '*dunamis*' and '*kratos*' power through us.

Demonic forces at work in this world to inhabit the minds of truthless men – and they are watching and observing the things of God with evil intent and hearts set on violence. "The kingdom of God is within you" is one of the keystones for understanding mankind and the world in which we live, but this kingdom does not come by observation… it must be an actionable decision a person makes to be "all in" according to Christ to receive this wisdom! Examine one word Jesus uses in Luke 17:20-21 to put this into perspective…

> "Now when He was asked by the Pharisees when the kingdom of God would come, He answered them and said, "The kingdom of God does not come with *observation*; [21] nor will they say, 'See here!' or 'See there! For indeed, the kingdom of God is within you" (Luke 17:20, 21).

The word "observation" is '*parateresis*-G3907' (from *paratereo*-3906) and always implies sinister intent and insidious observation (Luke 6:7; Acts 9:24).[27] The individuals Jesus spoke of were not looking to see the kingdom so as to enter in, but rather, they were looking for the opportunity whereby they may seize it forcefully for themselves. So, then, there are two types of watchmen on this earth: those with insidious intent – and those who seek to establish the kingdom of heaven upon the earth… according to faith.

How can observers with insidious intent have the kingdom of God within them? What an excellent question! The kingdom of God within you is comprised of two subsets: the kingdom of heaven and the kingdom of darkness. Both kingdoms are under God's authority and both kingdoms are co-manifest and operational in man, but we must choose… to declare our allegiance one or the other. The war between good and evil is being fought – within us – and our soul is the prize.

---

[27] Strong's Concordance.

> "But seek first the kingdom of God and His righteousness, and all these things shall be added to you" (Matt. 6:33).

Jesus came to establish the kingdom of heaven upon the earth by establishing a forward operating position as living truth abiding within His disciples. Former things have passed away; the former things of Judaism and the law have been fulfilled in accordance through Christ, and now the law which was only a type and shadow of things to come has been rendered obsolete because the true Revelation of God has been revealed – in Christ Jesus.

Jesus *IS* the revelation of God Himself.[28] What more could be written to convince you that Jesus and heaven are synonymous? Heaven is wherever the Presence of Jesus is manifested!

> "No one has ascended to heaven but He who came down from heaven, *that is,* the Son of Man who is in heaven" (John 3:13).[29]

How can Jesus, who is speaking this as a Man standing upon the earth, tell us that He "is in heaven" at the same time? This is impossible, unless… **Jesus Himself represents heaven itself**; and now we know why He told us the kingdom of heaven is at hand, because **the kingdom of heaven is wherever Jesus is!!!** Jesus (Himself) brought heaven (itself) to earth to establish the kingdom of heaven upon the earth!

---

[28] Read, "Image – The Revelation of God Himself."

[29] Many of us in this present generation grew up with the NIV translation, but this verse "that is in heaven" is one of numerous verses omitted by the NIV, perhaps (in the author's opinion) due to its lack of comprehension by NIV scholars, including also their "less-than" alternative way to translate "Lord of Hosts." The word "heaven" is listed 691 times in KJV and 692 times in NKJV (the author's preferred version), and in comparison to other versions: JBPhillips-240, Message-326, NET-503, Hallman-599, *NIV-622*, NASB-637, ESV-692, Amplified-703, NABRE-705, ASV-712, Youngs-721, 1599 Geneva-729, RSV Catholic-744, NRSV-787, RSV Anglicized-791, NLT-912.

> "And they saw the God of Israel: and there was under his feet as it were a paved work of a sapphire stone, ***and as it were the body of heaven in his clearness***" (Ex. 24:10).

So let me ask you this: since Jesus is in your heart through faith, then where is heaven? Yup, *in* your heart! And if you, likewise, are standing upon the earth just like Jesus did, with heaven in your heart, then where is the kingdom of heaven? Yes indeed… at hand, it is *in* your midst! Go ye therefore! The kingdom of heaven is at hand! Preach this good news and make disciples of all nations.

"No one has ascended into heaven except He (Jesus) who has descended"… is a heavenly truth that should send shockwaves of revelation through the church – that is – unless you already understand who Jesus is, and who you are, as someone who existed in God's presence before the foundation of the world. Yet it is the Lord's fourth point within this single sentence of exquisite importance: Jesus is standing on earth when He says, "Who is in heaven." How can Jesus be on earth and in heaven at the same time? This is not difficult if you fully understand Who Jesus is – and what Heaven is.

The kingdom of heaven… is wherever Jesus is!

Jesus is the King of Heaven, and wherever King Jesus goes – He establishes His kingdom. Jesus is the Divine Doorway through whom the kingdom of heaven is being established – through you!

Jesus never promised us Heaven, the apostles never preached it and our creeds don't teach it. Spend a year or a lifetime searching this truth and it will liberate you from the bondage of numerous manmade doctrines and ordinances which contradict what Jesus purposed to accomplish through you – since the beginning! You were activated by grace through faith to operate as Christians (Christ in you) and as disciples of Christ to usher in a regime change on earth – from the kingdom of darkness to the kingdom of heaven! You are citizens of Heaven but your rightful place and proper '*oiketerion*' domain is – earth!!!

The kingdom of heaven is neither up nor down – but in. And now it's time to let heaven out!

"God is in us. God is everywhere and He is already in us. We do not have to go anywhere or go into any special building in order to find God; the kingdom of God is neither up nor down… but in. The God who is all in all – is already within you. "The kingdom of God is in you" (Luke 17:21). "He put eternity in your heart" (Eccl. 3:11). Why do we insist on making this too difficult to understand?"[30]

God is everywhere, yet (sadly) most people are unable to find Him.

You are a citizen of Heaven, and yet… you are a resident upon earth as "the host of earth" for one reason: to have dominion over God's enemies and redeem the earth – in Jesus' name!

God is everywhere.
God is in you!
God is with you!
God placed eternity in your heart!
The kingdom of God is in you!
Dunamis power is resident within you!
You are the offspring of God!
You are the image of God!
You have a divine nature!
You were created a little lower than angels,
Crowned with glory and honor!
You are more than conquerors!
You are *elohims*!!!
And you were never alone!

When are we going to believe God's truth and start living according to it?

---

[30] Excerpt copied from "Image" section titled "The Message."

> The fullness of the Godhead dwells within you.
> The dominion of the earth has been placed under your feet, and yet...
> The choice is yours.[31]

Once we thoroughly comprehend our mission is not to escape earth, but rather, convert it from darkness to light and establish the kingdom of heaven HERE... then we will thoroughly comprehend why we are here to begin with.

> "Do not fear, little flock, for it is your Father's good pleasure to give you the kingdom" (Luke 12:32).

> "And I will give you the keys of the kingdom of heaven, and whatever you bind on earth will be bound in heaven, and whatever you loose on earth will be loosed in heaven" (Matt. 16:19).

Jesus granted us dominion over the earth and He gave us delegated authority with power to effect a regime change on earth. This is your primary reason for being on earth: have dominion – in Jesus' name! It seems the enemy has tricked us to take our focus off our true mission in life.

Man's Purpose On Earth

There was a war in heaven and Satan was cast down to earth. God created man in His image and placed him in a garden to begin the "clean-up process" and to take this kingdom of earth back, but man forgot who He was, he lost His way and then He forgot who God is, so Jesus came to teach us, reminding us who we are and to show us the way, and now we are of this new age generation whom Jesus will use to finish the job. We are world-changers for Christ, not for our glory, but to redeem and rebuild and restore His kingdom for the praise of His glory!

---

[31] Excerpt copied from "Commission" section titled "We Need The Mind Of Christ."

Palingenesia! Regeneration! *Regenesis*! Genesis again!

All kingdoms of this world will be removed. All of them! All kingdoms will pass away, including the wimpy kingdom of institutional christianity. He who has ears to hear, let him hear.

> "Then the seventh angel sounded: And there were loud voices in heaven, saying, "The kingdoms of this world have become the kingdoms of our Lord and of His Christ, and He shall reign forever and ever!" (Rev. 11:15; read the entire verse).

This is who we are now: sons of men. This is our mission: to have dominion over the earth. This is what we are going to look like: the glory of God made manifest in resurrection power within resurrected bodies - *as sons of God*. And what will the earth look like? As His kingdom *"on earth as it is in heaven."* Earth will no longer be a type and shadow of the true Heaven; earth will become an exact copy of heaven itself in the kingdom of God. Earth will become like Heaven – again. *Palingenesia* - Regenesis! The kingdom of earth will be restored to its former glory before the prince of darkness came and brought chaos and destruction to earth, temporarily taking earth's glory captive. Time has been shortened, the end of this age is upon us even now, and another age has already begun, but much tribulation will occur before the New Earth age begins, when the glory of resurrected man upon the earth begins, living as sons of God, just like angels that are in heaven, with Christ in us and resurrection power operating through us.

The new age of greater works – with greater grace – is about to begin.

Listen up! *God does not compromise His truth to accommodate our theology*!

The truth of this matter has always been made known, but we prefer to defend our doctrines about Heaven rather than defend Christ and advance His kingdom upon the earth. We seem more interested in escaping the dark realities of life on earth rather than changing it with the light of truth; and we are more interested in entering pie-in-the-sky Heaven than to accept our God-given responsibility to be the world-changers and dominion bearers that we were commissioned for and sent here to accomplish (and, oh yes, for our salvation and sanctification).

> "You are the salt of the earth; but if the salt loses its flavor, how shall it be seasoned? It is then good for nothing but to be thrown out and trampled underfoot by men. [14] "You are the light of the world" (Matt. 5: 13, 14).

Jesus is the light of the world, and He sent us here as His representatives – as the light of the world – to overtake the darkness with light. We are the salt of the earth, sent from Heaven, to season this planet with light and truth.

> Jesus said, "My kingdom is not of this world. If My kingdom were of this world, My servants would fight" (John 18:36; 17:14).

The earth already belongs to God, but "this world" which is under the demonic dominion of Satan is OUR proper domain that we have been granted dominion to govern, but we prefer to fight against one another rather than fight on behalf of Christ – and against all enemies of God. Jesus came unto His own and they rejected Him, and now, it appears we are falling victim to the same broken theology. If Jesus is your Lord, then it's time to fight like one of His servants!

The Jews wanted the kingdom restored upon the earth, but they rejected the King of Heaven, and now it seems the church has accepted Jesus as the King of Heaven in their hearts, but they are rejecting His kingdom of heaven upon the earth. Anathema!

> Jesus said, "Or how can one enter a strong man's house and plunder his goods, unless he first binds

> the strong man? And then he will plunder his
> house" (Matt. 12:29)

The kingdom of heaven is upon the earth. Earth is not Heaven, yet the kingdom of heaven *is* wherever Jesus is. And Jesus has already bound the strong man (Satan) so that we (with Christ in us) may plunder his house. The full resource of heaven's storehouse and war-chest is waiting for us to get this conquest started, which also includes angelic visitation.

Adam and Eve fell from grace on account of disobedience and unrepentance – into the reality of sin; yet we, as their offspring, may enter into grace – again – on account of repentance and obedience through faith in the last Adam, Jesus Christ. ***Through faith – we are able to enter into the reality of Grace – to begin anew!***

We are not going to Heaven, yet Paradise upon a New-Earth is available – *if* you want. Jesus told the repentant thief on the cross next to Him that "Today you will be with Me in Paradise" (Luke 23:43), and the Apostle Paul told us about his experience in the third heaven where "he was caught up into Paradise" (2 Cor. 12:4). So, what does Christ Himself say about Paradise?

> "He who has an ear, let him hear what the Spirit
> says to the churches. To him who overcomes I will
> give to eat from the tree of life, which is in the
> midst of the Paradise of God" (Rev. 2:7).

It seems the very last place we might think about going, after the resurrection, is right back here... back to the beginning... into Paradise. Well, the original Garden of Eden and the Tree of Life are still here upon the earth – and that is where we must begin again. *Palingenesia*!

Are we going to consult religious clerics, theological man-made doctrines – or the words of Jesus Christ Himself regarding our eternal dwelling place? Focus on Jesus! Our great reward is the "Tree of Life" in the midst of Paradise – *if* – we cling to the hope of our salvation, that is, Jesus Christ. Stop following blind leaders. Jesus only... you must follow and obey!

Now you know where we are going: back to Paradise. The Garden of Eden is the Paradise of God, where the "Tree of Life" resides, and we are going back to "that place Jesus left to prepare for us" in order to fulfill our mission and commandment mandate: have dominion over the kingdoms of this earth. Eden is a spiritual garden that cannot be discovered in the natural; this, again, is a work of the Spirit for saints to perceive and comprehend... and enter in.

Isn't it just like Jesus, who dined with tax collectors, prostitutes and sinners, to tell everyone the most important aspects of the kingdom of God to the least in the kingdom; He told the thief on the cross where Christ is setting up His kingdom (in Paradise), and His first resurrection appearance was to Mary Magdalene, a prostitute out of whom He cast seven demons – whom she supposed to be the Gardener in the garden, no less.

Paradise – on earth – is our eternal destination!

Many intrigued at this point may ask – but didn't Jesus say to the thief: "Today you will be with me in Paradise"? That is what our bibles tell us, but that is not exactly what Jesus said. The word translated "today" is '*semeron*-4594' and implies "on this day; at present hitherto" – as in *NOW*! In that moment... when the thief entered into faith, Jesus told him "*Now* you will be with Me in Paradise," not that the thief can actually go to Paradise because this place will not be available until after the regeneration, but the first part of this statement is what we need to focus on: <u>in this moment</u>... "*Now* you are "*with Me*"![32]

---

[32] Many death-bed conversions with genuine faith have happened and will continue to happen, but let me say two things: 1) we do not know the hour or 'now' of our death whereby the 'day' may come upon many unaware and suddenly without advance notice; and 2) the thief did not die instantly after his confession... he endured tremendous torment for many hours before the soldiers

When we come to faith in Christ Jesus as our Lord and Sovereign, we are no longer working against Him; "now" we are "with Him." We have all been tempted to sin and have freely entered into sin whereby we entered into spiritual death... "In the day you eat of it, you will surely (spiritually) die" (Gen. 2:17), but when you come to faith in Christ, when you 'eat' of the Son of Man and enter into a personal relationship in oneness "with" Jesus, you will surely (spiritually) live. Jesus is "the Life" and when we enter into Him, by grace through faith, His life enters into us! Our bodies will most certainly die, but we will never (spiritually) enter into that wretched place called Death.

By grace, through faith in Christ Jesus, you are "*Now*" in the kingdom of heaven because if you are with Him, then you are wherever Jesus is –in Paradise (as already now... but not yet).

> "***Now*** salvation has come to this house" (Luke 19:9).

But, how many times have we heard the faithful and elderly say, "I can't wait to go to Heaven" or "I just want to die and go home to be with Jesus"? Well... if you have been born again, then you are already with Jesus; however, if you believe that you were "born saved" and will go to Heaven when you die, then *this* holy truth from God should stimulate a conversion to seek the truth regarding who Jesus is. If you are ordinary, *you aren't going to heaven.* **<u>None of us are</u>**!
If you want the Heaven that is, then start living an extraordinary life devoted to Jesus.

It seems we have made a great many assumptions about who is going to Heaven, which religion is right, and where we go after we die. For thousands of years, religious leaders have debated the doctrine of salvation regarding who attains Heaven – and it has distracted us from keeping our eyes upon Jesus and the mission He

---

broke both legs whereby he suffered excruciating agony until he suffocated slowly under the weight of his own body.

gave us: have dominion over the earth. In all our fighting and devouring of one another, we never asked the simple question: does anybody go to Heaven?

All religions have made false assumptions, but this false assumption has been adopted by all religions without knowing it! We need ears to hear the Spirit of truth now more than ever.

We have been killing and conquering and tearing one another apart to inherit Heaven and Earth in the name of religion, but this must stop now! Jesus Himself is our inheritance. Focus on Jesus! But if you are not saved according to the true gospel of grace according to faith in Jesus Christ of Nazareth, and if He is not abiding in your heart-house speaking truth to you within a divine relationship that is born of the Spirit, then you are not even counted worthy to return here.

We do not go up to or ascend into Heaven – heaven comes into us!

How utterly foolish we have been all these centuries.

This revelation is just one of many false pillars within institutional christianity promulgated by the spirit of religion and the spirit of fear that is being torn down – with others to follow.

We do not go to Heaven; rather, heaven has come down to us in the God-Man, Jesus Christ. Believe Him! Hear Him! We do not go home to be with Jesus. Jesus is our home, our eternal place of rest – **and He made His home in us**! Read this again – and again… and again!!!

Home – Is Where Your Heart Is

If you have not offered your heart-home to Him as a sanctuary and Jesus has *not* made His home in you, then you are already among all people – utterly vanquished! Is Jesus the center of your life? If He is, then put Him in the center of your heart and redirect all your efforts toward loving Him, serving Him and giving Him glory.

There is yet another scripture to seek truth regarding this matter...

> "Let not your heart be troubled; you believe in God, believe also in Me. ² In My Father's house are many *mansions (mone)*; if it were not so, I would have told you. <u>I go to prepare a place [*topos*] for you.</u> ³ And if I go and prepare a place for you, *I will come again and receive you to Myself*; that <u>where I am, there you **may** be also</u>. ⁴ And where I go you know, and the way you know. ⁶I am the way, the truth, and the life. No one comes to the Father except through Me" (John 14:1-4, 6).

Layer upon layer, the Holy Spirit has been revealing this truth to me – that men do not go to Heaven, but here now is a scripture that seems to contradict all other scriptures. The Spirit began this teaching with a question, so I went back to Him in prayer and asked: what question will you ask me now? And He said, "Who is doing what and why?"

So I looked and I listened. "I (Jesus) go to prepare a place for you." This is the key to understanding our eternal destination. The "Who and what" have been answered by scripture, and as for why, Jesus continues... "I will come again and receive you to Myself; that where I am you *may* also be." And if "where" is not in Heaven, then where? Where else can we be with Jesus to go to "a place" that He is preparing for us? Get ready...it's a place called Paradise.

Jesus said, "Where I am going you cannot come" and then "Where I am, there you *may* be also." Jesus is telling us we cannot go and be with Him in Heaven because Heaven is not the future home that He has been preparing for us. We will follow Him in the judgment and be raised in glory when He receives us to Himself in the resurrection, so that "where He is we may also be." Jesus told us He desires "that we *may*" be with Him in glory because this is how intensely Jesus loves us, but He knows that this cannot happen in Heaven. Why not? Because we are "the host of earth" and residents *for* the earth and we were commanded to deliver "the kingdoms of this earth" into His hands. This is our mission! This is our eternal purpose in life! We will meet Him in the resurrection and we will be with Him forever, and yet, we are already with Him "***now***" – and forevermore. Nothing can separate us from His love.

We cannot go to Heaven, so Jesus brought Heaven down to us. Selah.

Examine closely: the word that Jesus used for "house" in John 14:2; it is '*oikia*' (3614) meaning a dwelling or house, and this is the same word that Jesus used for house in John 8:35. However, this is not the same word for "My Father's house" in John 2:16, which is '*oikos*' (3624) and "in Attic law *oikos* denoted the entire estate, while *oikia* stood for the dwelling only."[33] There are many abodes (*mone* -3438-dwelling places) in the Father's *oikia* house; however, Jesus is going to prepare a '*topos*-5117' (topography) place for us – a garden place in Paradise alongside His '*oikos*' estate for those judged worthy of life eternal. Let's segregate this sentence (for a moment) and look at is as several facts inserted into the mainstream of His many thoughts, whereby we are able understand several things:

1. The Father's *house* is the Father's dwelling place (v.2a)
2. There are many '*mone*' (*abodes*) in His house
3. Jesus is going to prepare a *place* "*topos*' (Eng. topography) for His followers (v.2b)
4. Verse 2a and 2b represent two distinct concepts within two separate sentences that theologians have erringly unified to endorse Heaven as our eternal home. [Note: chapter and verse notations are not "*inspired*."]
5. The place 'being prepared' is not the same place as the Father's house that *already* exists
6. And after He has gone to prepare it, Jesus will come again to receive us to Himself so that, ***now***, "where I am you may

---

[33] Vine's Expository, word study on house, OIKIA.2.

also be" (v.3) – in Paradise. The "place" is a *'topos'* garden in Paradise: the Garden of Eden (Gen. 2:8)
7. And another proof of this concept "men do not go to Heaven" becomes crystal clear in the next verse: "And where I go you *'oida' know*, and the way you *'oida'* know." Do men know the way to get to Heaven or the Father's house? Absolutely not. Only Jesus *'oida'* perfectly, completely and experientially knows the way to Heaven because He came from Heaven. So how, then, can Jesus tell His disciples, "where I go you *'oida'* know, and the way you *'oida'* know"? They don't. The host of heaven (angels) *'oida'* the way to Heaven, but the host of earth (men), absolutely not! No *oida*!

Man is completely unfamiliar with the things of Heaven and heavenly places, but can you tell me where, in this vast universe, is man familiar? Upon which of all the celestial bodies that orbit the "heavens" is man *'oida'* most familiar with? This is not a trick question, but somehow we have been tricked into thinking we are going to Heaven by a false heaven doctrine.

We cannot ascend into Heaven – so heaven comes into us!

One reason for this confusion is because our general understanding is that houses have rooms, which is true, but A) the Father's dwelling place has abodes; and B) Jesus uses the word *'topos'* that has been translated 'room,' but within the larger context, we need to see it as a topographic place within the *'oikos'* estate that surrounds the Father's *'oikia'* dwelling place.
The *'topos'* place that Jesus is preparing for us – is the garden you are cultivating in your heart even now!

Consider, now, *'topos'* as a type and shadow of the Jewish Temple with outer court, inner court and Most Holy Place. The Father's *'oikia'* Most Holy Place (the secret place in your heart) is surrounded by an inner court and outer *'oikos'* estate, and this future dwelling place for the saints is the *"topos" place* that Jesus went to prepare for us, which is distinctly different from the Father's house that is already established. Jesus left earth to go and prepare "the New Earth" as the eternal dwelling place for His disciples who hear His voice and obediently follow Him.

Our Heaven doctrines have been completely backwards because this is how man and "his religion" thinks it will happen. But – we are not going to Heaven to occupy an abode in the Father's house – They have come into each of us to make Their abode "with/in" us… and we are going to the *topos* place prepared for us. Heaven is the Father's house and He established a heart-house in us for the Godhead to dwell.[34]

Truly, men are tabernacles for the Divine!

Jesus left earth to prepare a place for us and He is coming back to receive us to Himself. Where is Jesus coming back to? And for whom? And why? This place He is coming back to is called earth, and we *oida* know it very well, and now it should also make sense "why" as well.

Jesus must still work the works of the Father before we can enter into His rest. There is a tribulation period, millennium period, a final conflict, the rapture, and resurrection yet to be fulfilled. We do not know what each moment will look like or if these events are in the correct order because not all of it has been revealed (i.e. we do not know what the seven thunders said to John). Yes, the saints will be resurrected into the glory of Christ in the clouds and there we will be received by Him, so that "where He is we may also be." But what is the place that He is preparing for us? The "where" is upon earth, in a place called Paradise, and the "what" is a glorious

---

[34] A greater understanding of this can be found in the Garden of Eden narrative wherein the Lord built "two" gardens; God planted one garden for Adam to tend eastward of Eden (Gen. 2:8) and "then" the Lord brought him into His presence to visit with the Lord and tend His Garden called Eden (aka Paradise; Gen 2:15) where the Tree of Life resides (Rev. 2:7). In Paradise, we will be given a *topos* place to tend six days, and "then" we will spend one day in the Father's house (as a type and shadow of the Sabbath) to maintain intimacy with Him. Read "Gateways" section titled "Paradox – Glory Alongside" to understand more about what you will be doing in Paradise.

banquet table and victory celebration that is prepared *for us* in the presence of our enemies.

Jesus said, "I have overcome the world" (John 16:33). Now, He has left the remainder of the overcoming part to us – His triumphant bride, the true and faithful church that worships Jesus in spirit and in truth. "As He is in this world, so are we." He told us to expect tribulation, but this contradicts our rapture theology. *Well, it looks like we need a new rapture doctrine and open-heaven doctrine to compliment our new-earth theology.*

Let me ask you ONE question:

1. If people go to Heaven when they die, then how does Jesus send you back to earth so that you may participate in the resurrection?

You cannot have it both ways. That would be redundant – and God is never redundant!

If you are already in Heaven, that means you are one of earth's four outstanding people groups, and if you are a martyred saint, you are only temporarily under the altar in Heaven waiting patiently for the first resurrection whereby Jesus will send you back to earth to rule and reign with Him in the millennium (Rev. 20:4, 5). Saints of God... by grace, we are all coming back! (Rev. 21:10, 24)

Listen up! We have made a great many assumptions about spiritual matters and heavenly things.

Listen up! Jesus is not coming back to make all new things... *He is coming back to make all things new - again*! There will be a new heaven and a new earth, as well as a New Jerusalem, and the dimensions of this new Holy City are cosmic in proportion. It has been calculated that the total square area of this city of 1400 miles long by 1400 miles wide by 1400 miles high is approximately 2 billion 700 million cubic miles of city – or roughly 15 times the surface area of the earth's land and water combined.[35],[36] This is roughly 69% the size of the continental United States or of Australia. Amazing! Are you willing to trade your birthright and inheritance for a meager bowl of stew like Esau, or are you going to man up and finish the race that has been set before you? Do you want to rule as a king like Joseph in Egypt or lament your slavery at the hands of your brothers in a country that is about to experience extreme famine? Do you really know what you are willing to forfeit on account of cowardice? Do you expect to inherit a room in the Father's house (which, as matter of fact, was never promised) – or do you desire an entire city that Jesus has spent the past 2,000 years preparing for those who obey His commandments?

O ye of puny confidence! Do what He tells you! Listen up – obey His voice and follow Him!

Grace, Lord Jesus, we need the Spirit of wisdom, understanding and grace for this living truth.

And now this brings us full circle to Jesus once again. Jesus said, "I am the way, the truth and the life. No one comes to the Father except *through Me*" (John 14:6). Jesus is the only way. Period! The only way to find Jesus is to seek Him as the one who stands as a Door in the gateway of your heart and bids you, "Come." We do not invite Jesus into our heart, but rather, He is already standing as the Door of your heart and you must enter into Him – on His terms

---

[35] Willmington's Guide To The Bible, p.686. This is true, if - it is in the shape of a cube. It could be a pyramid or a dome, so let's not make assumptions.

[36] This figure seemed unrealistic, so I ran the calculations for Rev. 21:16: the dimensions of the New Jerusalem are 12,000 furlongs long, wide, and high – each, a furlong is 660' and a mile is 5280' in length = 1500 miles, which makes the volume of this Holy City 3 billion, 374 million cubic feet. The surface area of the earth is nearly 200 million square feet, which means it is actually 16.75 times larger than the surface area of the earth. Truly incredible! Continental America (without Alaska and Hawaii) is 2.96 M mi^2; Australia is 2.97 M; the New Jerusalem is 2.25 M. This city is surrounded by a 240' tall wall for reasons I do not comprehend as yet, or why this city even needs one.

– according to Galatians 2:20. And once you enter into Christ, He leads you to the Father in His dwelling place, which is (and always has been) in the secret place in your heart, and They begin building a *'mone'* permanent home "with you".

But, you say, the Father's dwelling place is in Heaven, right? Yes, God's throne is in Heaven, to be certain, but let me ask you this... where is His house and dwelling place with many abodes (*mone*)? Get ready... Jesus said:

> "If anyone loves Me, he will keep My word; and
> My Father will love him, and We will come to him
> and make Our *home [mone] with* him" (John 14:23).

Wow! Did you perceive it on your own? *They come to us*! There are many abodes (*mone*) in the Father's house and "now" you are one of His (*mone*) permanent abiding places *in Him. The Father abides in you – and now you abode* with *the Father*. And now we have one essential key to unlocking many mysteries in the Bible...

With Christ in you, you are united to the Father – and you are home!

Allow me to reiterate this point. The word *'mone'* appears only twice in the scriptures!!! And both times (v.14:2, 23) Jesus spoke regarding our eternal habitation, not as a "where" but as a Divine relationship in which we abide "with" the Father "in one abode" to share with one another "the what of His glory" within "the secret place" of your heart (Matt. 6:18; Jer. 23:24).

"There is an interesting correlation between two terms that Jesus used in John 14 to teach truth with understanding regarding the kingdom of God: *'mone'* (3438) and *'meno'* (3306). *'Mone'* is a permanent abode and *'meno'* is a dwelling place to abide temporarily, which is similar in meaning to *'katoikeo'* (2730) as a quasi-permanent place to dwell while temporarily living as a sojourner (*kata*-2596-down + *oikeo*-3611-house) down on earth

(Eph. 3:17) i.e. dwelling under '*oikos*' the Father's estate."[37]

The Father dwells in everyone – even apart from faith – in the '*meno*' temporary staying place of your heart, but through faith in Christ, it becomes '*mone*' a permanent abode. This is what God meant when He asked: "Where is the house that you will build for Me? says the Lord, or **what** is the place of My rest?" (Isa. 66:1; Acts 7:49). Once you've made a permanent abode in your heart as a dwelling place for the Father, the "Now" has happened in you and your eternity with God as an adopted son or daughter is steadfast and true. Beloved, through faith in Christ – you are now home with the Father – and **home is where your heart is**! You have entered your rest.

Beloved, the kingdom of heaven is neither up nor down… it's IN!

This is the essence of the divine relationship! Through faith in Christ, Jesus abides in your heart and you abide with Him, and They make an eternal abode in your heart-home so that you may enter into His rest, and "now" – the Holy Spirit within you enables you and empowers you to live according to your mission mandate: have dominion.

It doesn't matter where you go or what happens to your earthly body (home, tent) from this point forward; wherever you go, you are already "at home" with the Lord. Eternity has happened and is now operational in you! Time is somewhat irrelevant at this point; whether you have fifty seconds or fifth years, you are "now" operating in eternity!

Heaven is just as much an eternal "place" as an eternal "state of being in the Lord's presence" – within your heart. When you are living for Jesus, then you are already walking in eternity!

---

[37] Excerpt copied from "Dominion" section titled "Mone and Meno."

Beloved, we have been waiting for something that has already happened – and all the while – seeking to go up into Heaven that is already within us according to faith!

Is Jesus the center of your life? And this is why hard-hearted, spiritually dead people will never come to know Jesus, or understand the things of God – or live in eternity with Jesus. **The undiscovered country called heaven is within your heart and you must open the door of the Divine to enter in. You cannot ascend to it – <u>you must enter in</u>!** It's your choice… so I hope you soften your heart to make the right choice, as an eternal choice, that you must live with, both now and forevermore.

Now, through faith, you have a permanent room in your heart where eternity dwells and the Father abides, so let me ask you: are you content with just this room… or do you desire to build more upon more in your heart, like a city on a hill or perhaps a nation like Abraham? When eternity exists in your heart, you have unlimited time… and space. Ask God to open the storehouse of Heaven so you can start building cities – in the name of Jesus!

The heavenly pattern for the Temple was given to us according to the design which was seen in Heaven, however… God does not dwell in houses or temples made by human hands. So, why did He tell us to build in this manner? So we may learn about the Heaven that is. Man is unable to comprehend spiritual paradigms unless he is shown patterns, templates and examples in the physical realm. The Holy of Holies, the Lord's Most Holy Place, resides within the inner court of your heart-home, and your body (as a temple, tabernacle and sanctuary for the Divine) represents the outer court and interface within the local world community in which you live. Wherever you go with your inner court, you are hosting God's presence within your most holy place (in your heart) and you are releasing the presence of heaven into the outer court (the world) – through you. God is in you! Heaven is in you! Go ye therefore – and establish the kingdom of heaven on earth. Is this beginning to make sense now?

The spiritual pattern for earth is Heaven, and the spiritual pattern for man – is Christ Jesus

> "From that time Jesus began to preach and to say, "Repent, for the kingdom of heaven is at hand" (Matt. 4:17).

Jesus never promised us Heaven, the apostles never preached it and our creeds don't teach it!

The enemy played a deceitful trick on us about 1,600 years ago. By getting us to believe in the heaven-home doctrine, we took our eyes off the prize: earth! The time has come for the "host of earth" to turn the tables on our adversary, Satan, and take this battle to the enemies of God – in the name of Jesus!

> "Your kingdom come. Your will be done *on earth* as *it is* in heaven" (Matt. 6:10).

"We all know the tribulation is coming that will be followed by a tremendous battle of flesh and spirit, but Christians would rather adopt a policy of appeasement, pacification and cowardice called "the rapture" to escape this conundrum, but the going up into the first heaven does not even mention saints continuing into the third heaven. Even though we are dual citizens of heaven and earth, the earth is our home; we are the host of earth. ***We were formed here, we were born here, we will die here and we will all be resurrected from here – and our responsibility is to have dominion – HERE!*** This is who we are and this is what we are supposed to be doing, but we keep trying to run away to heaven when we were commissioned to bring heaven to earth. Anathema! We have been commanded to bring the atmosphere of heaven into the midst of earth, just as Jesus did, in order to take back from the enemy what has stolen from our Lord and King, Jesus Christ, and our fellow brethren! Follow our Victorious Leader and let's get this revival party started because I want to kick some demonic donkey. He insulted my Daddy, he stole my best Friend's dominion, and he has been waging war against all my brethren – the sons of men – in slaughterhouse envy, beguiled hatred, villainous arrogance and heinous evil, but his time has come to an end – and now it is time for the sons of God to awaken and arise to take their place as watchmen upon the wall. It's time for us to remember who we are: we are watchmen, intercessors, worshippers, warriors, kingdom builders, and Holy Spirit empowered saints who are getting ready to awaken from a long slumber into the glorious moment prepared in advance for all of us – and we are the generation that gets to see it happen by making it happen."[38]

Hallelujah!

With every step you take and every breath you take, you are releasing the atmosphere of heaven wherever you go! Beloved, the earth is your birthright! Earth is your inheritance! When you come against the darkness, you are taking back what the enemy stole from you. We are partners with Christ in the redemption of this earth as your rightful inheritance among the saints. So, disregard the darkness; *kabash* the darkness and continue advancing forward with the light of Christ within you. Expose the darkness… with truth! Advance the kingdom… with love!

> From this time forward [*fill in your name*] began to preach and to say, "Repent, for the kingdom of heaven is at hand!"

Your heart-home is a garden in which you plant either good seed or bad seed. Either you are cultivating the kingdom of heaven in your heart with pearls of truth, or you are contaminating your garden with the deceitful tares of this world. You alone are the guardian gardener of your heart. This is not about your pastor or priest or anyone else… this is about you and your personal relationship with Jesus Christ, who desires to abide in your heart through faith.

Truly, we are tabernacles and sanctuaries for God Most High, through Christ Jesus, our Lord.

---

[38] Excerpt from "Gateways" section titled "Bifurcated Kingdom."

Truly, by grace, eternity resides within your heart – and the kingdom of heaven, as our eternal *resting* place, is located in your heart-home as well. So, I say again, what kind of a house are you building as a holy habitation for the Divine? Your body is a temple for the Holy Spirit and you are a living tabernacle for Jesus. Are you building up or tearing down the kingdom of heaven in your heart? Do you want to stay connected to your heavenly Father, through Christ, or do you still desire to do your own thing? Your eternal soul will experience emotion and pain in the hereafter, so, do you desire eternal *rest* – or eternal anguish? Again, I ask, what on earth are you doing here!!!

> "Heaven is My throne, and earth is My footstool. Where is the house that you will build for Me? says the Lord, or **_what_** is the place of My rest?" (Acts 7:49)

Men are houses for the Divine wherein heaven resides – and we are gateways through which heavenly things pass through, so that the kingdom of heaven may be established in our midst as we reside upon earth for one season of eternity and for this reason: to overthrow the kingdom of this world by overcoming *Satan's* dominion – with truth and love – by God's grace.

Now, read Gen. 28:11-17 to gain wisdom and understanding regarding "who" and "what" the house of God is.

> "So he came to a certain place and stayed there all night, because the sun had set. And he took one of the stones of that place and put it at his head, and he lay down in that place to sleep. [12] Then he dreamed, and behold, a ladder was set up on the earth, and its top reached to heaven; and there the angels of God were ascending and descending on it. [13] And behold, the LORD stood above it and said: "I am the LORD God of Abraham your father and the God of Isaac; the land on which you lie I will give to you and your descendants. [14] Also your descendants shall be

as the dust of the earth; you shall spread abroad to the west and the east, to the north and the south; and in you and in your seed all the families of the earth shall be blessed. ¹⁵ Behold, I am with you and will keep you wherever you go, and will bring you back to this land; for I will not leave you until I have done what I have spoken to you." ¹⁶ Then Jacob awoke from his sleep and said, "Surely the LORD is in this place, and I did not know it." ¹⁷ And he was afraid and said, "How awesome is this place! ***This is none other than the house of God, and this is the gate of heaven!***" (Gen. 28:11-17)

Jacob had a dream (in his mind) where he saw the Lord Jesus standing above a ladder with angels ascending and descending. The ladder was set "on earth" and its top reached to heaven. When Jacob awoke, he proclaimed, "Surely the Lord is in this place. How awesome is this place. This is none other than the house of God, and this is the gate of heaven."

Jacob was sleeping under the heavens with his head upon a rock – and he encountered the Lord. He was not in a building, but he called the place Bethel, meaning "House of God." Now, examine closely and see that "the place" within a certain geographic area is somewhat irrelevant, but the person is exquisite. Jacob had the dream in his mind, and Jacob's heart "is" the house of God, so… where is the gateway of heaven?

The gateway of heaven is through the renewed mind of man! (Rom. 12:1, 2)

God does not dwell in houses made by human hands…
He dwells in houses that have human hands!

We are the host of earth for a reason. *Men are dominion bearers and kingdom builders. We are gateways so heaven can be released through us.* Selah.

The battlefield between the kingdom of heaven and this present darkness – is within the mind of man. Our weapons in this war – are: A) the word of truth, B) the word of our testimony, C) the gospel of Jesus, D) the indwelling Holy Spirit, and E) His promise of life eternal with glory that already resides within us, through faith.

Now, look again at Acts 7:49. The house (tabernacle) we are building unto the Lord is our "new spirit man" that is being transformed through faith as a work of grace by the Holy Spirit. Our redeemed soul, that operates with a renewed mind, becomes a gateway of heaven whereby heavenly things pass through, but the new spirit man we are constructing in our heart becomes a "living stone" that is temporarily placed in Heaven until the resurrection ... which comes down to us "from out of" Heaven at the regeneration.

In simple terms: you are building your future *oiketerion* – the future house you shall dwell in.

So, where is the place of "the Lords" rest? Think it through... other than the body and mind, what is the third element of your person whereby we may enter into His rest? Is it not your heart? So then, where is your eternal place of rest? Is it not in the heart – which (hopefully) you have sacrificially yielded to Him, that is, ***if*** you have totally surrendered your soul (mind, will and determination) to Him and you have exalted Him upon the throne in your heart-home!

The reason we remain spiritually unconverted is because – our hardness of heart!

The spiritual paradox of the heart is: hard hearts won't let God in ... or out! The very walls people construct to keep God from getting in – become the walls that prevent love from getting out. The sad thing is: God is already in us, yet we somehow created an alternate reality that says He isn't... which may explain many psychotic behaviors... and many loveless, graceless actions.

The King of the universe wants to live in your heart to build "the kingdom of heaven" in you – and release the kingdom of heaven through you. This is really Good News! If you believe this, then allow the Lord to build and establish and expand His kingdom of heaven in your heart, through a renewed mind, with the mind of Christ reigning sovereign in you, and the mind of the Spirit flowing through you – and let's have dominion as we have been commanded.

Again, I say… we cannot go to Heaven, so heaven came down to us.

The undiscovered country called Heaven which sons of men cannot go to or ascend into has been placed within our hearts, by grace through faith, according to the Spirit of life in Christ Jesus. According to true faith, Jesus put heaven and eternity into your heart and *He* wants to have a Divine personal relationship with you – as *They* live in oneness "*with*" you. You are not only saved – you have been restored to "life anew" in the Father's abode (i.e. within the abode of your heart). Once you believe, then you are already living in eternity right "now." AMEN!

But, you say, how can Jesus rule upon His throne in heaven and in my heart-throne also? Read Zech. 6:12, 13 and Rev.5:9, 10. Jesus is both Priest and King and He can do whatever He wants in His kingdom. Jesus is God, so being in multiple places is easy since He is – all knowing, all powerful and everywhere, and He is the First and the Last, and also the Beginning and the End. (And besides, He built a ladder for us to get back and forth, with angels in attendance.)[39,40]

---

[39] There are some who are already thinking logically about this, so let me explain more. The second element of our *person* (the heart) hosts His presence, but the third element of our *being* (body, soul and *spirit*) is the "part" of us that experiences heavenly things as we stand upon the earth. Soul travel is a false teaching, but our spirit which was given to us by God to compliment our soul can travel within heavenly places, as the Apostle Paul experienced (2 Cor. 12:2), as have many people even recently, though not into Heaven, per se, but within paradisiacal earth. Also consider Philip *being* physically translated (Acts 8:39).

> "Just as He chose us in Him before the foundation
> of the world" (Eph. 1:4).

All things of Christ resided "in Him" before the world even began, and He lives in oneness with the Father to make the glory of the Father known – in this world – and in the lives of all men.

Oneness With The Father

> Jesus said, "Believe Me that *I am* in the Father and
> the Father in Me, or else believe Me for the sake of
> the works themselves" (John 14:7-11).

When believers operate according to the paradigm of "Christ in you," then we are able to make this declaration as well: I am in the Father and the Father is in me. The biggest problem Jesus had teaching us about the Father is – the Father is already in us. God is in us and with us.

The disciples asked Jesus, "Show us the Father." It seems the disciples heard the message, but still did not *'suniemi'* understand. It seems we have studied the same message for the past two thousand years, but we do not *'suniemi'* either because we have built a great many glorious cities and cathedrals upon the wrong hill. Heaven is neither up nor down, but in. The people of Jesus'

Consider the angels that ascend and descend on Jacob's ladder, and now consider the Biblical term for angel implies "messenger" and "spirit" or "spirit messenger" if you will. These "spirit messengers" were ascending and descending in Jacob's mind from heart to heaven and back again with spiritual messages and revelation truth "through the mind." Now consider, also, that "in heaven their angels always see the face of My Father who is in heaven" (Matt. 18:10), and yet they are also with us all the time as we stand upon the earth. There is only one condition whereby our guardian angel is with us and is also before our heavenly Father... and that is if we are all "in" the same "place" – at the same time (i.e. your heart). And finally... "are they not all ministering spirits, sent forth to minister to them who shall be heirs of salvation" (Heb. 1:4).
[40] The soul and spirit can be more than just distinguished, which Vine's seems to underestimate (Vine's, soul, p. 1068), they can be divided and discerned, just as Hebrews 4:12 teaches.

generation had actually seen God Almighty – and talked with Him! And if you have ears to hear, so have you. Jesus said:

> "I and My Father are one" (John 10:30).

> "And he who sees Me sees Him who sent Me" (John 12:45).

> "He who has seen Me has seen the Father" (John 14:9).

Jesus is God who came to us as God incarnate (in the flesh). Jesus was trying to teach His disciples – and every one of us – about the oneness the Son shared with the Father which is also available to everyone according to grace because… the Father is in us. The mysterious oneness of the Father and Son is available to every one of us! Once we grasp this truth and thoroughly comprehend the implications of God's presence dwelling in us – we are then, through faith in Christ, able to say – I and my Father are one! So perfect was this mysterious Oneness by Jesus in word and deed that He could say – I exemplify the Father – and He who has seen Me has seen the Father.

When we live our life like Jesus, people will be able to see "God in us" and, yet, if not for the sake of our character, mannerism and life of grace, then for the sake of the works themselves when we host God's presence in such a tangible way whereby the outward manifestation of God's presence is being revealed through us – in word and deed.

What, then, is the purpose of any building if the Father is already in us? That is precisely the right question to ask. The Father has a temporary place of staying that He wants converted into a permanent '*mone*' home in our heart – through faith in Jesus Christ. To be candid, we do not need to go anywhere or to wait any longer because the process of our salvation has been made complete in Christ; we are already – not yet; however, we must tarry in these earthen vessels through sanctification before we experience glorification in order to increase the size of our eternal house and estate. The type of "new man" house you are building in your heart becomes your eternal '*oiketerion*' habitation dwelling in the New Earth. How large or small your new man becomes – is entirely up to you.

There is a spiritual purpose for those buildings we build on earth where we gather once a week: to be united in oneness of praise, worship and prayer. Brethren, this has become the source of much broken-heartedness for me because… I have attended a multitude of churches where the worship program starts at a specific time… but worship never happens. The man show includes a pre-programmed agenda of music with singing that is systematically followed with religious regularity, but it doesn't look or sound anything like what angels are doing in heaven; theirs is done in reverent adoration, while ours has become a mere checkmark to get to the next item on the agenda. Let me ask you: when was the last time you saw and heard anointed rejoicing and thanksgiving with holy hands lifted up in loving adoration to our Lord and King? When was the last time you wished the worship would keep going and going because you entered into oneness with the Spirit? When was the last time you felt the heaviness of God's glory upon you that caused you to bow down in prostrate, obeisance worship? Why do we go to church or synagogue if all we offer up to God is obligatory lip service with lemming-like performance? Are we worshipping God or are we satisfying the rules we were taught to obey from other men?

Of the three reasons mentioned above for gathering together weekly, what do you think is the most important of these from God's perspective… and yet we do it the least? Our religious buildings should be houses of prayer for the nations!

> "Has this house, which is called by *My* name, become a den of thieves in your eyes? Behold, I, even I, have seen *it*," says the LORD" (Jer. 7:11)

> "Then He [Jesus] taught, saying to them, "Is it not written, '*My* house (*oikos*)[41] shall be called a house of prayer *for all nations*'? But you have made it a 'den[42] of thieves'" (Mark 11:17).

I could re-quote many sayings by Jesus in the New Testament as prophetic words that were uttered by prophets of the Old Covenant, *but Jesus wasn't quoting the prophets*... **He was repeating Himself!** When are we going to '*suniemi*' assemble these thoughts in our mind so as to *thoroughly and completely understand* that it is all about Jesus. Listen up!

There is only one way to ~~heaven~~ "the Father" and that is through Jesus Christ! Follow Him!

> "Jesus said to him, "I am the way, the truth, and the life. No one comes to the Father except through Me" (John 14:6).

Jesus taught us: "Believe in Me." Focus your eyes upon Jesus only – and nothing else – not even the Father. "Who" is the Name above all names?" Jesus!!! (Eph 1:21; Phil. 2:9).

> Jesus said, "And the Father Himself, who sent Me, has testified of Me. You have neither heard His voice at any time, nor seen His form" (John 5:37).

No one has seen the Father or heard His voice at ANY time! But we have seen and heard Jesus! Focus not on the Spirit, Mary, saints, sacraments or any man-made traditions or religions. These cannot offer you life eternal![43] Jesus only! Jesus is the

---

[41] Whenever Jesus uses the term house in reference to "the house of God" or "My house will be a house of prayer," '*oikos*' (estate) is used, but when He refers to His Father's house as His dwelling place, it is '*oikia*.'

[42] The word den is '*spelaion*' (4693, Lat. spelunca) meaning: a cave, grotto, or grave, as in 'the grave of Lazarus' said by Jesus (John 11:38).

[43] Do not misconstrue this teaching. When we reverence the Son, we glorify and honor the Father who entrusted *all things* to Jesus who has ALL authority in Heaven and on Earth, but the church has minimized Jesus in favor of

Resurrection. Jesus is the Life. "Jesus is the resurrection and the life" (John 11:25). Jesus is life eternal! If, by now, there remains even the slightest shred of religious dogma and tradition that you embrace in place of Jesus, then "the place" Jesus prepared for you – has now been forfeited by you. Jesus is jealous for you – and His glory He will not give to "any other." Jesus is Lord God Almighty; His disciple you must become – with Him exalted upon the throne in your heart!

King of kings and Lord of lords – Jesus – the Name above all names!!!

Jesus is God Most High, in Oneness with the Father… and there is no other God! And He is the only God anyone on this earth has ever known![44]

For 2,000 years, the church has been selling and preaching Heaven… but we have been promoting the wrong product. We should be preaching Jesus only – and Him crucified[45] – and the indwelling Holy Spirit to continue Christ's work upon the earth – through you and me.

It's all about Jesus – and God gets the glory!

Heaven is not the prize, it is not our focus, it is not our inheritance or great reward, or the place where we go in the hereafter - - - - Jesus is our focus, our prize, our inheritance, our very great reward, and our eternal home and country where we reside forevermore. Jesus is our first love, and when the church returns to her first love rather than pushing Him outside the church (Rev. 3:20), this world will be shaken to its very core and all will know

---

fatherology. "No one has seen the Father or heard His voice at any time," but we have seen Jesus! Seek Him! This is what the Voice (of the Spirit) from Heaven told us: "Hear Him!" In this, God is glorified: Follow Him! Jesus is our Lord and Master, now go, and do what He says! Jesus is Lord! Serve Him!
[44] Excerpt copied from "Image" section titled "The Lord Your God."
[45] Crucified, yes, but left hanging upon the cross, NO! Our hope is in the resurrection; look forward, not backward!

that Jesus is Lord – from least to the greatest. The earth is a spiritual crossroad and man is "the intersect" between Heaven and Earth; we need to understand that those things happening around us – are happening for a very good reason. We need spiritual understanding and divine revelation asap.

> Jesus said, "Unless you are born anew you cannot *oida* the kingdom of God" (John 3:3; *oida*, to perceive so as to completely comprehend and understand).

You must be born (*anothen*) *anew from above* by the Spirit in order to understand how the kingdom of God operates… whereby you are given a new heart and a new spirit (Ezek. 36:26) wherein the Holy Spirit is deposited into your spirit as well (v.27) to accomplish perfectly the specific work the Lord predestined you to accomplish. This is the working of the Holy Spirit: be converted. You are now an official representative of Heaven and a true citizen of Heaven as you sojourn as a resident upon earth to establish the kingdom of heaven wherever you go.

Now, read John Chapter 17 to see how this makes sense – as we operate *in oneness with God* while we are upon the earth "to make the glory of the Father known to all men" (John 17:4).

Listen up! *Perhaps the greatest mystery upon the earth is not that resurrected man may ascend into Heaven, but rather, heaven already resides within regenerate man and we have the spiritual capability, through the Spirit, to release heaven into this world in the same manner that Jesus our Lord did.*

He came as the King of Heaven, He established the kingdom of heaven among His disciples and now heaven continues to be released through all His disciples who acknowledge this truth: Jesus Christ is Lord of All – and we must therefore… live accordingly!

Jesus placed heaven in your heart, now, go ye therefore… *and let heaven out!*

Christ in you. Tell the world there is hope!

Stop trying to fix the world. Change it!!!

Now, imagine the Father's delight when the glory of God is released in '*dunamis*' power through yielded, fleshy-weak humans while His enemies stand opposed in their own self-made "kingdoms of this world" that they stole from Him. They killed His Son, but they could only trade flesh for flesh. And now, Jesus resides within you and me and this is why the enemy hates you, not because you are anything, but because Jesus Christ is everything. Jesus is all in all, and Lord of all – and Lord over all His enemies. As He said, "My power is accomplished perfectly in weakness" (2 Cor. 12:9). *His victory is accomplished in us and then it will be accomplished through us*! And what kind of reward awaits those who have sacrificed all on account of Christ? Read Rev. 14:13 and 20:6. So, what happens to the rest of us?

> "Behold, I tell you a mystery: We shall not all sleep, but we shall all be changed – [52] in a moment, in the twinkling of an eye, at the last trumpet. For the trumpet will sound, and the dead will be raised incorruptible, and we shall be changed" (1 Cor. 15:55, 52;

> "For the Lord Himself will descend from heaven with a shout, with the voice of an archangel, and with the trumpet of God. ***And the dead in Christ will rise first***. [17] Then we who are alive *and* remain shall be caught up together with them in the clouds to meet the Lord in the air. And thus we shall always be with the Lord" (1 Thess. 4:16, 17).

Through faith, we enter into the Lord's rest and wait – clothed in Christ. Death is just an intermission between one age before another age begins.

The scriptures never tell us we go to Heaven, not once, not even after the trumpet sounds when we are raised with Christ in the clouds. There is no mention by Paul (at this point) of the body or a resurrection unto judgment – either for those who have forsaken Christ or those with life, so perhaps we should consider carefully what is going to happen next – and why. Jesus said:

> "For as the Father has life in Himself, so He has granted the Son to have life in Himself, [27] and has given Him authority to execute judgment also, because He is the Son of Man. [28] Do not marvel at this; for the hour is coming in which all who are in the graves will hear His voice [29] and come forth—those who have done good, to the resurrection of life, and those who have done evil, to the resurrection of condemnation" (John 5:26-29).

The resurrection – includes judgment.

When the Lord returns, we will be in various states of being: some have fallen asleep, some martyrs have been received up into Heaven in victory, and some saints will still be awake (alive in the body). However, what happens to the vast majority of us who have fallen asleep? Where are we waiting and what are we doing? This will be discussed in greater detail in Chapter 6: we wait in Hades (no, this is not Hell; from a worldly perspective, your body is dead, but from God's perspective, your soul – which is who you really are – is still in a state of existence). A great number of Christians have been taught there is no such thing as soul sleep, and I agree, so let me put this in context because many people have asked the same question that is running through your mind right now: where do we go and what happens to us? Because Jesus is *alive in us*, through faith, those who have already entered into Him will enter into *His* rest *where* we wait upon the Lord, "Who has become the firstfruits of those who have fallen asleep" (1 Cor. 15:20). We are not "waiting" in the human sense of waiting, per se... because a day is as a thousand years to the Lord, so conceivably, those who have fallen asleep 6,000 years ago may awaken with the sense of only a few moments having passed.

Yet I have heard many saints utter, "I just want to go home to be with Jesus" yet they have somehow failed to comprehend – if they have offered their heart as a home to Jesus and He has made His home (abode) in you, then *you are already home* "in Him and with Him." We do not go home to be with Him – He came to us and made His eternal home in us! Eternity is in our heart! But if some people have not made a home in their heart for Jesus, then they have already condemned themselves to judgment before they even depart from this mortal life. The dead in Christ shall wait in peace, having entered into His rest, but I doubt unregenerate souls who rejected Christ will be resting – or waiting in peace.

Is an epiphany happening within your mind at this moment? This is the mystery of God that was hidden in Christ all along. Church, listen up! It's time to throw away the old worn out man-made, lukewarm, heaven-only doctrines and begin walking in the light of *truth*: **Jesus only**!!!! Believe in Jesus. Trust in Jesus. Rest in Jesus. Be raised in Jesus. Reign with Jesus.

Jesus said, "I am the resurrection and the life." Jesus is the resurrection. And Jesus is the life. We have life within us because Jesus breathed life into us from out of Himself, such that, the life within us is already a living testimony that Jesus is Lord (Gen. 2:7). All life came from Him and all life belongs to Him… which resides within His manifold expression that He manifests within this world. Jesus is life eternal. Jesus is our life, our joy, our hope, our truth, our salvation, our provider, our strong tower, our deliverer and yes, even heaven itself. He is our eternal King and country; wherever He goes, we go. We need to see Jesus for who He really is, not just as the Son of God, but as Lord God and Lord Almighty, who has All power and All might, as the Creator and sustainer of all life, and who is All in All. "And *IN HIM* all things consist" (Col. 1:17).

Wherever He goes, I go; wherever He is, there i̲ am… in the midst of Him.

For this reason, another book in the "Image Bearers" series was written to share kingdom truth with you regarding "the Dominion."

I cannot begin to describe how wonderful Paradise will be, as a heavenly place amidst heavenly places, which is perhaps why we defaulted by calling it Heaven, and in one sense, despite getting off focus (i.e. not keeping our eyes upon Jesus) and off task (not having dominion over principalities and powers on earth) the old terminology is still valid… the pains and troubles and torments of this life will be long forgotten. And, as the scriptures seem to indicate, this newness will be so wonderful that:

> "There is no remembrance of former things, nor will there be any remembrance of things that are to come by those who will come after" (Eccl. 1:11; Isa. 43:18).

> "For behold, I create new heavens and a new earth; and the former shall not be remembered or come to mind" (Isa. 65:17).

And now, for all people and all tribes and nations and ethnicity, the real choice is this – either eternal bliss *with* Jesus in Paradise (our eternal home) … or eternal torment in a hand-dug hell. Your soul is alive even now for all eternity… and this choice is very, very real… yet only *you* can make this choice by deciding how you are going to live – right now and forever more. If Jesus is your Lord, then tell Him now, even right now, and tell Him you commit your entire life to serving Him… no longer standing between two ways. Declare your sovereign allegiance to His Lordship as the Master and Savior of your eternal soul. Bow before Him, repent, confess your sins and be converted as a changing and turning away from your way – to walk in His way.

For some people, this earth will be the only heaven they will ever know… and for others, this earth shall be the only hell they will ever experience. Selah.

Read the entire Beatitudes to see what Jesus is really telling us – now that we know the kingdom of heaven we were told to establish as we live according to His truth – is on Earth.

> "Blessed are the poor in spirit, for theirs is the kingdom of heaven! (Matt. 5:3)
>
> "Blessed are the meek, for they shall inherit the earth!" (Matt. 5:5)
>
> "Do not fear, little flock, for it is your Father's good pleasure to give you the kingdom" (Luke 12:32).

Jesus is in Heaven – and Jesus is in us, through faith, as is heaven itself – and we are His image bearers to continue His work upon the earth, as gateways for heaven's glory operating within us and flowing through us to establish His kingdom "on earth as it is in heaven."

Some of the kingdoms and nations that are established in the New Earth are being built in your heart – even now. If you desire more, then allow the Lord to expand your heart.

Read "Image" to learn more about "who" you are according to "Whose" you are – and your wonderful declarations of faith as a child of the Most High God. This is who we really are when we live according to the truth. Read it till you own it.

Life is not about who you are – but about what you are becoming… as a likeness of Jesus!

Faith in Christ is something worth dying for. Establishing the kingdom of heaven upon the earth is something worth living for.

> "Therefore we also, since we are *surrounded by so great a cloud of witnesses*, let us lay aside every weight, and the sin which so easily ensnares us, and

> *let us run with endurance the race* that is set before us" (Heb. 12:1).

It's time now to start living like we have something worth inheriting on this planet!

Darkness hates the light! Sons of God, it's time to get to work! You are the light of the world!

> It is all about Jesus – and God gets the glory!

> "For *this commandment* which I command you today is not too mysterious for you, nor is it far off. [12] *It is not in heaven*, that you should say, 'Who will ascend into heaven for us and bring it to us, that we may hear it and do it?' [13] Nor is it beyond the sea, that you should say, 'Who will go over the sea for us and bring it to us, that we may hear it and do it? But the word is very near you, in your mouth and *in your heart*, that you may do it. [15] "See, I have set before you today life and good, death and evil" (Deut. 30:11-15). *Selah*!

It is not about you – it is all about He Who abides within you, namely, Jesus Christ.

Live by the Spirit. Love one another. Let heaven out. Have dominion in Jesus' name.

> "For nothing is secret that will not be revealed, nor *anything* hidden that will not be known and come to light" (Luke 8:17).

> "The church age is over… the kingdom age has begun."

> Go now, therefore… and live like you mean it!

Grace and peace to you, with brotherly love toward one another.

It's all about Jesus – and God gets the glory!

AMEN

4) Nigh, At Hand

> "From that time Jesus began to preach and to say,
> "Repent, for the kingdom of heaven *is at hand*."
> (*eggizo* 1448 – to make near; Matt. 4:17)

What did Jesus mean when He said: "Is at hand?" Did He use this exact phraseology as being unique to that situation only or was He pulling from other Old Testament utterances that He communicated previously to the prophets? We may never know by looking at the original texts because there are often translation and transliteration problems when attempting to communicate certain values said within a certain context that may have become misunderstood when passed back and forth between language barriers and generations. When this occurs, as in this instance, we should ask the Holy Spirit to guide us into all truth. So I asked Him what "is at hand" means, and with just one word, He answered: "Embrace."

It was not the word I was expecting, but it made sense as I contemplated it. Let me explain.

The best 1:1 comparison for "is at hand, to draw near" is Isa. 29:13 (5066) and Matt. 15:8 (1448) as complimentary texts within both testaments, but this does not bring us closer to understanding what Jesus meant by "is at hand" even though Matt. 4:17 and 15:8 employ the same word '*eggizo*' or as it's pronounced '*eng-id-zo*' (1448). It is difficult to tell whether it means:

- Has come close, to make near in proximity, in regard to space, place, time, person or event
- A contact has been made and established, as in spiritual heaven touching physical earth
- Is now here, as having been manifested and can be experienced by the senses (sight, sound, and can be touched "by hand" by reason of nearness and close proximity)

- Can be experienced as an intimate and intentional personal encounter, not as a chance encounter by happenstance or as an opportunity available without foreknowledge
- As in the King of Heaven making a decree that earth "now – is" the kingdom of heaven

Much of this discussion has already taken place between theologians in an attempt to place clarifying light between two very similar words. If <u>*the focus of the phrase is on the distance*</u> and *nearness* of this kingdom "*at hand*" as having drawn near '*eggizo*' (1448) as a lessening in distance, which the scripture seems to indicate, then we are well and good with the translation, but if <u>*the focus is on the subjects*</u> (heaven and earth) wherefore the kingdom of heaven '*eggus*' (1451) is nigh, as more attainable and closer on account of Christ, does this necessarily contradict the implied meaning? Not really, unless you think of Heaven as a physical place (only) instead of a spiritual reality not bound by space, place, time, persons or events. Such was the case of Vine's interpretation "at hand" as being an element of time, as something imminent[46] that approached and drew near rather than a spiritual reality exceedingly far and above the limitations bound by any physical reality, such as time itself.

You can come close, approach and draw near '*nagash*' (5066) to God, as Moses did upon the mountain (Exodus 19) and also, come into the presence of God (Ezek. 44:13) so as "*to come in contact with*" God, but this does not imply intimacy – it merely implies nearness and proximity. So, let me ask you this: how would you describe your relationship with Jesus?

Did Jesus invite us to enter into a personal relationship with Him yet do so without spiritual intimacy? Absolutely not! Verily, He wants to abide in your heart, as you abode with Him, and while He can feel your heartbeat, He really wants *you* to feel His heartbeat and deep affection for you, much like the disciple John felt at the Last Supper. The heart of man, it seems, is the best place for intimacy between God and man to occur.

---

[46] Vine's Expository, word study on "at hand, near" see Approach, A.

Perhaps the KJV (c.1611) was projecting a certain level of properness and propriety in this translation as would have been expected in Jacobean England whenever a servant beholds their sovereign whereby the lesser one greets the greater with a polite curtsey; today, it would be a firm yet formal handshake in American culture or a bow from the waist in Asian culture. Did Jesus want religious formality – or did He desire spiritual intimacy?

The Holy Spirit said, "Embrace," so with this term in mind, let's continue in this discussion.

It would be nothing less than anti-climatic for God to manifest Himself, as the Son of God who is the King of Heaven, to tell us the kingdom of heaven is at hand, and yet, withhold this manifest expression as something intangible, unattainable, unthinkable, untenable, untouchable, and even obstructed (veiled from perception) until a later date or moment occurs, which might be akin to being invited to your own birthday party without cake, candles, gifts or anyone therewith to celebrate. This, most certainly, is not the loving and intimate Lord Jesus that I '*oida*' know intimately.

If "is at hand" may be interpreted as "has come near" as a general nearness *apart from* personal experience, then we among all men are living with the greatest of disappointments; however, if "is now here" or "is here now established" is a statement of "being upon us now and is approachably manifest" which can be tangibly experienced, even embraced, then this is quite a revelatory moment in human history that seems carelessly overlooked or perhaps misunderstood due to some lack of spiritual comprehension or insight, much like living within a "*thoroughly open*" Heaven '*dianoigo*-1272' (*dia*-1223-thoroughly, *anoigo*-455-open) for 2,000 years yet all the while praying for the gates of Heaven be opened unto us in our times of great human need… when Heaven has been open to us the entire time.

And yet, Jesus may have simply meant: "I have established the kingdom of heaven on earth," which is intensified by '*gar*' (1063) a word that assigns a reason of explanation to the verb "is here, now is, at hand, has approached" to His bold declaration. '*Gar*' is most often translated as "for" as in "for this reason," so if we insert this idea into the flow of Greek text, it reads:

"Repent, for this reason (*gar*) the kingdom of the heavens (*ouranos*) has come near (*eggizo*)."

What would be the primary reason for the kingdom of heavens to come near? For what reason did Jesus come to earth this time that was different from all the previous 30 visitations?[47] Was it not "for this reason" that Christ came to earth as the Messiah and conquering King: to overthrow the kingdom of darkness (of this world) and thus liberate earth from this bondage, and *not only* "upon those living in the shadow of death" (Matt. 4:16), but the very land upon which they dwell as well? It is for this reason that we are called to repent: to become unbound to the darkness that surrounds us so the kingdom of heaven can be established *in our midst*. Man is so self-centric, narcissistic and narrow-minded that we only seem to comprehend the reason for Christ's coming... was to save mankind from his sin and take him from the earth and into Heaven, but (get this) Jesus also came, "to take away the sin of the world" (John 1:29). Not only does sin desire to have us, but "it" also desires to have this world by taking God's glory captive so Satan can exalt himself over the Most High. This was the third reason for Christ's coming to earth, as the Life – to offer redemption and life eternal to us, and the other two reasons are as follows:

> "I am the way, the truth and the life. No mans comes to the Father except through [by way of] Me" (John 14:6; to show us the way to the Father and by being the example to follow.... ***the Way***).

---

[47] Read "Image" section titled: "Theophanies."

> "For this cause I was born, and for this cause I have come into the world, that I should bear witness to the truth" (John 18:37; ***the Truth***).
>
> "I am the resurrection and the life" (John 1:23; ***the Life***)

Jesus came to restore everything in newness of life beginning with the new birth for man according to the Spirit and will end with the regeneration of Heaven and Earth at the last day.

> "Nevertheless I tell you the truth. It is to your advantage that I go away; for if I do not go away, the Helper will not come to you; but if I depart, I will send Him to you. [8] And when He has come, He will convict *the world* of sin, and of righteousness, and of judgment: [9] of sin, because they do not believe in Me; [10] of righteousness, because I go to My Father and you see Me no more; [11] of judgment, because the ruler of this world is judged" (John 16:7-11).
>
> And Jesus continues, "I still have many things to say to you, but you cannot bear them now" (v.12).

Even now, heavenly wisdom is being released for such a time as this – and heavenly resources are being made ready and available in preparation for the completion of "Christ's" mission upon the earth. It seems to me that any General or Commander seeking conquest over an enemy never travels without an arsenal and enough resources to accomplish the mission. If this is true, then how could we have missed this for the past 2,000 years? Perhaps it is because sin merchants and faith merchants, enjoined with the spirit of religion, made a lively industry of selling Heaven at the expense of Christ and His marvelous, amazing grace – and regenerative work in the earth.

Well, what's past is past – so now I implore you… let's move forward. Let's stop overly interpreting what it says and believe it in simplistic terms on the level of childlike faith: **the kingdom of heaven is here**, and with us, right here and now! *Embrace it!* Believe it! *Embrace Christ!* Live with this exceedingly great promise and heavenly assurance abiding within you, through faith – to change the world!

If you believe heaven resides within you, then by grace – through faith in Christ, let heaven out!

The kingdom of heaven has come down to earth and unto men – and the King's name is Lord Jesus Christ. Hear Him! Do what He tells you.

Jesus is the King of Heaven and Earth and He didn't just establish Himself as the bridge between heaven and earth; rather, He brought the world-changing atmosphere of Heaven onto earth and imparted this divine truth into the hearts and minds of His disciples to restart the regeneration process (in renewed minds) whereby men shall have dominion over the kingdom of darkness! But before they could get started, Jesus told them to wait fifty days while He binds the strongman, prepares the way of righteousness in the earth to advance through gateways of heaven called sanctified saints, and then release the most formidable spiritual weapon upon the earth: men filled with the Holy Spirit. You… are a weapon!!!

And this is why Jesus gave us the keys of the kingdom: to unlock, open up and unleash a holy army of righteous listening disciples who hear His voice and follow Him. Incredible!

Stop thinking about what Heaven means to you – and start thinking about what the kingdom of heaven upon the earth means to Jesus and the restoration of His kingdom.

Let revival begin – now! Let's get this kingdom party started – in the mighty name of Jesus!

It's all about Jesus – and God gets the glory!

Jesus said, "My kingdom is not of this world" (John 18:36). Jesus also told us, "The kingdom of God is within you" (Luke 17:21) and Jesus came preaching, "The kingdom of heaven is at hand" (Matt. 10:7). There is only one condition whereby all three of these proclamations by Jesus are consistent: the kingdom of heaven goes wherever you go. Jesus did not come to build a kingdom upon the earth, per se. Jesus created everything in the universe – and the earth already belongs to Him, but the kingdom of darkness upon this world is not His… at least not yet, anyway. Jesus came to establish His kingdom *in* us as a testimony against the kingdom of darkness around us, with the holy presence of Jesus residing within us, so that wherever we go, the kingdom of God and the presence of Jesus is being revealed – in us and through us.

The presence of Jesus – is heaven to us.

Selah.

One last thing to consider for those who may still be struggling with translations and meanings…

In Hebrew, the word 'near' implies: "to come near, or to be at." In Greek, the word 'near' implies: "has come near, to make near, or be at hand." However, if we were to translate the Greek meaning back into Hebrew, we might get something quite unexpected with the word '*qarab*' (7126) that implies: "to approach, to come up to" which is what our tradition regarding man's ascent into Heaven has taught us. Is this really so important to parse it in this manner? Well, yes, absolutely… especially if the inherent meaning of '*qarab*' is also the same word to imply the intimate drawing near for sexual relations between a man and woman, as something so close to the subject that it can be experientially seen, heard, touched *and embraced*, and in this manner, '*qarab*' and "to draw nigh" may thus be interpreted as: "it is here, it now is" … and in the present tense – ***IT NOW IS!*** The kingdom of heaven – is not there for us to come up to, but… ***"HERE NOW IS!"***

The kingdom of heaven 'concept' has been wrapped up within a predominately Greek mindset and consciousness complimented by a "heaven-only" eternal destination "lens" that appears to have confused the meaning of "is at hand, here and now" to a much delayed second-coming of the Son of Man, whereby we have been waiting "to come up to and ascend into" Heaven to be with Jesus Christ – *when in reality – He is already with us and "here now is"* according to faith, not saved for an eternity to come, but saved within – and operating in – eternity right here and now (in our heart) with full jubilant expectancy of the promised resurrection and the promised land of "the world to come" in the regeneration of all things.

> "For He has not put the world to come, of which we speak, in subjection to angels" (Heb. 2:5).

Jesus placed the subjection and dominion of this world and the world to come into the hands of men. Do you want the Heaven you want – or the kingdom of heaven that is already within you?

Jesus wants you to embrace the King who is – and embrace the kingdom of heaven "here now is," literally, "on earth as it is in heaven" within you.

Revival happens when revelation intersects epiphany to initiate newness through truth, change and oneness. When newness happens, then revival begins!

Be the head… and not the tail. Do you still want to be joined to the best the "old tail" has to offer or do you want to be part of the "newness head" to walk in victory with dominion authority? Soften your hardened hearts to believe and understand what is happening as "here now is… on earth as it is in heaven."

Revival will happen – and our defeated enemy hasn't got a clue what God has prepared in advance for this great and awesome manifestation of God's strong right hand being mightily demonstrated through gateways of grace called sons of God! Get ready... another Exodus is about to happen. The jubilant message of the gospel is this: Christ is victorious, and we have the victory with Christ in us.

Alleluia! Let freedom ring! Let liberty rejoice! Spirit anointed and empowered saints of the Most High God... we have a kingdom to '*kabash*' and overcome – in Jesus' name!

It's all about Jesus – and God gets the glory! AMEN!

And now we shall comprehend what Jesus meant by "is at hand" as being perhaps the boldest declaration that Jesus has ever made in regard to His Divinity...

> ***"Am I a God near at hand," says the LORD,***
> ***"And not a God afar off? (Jer. 23:23).***

Jeremiah recorded this prophetic utterance from the Lord Jesus. When we look up the meaning of "at hand" we see the Hebrew word 'qarob' (7138, coming from the word 'qarab' 7126) and it means, "near in place, kindred or time: – allied, near of kin, neighbor, them that come nigh at hand." [48]

Jesus is telling us with an impassioned heart exploding with love toward us in fervent hope that we embrace Him as Lord God and return toward Him with softened hearts. Jesus does not desire that anyone perish; He desires that we all be saved from the dragnet of judgment by coming to our senses to seek a new life that can only be found in Him through repentance. But it is vitally important to see these words of Jesus within the context that He spoke them – as words spoken to His kindred people! This is not Israelites only... but everyone. Jesus created us and we are all His kindred family... every one of us!

His salvation message was first to the Jew; He came to a people that He covenanted with, but they rejected Him; and even though

---

[48] Strong's Concordance.

He warned them about His coming and the ensuing judgment if they rejected Him, they refused to soften their heart and listen to Him. My heart breaks for the nation Israel because they did not recognize their Savior on the day of visitation; and now my heart breaks for His Bride, the church, who would not be able to recognize the Bridegroom if He were to sit on the front row and speak a word of prophecy in their midst.

Other than Jeremiah 23:23, there are only four times that '*qarob*' "is at hand" appears in the scriptures, and for this reason, we must pay careful attention to what the Lord Jesus is telling us:

> "Wail, for the day of the LORD ***is at hand***! It will come as destruction from the Almighty" (Isa. 13:6).

> "Alas for the day! For the day of the LORD ***is at hand***; it shall come as destruction from the Almighty" (Joel 1:15).

> "Be silent in the presence of the Lord GOD; for the day of the LORD ***is at hand***,
> For the LORD has prepared a sacrifice; He has invited His guests. [8] "And it shall be, in the day of the LORD's sacrifice, that I will punish the princes and the king's children, and all such as are clothed with foreign apparel. [9] In the same day I will punish all those who leap over the threshold, who fill their masters' houses with violence and deceit…
> [14] The great day of the LORD *is near*; ***it is near*** and hastens quickly. The noise of the day of the LORD is bitter; there the mighty men shall cry out. [15] That day is a day of wrath, a day of trouble and distress, a day of devastation and desolation, a day of darkness and gloominess, a day of clouds and thick darkness, [16] a day of trumpet and alarm against the fortified cities and against the high towers" (Zeph. 1:7-9, 14-16).

Read all of Deuteronomy 32 with attention to verse 35.

> Selah

Jesus came to His Jewish brethren as "a God near at hand" so they may draw near to Him, but they rejected Him (Zeph. 3). Jesus came as "a God near at hand" and they crucified Him on a cross, so that, through His death, He became the sacrificial Lamb to satisfy ALL requirements of the Law, whereby He made atonement for *all* sin thereby rendering the Law *obsolete*. There is no longer any need for temple or ritual obligations to be performed, or sacrifices, because *that* temple will never be rebuilt. Never Ever! Why? Because you... are the temple of God!

Why do you think Jesus allowed the temple to be destroyed in 70 A.D.? Why do you think He allowed a Muslim Mosque to be erected upon the very spot that prevents another Jewish Temple from being constructed? "God does not dwell in temples made by human hands," nor does He favor one hill over another. The entire earth is His, and Jesus desires to dwell within the temple we build for Him *in our heart* whereby we shall live with Him upon a holy mountain called Mount Zion in His holy city called New Jerusalem that comes down to us "from out of" heaven.

Jesus promised to come – and He did. Jesus came to embrace His chosen people with the kingdom of heaven, but they rejected their Messiah. All the promises that Jesus made to the Jews have been fulfilled – except the one pertaining to them leaping over the threshold. There are no longer any special promises for being Jewish, or Muslim, or whatever.... everyone now has the exact same opportunity for salvation *as anyone else...*

> "Repent... and believe in the Lord Jesus."

Jesus is the Messiah for all people everywhere, first to the Jew, and now to everyone... and if you have ears to hear, the Muslim also.

Jesus shows no partiality; He is just as much a God who "is at hand" to Ishmael as He is to Isaac.

What more could a loving God who "is at hand" do to prove His love for *all* His children? Allow Himself to be crucified a second time at the hands of sinful, hateful, doubting men? NO!

Peace in the Middle East is not about Jews and Muslims co-existing together in peace – it is all about Jesus, who is the Prince of Peace, whom they both reject. Their squabble is between nations that do not want to live in peace; the people of Israel and Islam say they want to live in peace, but they prefer to live within exclusive enclaves with religious, nationalistic ideologies that reject Jesus as Lord of all, who came to establish the kingdom of heaven upon the earth. They both want Heaven, but it grieves Jesus to think they are willing to kill one another to attain something that is freely offered to them through faith in Christ – and Christ alone.

The kingdom of heaven is at hand!

Christ in us – the hope of glory!

Either we have been so heavenly minded that we have become no earthly good – or so earthly minded so as to be no heavenly good. Focus on Jesus – not Heaven! We need to return to our spiritual roots and become spiritually minded in order to be of earthly value to Jesus and the kingdom of heaven He established within us... as His kingdom... on earth as it is in heaven.

It's all about Jesus – and God gets the glory!

5) The Five Keys

Like all faith journeys, we must begin again by going back to the beginning to find the trail of truth. "The mysteries of the heart no one can comprehend" so we must rely on the Spirit of truth to guide us in all righteousness and truth to bring wisdom, understanding and revelation so we may return to our first Love and high calling in Christ; and by grace through faith, let us continue to listen, hear, obey and follow the voice of Jesus as He Himself leads us in "the way."

What are the fundamentals of faith in Christ? What is our guarantee of life eternal? What are man's two primary missions? How do we establish and maintain a love and trust personal relationship with Christ? And to repeat what Jesus said, "Who do *you* say that *I am*?" We have been taught to believe a great many doctrines, but now we must begin again with the basics of faith. Being guided by the Holy Spirit, we must search the scriptures to see if what we believe is consistent and defensible by truth as recorded in the New Testament, not considering the way of the obsolete covenant but looking only to Jesus as the Author of a New Covenant way of life.

The Five Keys

By now, the faithful have listened to many teachings about various "keys" and the rolling of the eyes is expected because we keep hearing about keys and more keys for understanding spiritual things, but the same doors remain locked. The author does not pretend to have all knowledge and wisdom, but these five keys will help us remember the beginning, focus on Jesus, examine God's truth and return to the basics of faith to help guide us into the kingdom age:

1. You forgot who you are
2. You forgot what to do
3. You do not understand or know Me (Jer. 9:24)
4. You believed things not Mine

5. Obey the commands: listen, have dominion, and love one another

These keys are not intended to cause us to look backward, as that is not the Lord's intent for us, but we must remember these things if we ever want to walk in the destiny God predestined for us to live according to.

The True Bride Awakens

The church, in general, has believed in a great many things, but over time, she has changed her focus from her first Love – to herself. Self-referential, self-reliant and self-indulgent are not godly character qualities, nor are they spiritual attributes that the Bridegroom seeks in His bride, the church. It seems like a long time since the bride heard the Bridegroom's voice, but the Lord is calling out to her once again to see if the oil lamps are being made ready and full of revival oil. The true light will shine in the darkness – as gateways of grace release love, along with many heavenly things and greater works – upon the earth.

By now, it seems clear, the church needs to spiritually understand and reexamine the following:

- Have dominion, host His presence and love one another in brotherly love
- Establish the kingdom of heaven upon the earth as we obey the Holy Spirit's guidance
- Eliminate conflicting end times theologies that are inconsistent with New Earth doctrine
- Embrace the "come-near" presence of the Holy Spirit's invitation for global revival
- Overcome evil with good

2 Corinthians 5:1-10

It seems very odd, and even surreal, that I am writing this momentous revelation regarding why man is upon the earth and what he is supposed to do. Man, as Christ's image bearer, was sent to reflect His image into a darkened world and to have dominion, by taking back and occupying the territory that was stolen from the Lord, namely, the whole earth. But now it seems that, rather than man establishing heaven upon earth as he was commanded by God, our religious traditions have erringly taught us we will go to Heaven when we die so as to abandon this wretched earth.

Perhaps even now, understandably, I feel a bit like Noah who had a message to save many souls alive whereby he preached truth for 120 years only to see his friends experience the first washing of regeneration. Approximately 4,000 years later, a second regeneration took place upon a cross on Calvary and the washing "of blood" set men free from their own worst enemy: sin and death. The third regeneration began 50 days later at Pentecost, as a washing of the Spirit, but the truth of revival came into bondage centuries later to the spirit of religion and the spirit of fear by well-meaning religious clerics who, rather than starting anew, put band-aids on an old, worn out, obsolete religious tradition that only one chosen people group was intended to live under, that is, the Law, and this simply because they refused to listen to God's voice and heed His commands.

Man was created by God to live under grace – and nothing else. In the weakness of our human estate, God never intended man to live life apart from His presence. His mercy understands all too well that we are dust, but even dust must learn to listen, hear, obey and follow.

Man has a divine nature which is able to imitate the Divine, but because he cannot comprehend his weakness, or the reason that he was sent to earth, he theorized the essence of a sinful nature at work within him to explain the bad things he does that he does not want to do. This is "our" enemy at work against us because we were put into his rebellious kingdom, as the Lord's servant soldiers, to have dominion over his kingdom so as to create a new kingdom of heaven where Christ's righteousness governs the earth. We were created with weakness, not because we cannot accomplish the impossible, the inconceivable or the unimaginable, but because God never intended us to do it without manifesting His presence while we do it – and this, in the face of His enemy! We are the weaker things of God, sent to earth to reestablish His heavenly perfection while abiding within imperfection itself, having been formed from the very dust that our nemesis created when the war he started in Heaven spilled over onto Earth.

Mankind is the clean-up crew whereby God is taking the fight to Satan to overthrow his kingdom and dominion upon the earth. Man was never sent to wage war against flesh and blood, but to have dominion over Satan's kingdom upon earth by waging war against principalities and powers seated in heavenly places – and earth is one of those heavenly places, but Satan lied to us and tricked us into killing one another for the sake of religion, not dominion. Saints, there are two kinds of people on this earth: those that are being saved and those who don't want God or His salvation.

God already knows whose are His – and He also knows that some here upon planet earth are children of darkness who will never bow the knee to Jesus Christ. Christ has His – and Satan has his – and Jesus sent the Holy Spirit to help us discern all things by looking through the lens of truth to perceive who is who. It is really quite simple: the enemy hates God and hates the truth of God revealed through Jesus Christ and this enemy seeks to rob God of all the glory He deserves, including the dominion of the earth as a kingdom of heaven. In the kingdom of heaven, there is only yes and amen. No does not exist! Maybe is a noncommittal "no" waiting for a better offer – but there is no other offer. The host of earth is Plan A and there is no other plan. Jesus only! Serve Him!

This is the big picture gospel at 40,000 feet: we are servant soldiers sent to have dominion.

We were created to have dominion – and there is no "Plan B."

- Either we are following Jesus by the hearing of His voice, or we are not His sheep
- Either we are committed to understanding this truth, or we are not faithful servants
- Either we are willing to surrender all to do the will of the Father, or we are not His children
- Either we are all in – or we are all out; in between is an illusion and a lie of the enemy

Consider how Hernando Cortez came to the America's under orders with a mission to inhabit, occupy and defend – for the sake of Spain. He eliminated any possibility of a "Plan B" by ordering his men to burn all the ships after they arrived; there was no going back – and there was no other way. When Elisha was called by Elijah, he burned his wooden oxen plows to cook his oxen – and then followed Elijah to take his place. There is a moment when we surrender to a higher level of commitment when we embrace the "all in" model for spiritual obedience and success. When we remove Heaven as our "escape pod" destination from the table of eternal options for ordinary believers (the extraordinary exception being martyrs), then our focused priority will become, once again, having dominion over evil and the kingdom of darkness upon the earth as an "all in" new-earth paradigm for kingdom age living.

As a servant, you can be a baker, homemaker, plumber, accountant, school board volunteer, engineer, carpenter, travel agent, inventor, farmer, student, industrialist, or whatever skills the Lord has blessed you with – to be the light of truth in a world immersed in darkness. You do not need "a calling" or a "five-fold ministry" title to do the things which He has commanded us to do (have dominion), but we must not do this "dominion thing" in our own strength; we must host His presence *with* the Holy Spirit dwelling in us. What good does it do to overcome the darkness of this world without the manifest presence of God living within you – and moving through you? Many great civilizations and cultures, both ancient and current, have already conquered the known world of their day, but they did not host the presence of God while they did it. God wants us to host His presence and then stand in the presence of His enemy – while He accomplishes perfectly in us and through us, as His wonderfully beautiful and marvelous imperfect ones, the redemption of this world that He already accomplished through Christ Jesus 2,000 years ago.

We are not waiting on God – He is waiting on us!

Regardless of who you are or what you do for a living, our earthly mission is simple: host His presence, listen to His voice, have dominion, and, in the spirit of love, establish the kingdom of heaven upon the earth in the name of Jesus Christ! Comprehending this truth is the key to understanding the reason we exist. We are spiritual beings having a human experience, having been created as image bearers, and were sent from Heaven as the host of earth to dwell upon the earth for one season in eternity. When we have fully accomplished our individual mission, we will be rewarded at the resurrection, either for good or evil. When we have accomplished our corporate mission as servants obediently following Jesus Christ as our Lord, Savior, Master and Sovereign, then this earth will have been transformed from this present darkness into the kingdom of heaven as a reflective likeness of the true Heaven of heavens.

If you do not want to love and serve God, then you are a child of darkness and a slave to rebellion and destruction. If you do not want to be the servant you were sent here to be, then God considers you a disobedient goat. If you want to be a servant but you are more interested in building your kingdom according to the cares of this world, then God considers you a tare (weed). If you profess to know the truth but inwardly desire glory for yourself rather than give all glory to God, then you are a vainglory wolf in sheep's clothing. If you pretend to love God with pretend faith while pursuing selfish ambitions, then I dare say that you have not heard His voice – because if you had, you would be following Him and not "your" best laid plans.

Life on earth is not about you – it's all about Jesus!

How do we host His presence? Let Christ dwell in your heart through faith. Put on Christ. Jesus not only wants to abide within our hearts through faith, but He also wants us to put on Christ, as a new edifice superimposed upon us, who also puts upon us the spiritual garments of love, righteousness, peace, joy, holiness, truth – and praise. Without faith it is impossible to please God; Christ in us is our hope of glory, but above all – wear love like a garment as you sojourn through this life because in the end only three things remain, faith, hope and love – and the greatest of these is love. God is love. Beloved, we were created as His image to host His presence and to put on the garment of love. We are godly sojourners with Christ in us. The enemy hasn't got a chance, unless you walk in doubt, fear and hate!

What more can I say about this big picture? We are the host of earth and we were sent here on a mission, not just to do a job and then get transferred elsewhere, but to occupy and possess the "land" as redeemed territory in the name of Jesus Christ. We are servant soldiers who have been activated for priestly service to declare the kingdom of "our" King is at hand. (Israel is a type and shadow of this earthly transition from out of this wilderness into a Promised Land). The kingdom of God was placed within us and, through faith, we have been given the keys to this earthly kingdom, not Heaven but rather – the kingdom of heaven we were sent to build upon the earth. Let me ask you something – why would God give us keys to His kingdom in Heaven? Really? Is that what we have been teaching for 2,000 years? Utterly ridiculous! Look at the mess we've made of *this* planet! Consider this: why would Jesus tell us whatever we bind on earth is bound in heaven, or loosed, or forgiven, or whatever "on earth as it is in heaven"… unless He has given us the power and authority to do it? Our words upon earth have the power of life and death, either to build up or destroy. Jesus told us His words are spirit and life, and likewise, our words are either life-giving spirit-empowered words to regenerate life anew as something birthed by truth according to the Spirit of life in Christ Jesus, or unregenerate, man-centric, demonic words that do not honor truth, life, creation – or the King of Glory and Heaven, i.e. Jesus Christ.

Truly, we have been given many wonderful grace gifts and talents to build the kingdom of heaven upon the earth that Jesus established as a continuation of the Father's works (John 5:17, 20; 9:4). And "this is the work of God, that you believe in Him whom He sent" (John 6:29). For better or worse, we are creating an eternal kingdom upon this earth, not for our personal pleasure, but for God's glory! Anything we do that does not give God all the glory will be burned away in the ensuing Holy Spirit's fire – and that includes many of our pious religious benevolent works that we did for our own vainglory. Anathema!

What more could I say to convince you that the earth is our eternal home?

Shall I remind you how the dark-age church began to sell "Heaven" by indulgences so that many may attain Heaven apart from faith? Or how the medieval church built glorious cathedrals to host God's presence even though He does not dwell in buildings built with human hands? Or how the renaissance church adopted this false heaven doctrine as an intellectual ascent so as to ascend higher than earth in the hereafter, much like Satan himself? Or how the post-renaissance church created kingdoms and dominions based upon various doctrinal interpretations without understanding why man is here to begin with – being zealously consumed with advancing their religious dogma through conquest, colonization, imperialism, absolutism and hundreds of other isms – all in the name of religion? Or how the industrialized church adopted a man-over-nature theology utilizing science and mathematics and politics to solve the world's problems – from a man-centric perspective with eyes looking around rather than up? Or how the modern age created world wars, ruthless man-killing machines, deadly poisons and earth-annihilating weapons to justify our human-engineered ideologies as superior in every way to what God freely gave us through Jesus Christ? And now, we are in a new technological age where the entire world's information is available instantaneously 24 hours of every day (well, actually, it is 23 hours, 56 minutes and 4.1 seconds on earth – and within 13 seconds you can find out how long the day is on every planet in our solar system thanks to computers and the internet). We have enormous amounts of information available to us, and yet, we are rapidly sinking into an intellectual dark age because we are being taught to remember, but not "how to think." We lack the tools to comprehend truth so as to understand "what is" truth. We are being taught the things of God without being taught how to think like God thinks – from His perspective according to Divine truth and the Spirit of life. Truth is what this world has needed since Day-1 and love is the answer, but more than ever before… we need faithful obedience to the truth according to the gospel of grace and truth spoken by Jesus Himself – because Jesus is the truth of God who came as the revelation of God Himself – to tell us the truth and to model for us "the true way" we were originally intended to live life upon earth, as in the Garden: in truth, grace, childlike meekness, hosting His presence, having dominion and establishing the kingdom of heaven upon the earth by disregarding the lies of the enemy. This is your purpose in life – and mine also. Be the light. Live the truth. Love one another. Go ye therefore!

The institutional church has tried to establish this kingdom for the past 2,000 years, and failed, but now a new kingdom age has begun and a new generation is rising up with an insatiable hunger for the truth of God and an uncompromising desire to host His presence. The Holy Spirit will be poured out upon these ones the likes of which this world has never seen before – nor will ever see again – until Christ reigns upon the earth. The generation in Noah's day did not believe a flood was coming, the generation in Jesus' day did not believe He was the Son of God and Savior of the world, and now this new generation will no longer accept the passivity and complacency of this current obsolete church-age paradigm as it foolishly expects the rapture into Heaven without any regard for the billions of fellow humans left behind to suffer in bitter anguish because "they didn't have faith." Hogwash!

If a worldwide tribulation calamity is going to happen, as was prophesied by the Apostle John, then our understanding of all prophetic scripture has demonstrated time and time again that all cataclysmic tragedies can be averted because God provides a way of escape for all people from any dragnet if they repent, return to

God, and put their trust in Christ alone (consider the city of Nineveh, Kings Ahab and Manasseh, the Apostle Paul, and 2 Chron. 7:14). The Lord God wants us to have dominion over the earth and this alone may initiate or prevent the tribulation as a last-chance means to accomplish His will and purpose upon the earth. Jesus has already won the battle and the victory has been shared with us – but we must believe, listen, trust, and obey the voice of the Lord. There is no other way around this "kingdom of darkness" problem upon the earth. We are servant soldiers and priests and kings and fathers and mothers and students who were sent to have dominion.

Man does not have a sin problem – he has an "obedience to the rhema truth" problem that results in tripping over the threshold of offense whereby we tumble free-fall into sin.

Man simply cannot fix the dominion of darkness problem upon the earth if we continue to disregard the Holy Spirit's mandate to change us and transform us into the likeness of Christ – or if we continue to embrace our current Heaven doctrines as a running home to Daddy when He commanded us to make our home where He planted us – as seeds of righteousness – on the earth.

He commanded us to have dominion – and dominion it will be!

False Heaven Doctrine

When I first realized that we have been living under an open '*dianoigo*' heaven for the past 2,000 years, I became overwhelmingly excited about knowing God and His truth hidden for us in the scriptures. Under the direction of the Holy Spirit, I looked up obscure words and phrases to capture the essence of God's truth revealed *within* His scriptures, not by consulting any of man's teachings or religious doctrines, but by listening to "His" voice. Not long ago, the Holy Spirit revealed to me the truth about Jesus from an "all in or all out" perspective. It was then that I began to see Jesus for who He really is: God's manifest representative for the earth. And Jesus created us, as His manifest representatives, whereby He sent us to earth as His image bearers in His likeness to have dominion in His name. Verily, it is all about Jesus – and God gets the glory!

All of my writings have been developed layer by layer as the Holy Spirit's pealing back truth upon truth to show this present generation how to spiritually move forward in grace, truth, delegated authority, power, obedience and love. It is not man's wisdom doing it – it is the Spirit flowing through us to transform us into the likeness of Christ Himself. We forgot who we are (read Regenesis) and we have forgotten what we are supposed to be doing on earth (the Image Bearer series), but most of all – we have forgotten how to host His presence and operate His miraculous power made available by the indwelling Holy Spirit to yielded servants – through their spirit. We need to remember!

So, where did this false-heaven doctrine begin? As I mentioned previously, it was taught to simple men who did not have access to scriptural truth hidden within "sacred Latin" that no one else could understand, which is perhaps why we call this time period "the Dark Ages." No light!

Consider this: was Heaven ever mentioned in the Apostle's, Nicene, or Athanasian Creeds as an eternal destination for man? No – not once! All three creeds agree in terminology that we "shall go into life everlasting and the life of the world to come" but never do we "go into Heaven." Our dominion doctrine appears to be good for the first three centuries… and then something happened. What happened is beyond the scope of this teaching, since it is not the author's motivation to point fingers, but to awaken a sleeping-church giant that has been strategically positioned to begin a worldwide revival whereby we have dominion according to the love and truth gospel that Jesus taught us.

The church was created to be a giant killer… not a sleeping church giant.

Jesus did not promise Heaven, the apostles did not preach it and the gospels do not teach it, so why, then, do we embrace it? There are two possibilities, and perhaps three:

- Once Heaven doctrines began, no one wanted to take a stand against it... not even now
- Perhaps it was hidden until such a time as now – for a time of extravagant revival – until the vehicle for worldwide dissemination of truth was established (the internet) and the infrastructure was established in every nation, tribe and tongue (the church)
- An ignition spark of unusual revelation would be needed to initiate global revival (such as this book, and others like it, that talk about the kingdom age we are in)

We are living in just such a moment of human history that is remarkably similar to the Roman Appian Way which was used to take the gospel out of Jerusalem into every nation – and now the truth of Jesus Christ can be received into every home via the internet – with homes and communities becoming united together in oneness to have dominion in the name of Christ. The final great harvest can now be multiplied exponentially by the advent of the internet as long as it remains open without restrictions. (He who has ears, let them hear this warning.) There are no longer any limits or boundaries or religious hierarchical structures that can restrict this message of love and hope from changing the world as Christ determined. Forward this truth to everyone!

But in order for this kingdom age to continue, the church must be born *anew* (*anothen*). The church needs to focus its' full attention on Jesus Christ and no "other," and be guided by the Holy Spirit into all truth. Christianity is not an organization, institution or religion; Christianity is a parenting "organism" that passes on identical genetic material of the parent to offspring, which enables them to remain in life-giving relationship with their parent, namely, Jesus Christ.

That which is Spirit – spirit is.

A born anew church will function as a truth-loving, life-changing, and oneness-working body of believers being guided by the transformational power of the Holy Spirit that enables and empowers the church to walk in the love of Christ as He intended – and to love one another as Christ loved the church.

The only evidence to this transformation is this: the church glorifies the Bridegroom and gives all its' glory to Jesus Christ – and no one else. If any action or program or teaching cannot give all the glory to Jesus, then it is not operating according to the gospel of Jesus.

Back to the Corinthian text…

The closest scriptural text we have to "men go to heaven" is found in 2 Corinthians 5:1-10.

It is interesting that Paul writes this section within his fifth book and, yet, never mentions this theology before or again, not even in his subsequent masterpiece: Romans. Since this is the primary scripture that our current "Heaven doctrine" is based upon, is there another message that could be construed apart from the "Heaven only" lens that we have looked through for 2,000 years? Below, you will find the original Greek (with some KJV terms denoted to help navigate through the text), with generous explanations in the footnotes, as well as the author's presentation of a scriptural alternative that does not espouse "Heaven as our eternal home."

Whenever we read scripture, it is important to read just that, scripture, and not other people's expository, commentaries or interpretation of scripture (including mine) or biblical translation interpretations because we all come to the table with predispositions and biases that may cloud our interpretation – and most certainly our understanding. For example, W.E. Vine (Vine's Expository, 1975) did not believe in tongues outside of apostolic times, and he was Dispensational and believed in the pre-tribulation rapture of saints into heaven.[49] These biases will cloud his understanding and influence his interpretation, as it will for all of us. This author's bias is this: men are the host of earth (Gen. 2:1), Jesus is the Lord of hosts, and I am post-trib.

So, how do we know what the scripture says, especially when some terms are historical, cultural and some individual phraseologies by certain persons are rooted within certain time periods, theologies or philosophies? Well, the short answer is… we don't, but I know who does, because it was the same Holy Spirit who inspired men long ago to write the truthful words of God. And I say again… what is the Spirit saying to you? "<u>*You are sons of God*</u> when you are guided by the Spirit" (Rom. 8:14). The Holy Spirit's job is to reveal truth to you, because He is the Spirit of truth! We need to listen to the Spirit of Christ.

Literal Greek (2 Cor. 5:1-10)

We must first understand foremost why Paul is writing this message.

For 1,550 years, the Jewish Law was given to "a chosen nation" to walk in obedience with God. While it brought a written code of morality into everyday practice, it was poorly observed – and rarely exported into a vast Gentile world. In the fullness of time, Jesus came to render the old covenant obsolete by instituting a new covenant in His blood. It was the new theology of "the resurrection" that began to sweep through civilizations as the most intriguing element of this new doctrine "according to faith in Jesus Christ."

Jesus was resurrected from the dead. No one had ever heard of such a thing! It was mysterious and miraculous, intellectually objectionable, and quite liberating to people whose freedoms had become enslaved; they became free, that is, on the inside. The disciples of Jesus proclaimed this gospel as having born witness to Christ's resurrection who is now Lord and Master of Heaven and

---

[49] Vine's introduction, p.vi.

earth. No theology like this had ever been preached before. One King, one kingdom and one dominion – on earth as it is in heaven. No more lording over one another – only one Lord and one Master, Jesus Christ. Truly earth-shattering!

So, what was the resurrection? How did it happen? When did it happen? What happened when it happens? Where does it happen? And why? Paul was teaching the world about a new heavenly paradigm called the resurrection of the dead into everlasting life – and now 2,000 years later – we think we are so enlightened about heavenly things that it seems we know even less than the first apostles; at least they did not assume Heaven is our eternal home. They simply preached the resurrection of the dead unto life eternal and the world to come. That's it!

Paul often used metaphors as a way to convey deep spiritual truth, much like Jesus did with parables. Paul used various analogies to communicate the truth of the resurrection and his greatest metaphor is found in 2 Corinthians 5. This was not his first attempt to communicate resurrection truth, as we can see in his first letter to the Corinthians, chapter 15.

If you had to communicate the truth of "the resurrection" to a group of people with a radically different way of life, like indigenous tribes in Papua New Guinea, how would you do it? Would you use body paint or tattoo metaphors? Well, Paul is preaching to a paganistic Gentile world and uses various terms for "buildings" they could comprehend. He also uses the "change of covering" as an excellent metaphor (not necessarily clothing, per se) as something "put on over" the inner person. What metaphor you might use is entirely up to you…

Paul is not getting into a discussion about the nature of their person (mind, will and emotion) and he is not discussing the nature of their being (body, soul and spirit), nor is he discussing their eternal dwelling place – he is just trying to explain the difference between the earthly body (as a temporary tent) and the future spiritual body as a dwelling abode (future home) that changes as a result of the resurrection. It's kind of like trying to describe a scuba suit to an Eskimo that he puts over his parka before he has even seen an ocean or understands snorkeling.

It seems the earth suit keeps getting in the way of man's ability to perceive spiritual matters – and what man truly is! We are a soul within a house (body); we are a soul within a temple (tabernacle). The reason we struggle with this concept is because we have been indoctrinated to believe our body was given a soul when we were born, when in fact… our soul was given a body! Our soul was given an '*oiketerion*' physical house-body for this life – and our soul will be given another '*oiketerion*' spiritual house-body for life eternal. This doctrine of the soul departing the body (and going somewhere) is what Strong's and Vine's mentions repeatedly, yet erringly, because it is the body that departs from the soul.

Before you begin reading the selected text, allow the Holy Spirit to guide you as you read these passages, first as Greek-English, and then with "New Earth doctrine" understanding. Pay attention to: A) the primary Greek words (*oik*-), (*enduo*), (*demeo*) as Paul "constructs" the building metaphor of man's body and his future transformation, B) the highlighted words in ***bold italics***, C) the significant change in translation of (1736) from "being at home" (v.6, 9) to "coming home" (v.8) using the same word, and D) the monumental use of the word "habitation" (3613-*oiketerion*) in (v.2).

One major piece of advice: the key to understanding this message is the word '*oiketerion*' in verse 2. ***The focus of Paul's message is about the body***, not Heaven – as taking off one earthly home-body and getting another spiritual home-body in order to teach ordinary people about "the resurrection."

2 Corinthians 5:1-10 (Greek-English)[50]

¹ Οἴδαμεν γὰρ (For we know) ὅτι (that) ἐὰν (if) ἡ (the) ἐπίγειος (earthly) ἡμῶν ⁴(of us) οἰκία ¹(house) τοῦ ²(of the) σκήνους

---

[50] Greek text copied from the SBL Greek New Testament.

³(tabernacle) καταλυθῇ, (is destroyed), οἰκοδομὴν (a building) ἐκ (of) θεοῦ (God) ἔχομεν, (we have,) οἰκίαν (a house) ἀχειροποίητον (not made by hands) αἰώνιον (eternal) ἐν (in) τοῖς (the) οὐρανοῖς (heavens). ² καὶ (Indeed) γὰρ (for) ἐν (in) τούτῳ (this) στενάζομεν, (we groan), τὸ ³(the) οἰκητήριον ⁴(oiketerion-dwelling-place) ἡμῶν ⁵(of us) τὸ (-) ἐξ ⁶(out of) οὐρανοῦ ⁷(heaven) ἐπενδύσασθαι ²(to put on) ἐπιποθοῦντες, ¹(greatly desiring), ³εἴ γε (if) καὶ (indeed) ἐνδυσάμενοι (being clothed) οὐ (not) γυμνοὶ (naked) εὑρεθησόμεθα (we shall be found). ⁴ καὶ γὰρ (For indeed) οἱ ²(the) [ones] ὄντες ³(being) ἐν ⁴(in) τῷ ⁵(the) σκήνει ⁶(tabernacle) στενάζομεν ¹(we groan) βαρούμενοι, (being burdened,) ἐφ' (inasmuch) ᾧ (as) οὐ θέλομεν (we do not wish) ἐκδύσασθαι (to put off) ἀλλ' (but) ἐπενδύσασθαι, (to put on), ἵνα (in order that) καταποθῇ ³(may be swallowed up) τὸ ¹(the) θνητὸν ²(mortal) ὑπὸ (by) τῆς (the) ζωῆς (life). ⁵ ὁ (Now) δὲ (the) [one] κατεργασάμενος (having wrought) ἡμᾶς (us) εἰς (for) αὐτὸ τοῦτο (this very thing) θεός, [is] (God,) ὁ (the) [one] δοὺς (having given) ἡμῖν (to us) τὸν (the) ἀρραβῶνα (earnest) τοῦ (of the) πνεύματος (Spirit). ⁶ Θαρροῦντες (being of good cheer) οὖν (therefore) πάντοτε (always) καὶ (and) εἰδότες (knowing) ὅτι (that) ἐνδημοῦντες (being at home) ἐν (in) τῷ (the) σώματι (body) ἐκδημοῦμεν (we are away from home) ἀπὸ (from) τοῦ (the) κυρίου; (Lord); ⁷ διὰ ²(through) πίστεως ³(faith) γὰρ ¹(for) περιπατοῦμεν, (we walk), οὐ (not) διὰ (through) εἴδους; (appearances;) — ⁸ θαρροῦμεν (We are of good cheer) δὲ (then) καὶ (and) εὐδοκοῦμεν (think it good) μᾶλλον (rather) ἐκδημῆσαι (to go away from home) ἐκ (out of) τοῦ (the) σώματος (body) καὶ (and) ἐνδημῆσαι (to come home) πρὸς (to) τὸν (the) κύριον (Lord)· ⁹ διὸ (Wherefore) καὶ (also) φιλοτιμούμεθα, (we are ambitious), εἴτε (whether) ἐνδημοῦντες (being at home) εἴτε (or) ἐκδημοῦντες, (being away from home), εὐάρεστοι (well-pleasing) αὐτῷ (to him) εἶναι (to be). ¹⁰ τοὺς (-) γὰρ (for) πάντας ²(all) ἡμᾶς ³(us) φανερωθῆναι ⁴(to be manifested) δεῖ ¹(it behooves) ἔμπροσθεν (before) τοῦ (the) βήματος (tribunal) τοῦ (of) Χριστοῦ, (Christ), ἵνα (in order that) κομίσηται ²(may receive) ἕκαστος ¹(each one) τὰ (the things) διὰ (through) τοῦ (the) σώματος (body)

πρὸς (according to) ἃ (what things) ἔπραξεν, (be practiced), εἴτε (either) ἀγαθὸν (good) εἴτε (or) φαῦλον (worthless).[51]

Line by line, verse by verse.

[1] For we know that if the earthly "house (3614-*oikia*) of the tabernacle (4636-temporary tent) of us" is destroyed, a building (3619-*oikodome*)[52] (ἐκ) ~~of~~ from God we have, a house (3614-*oikia*) not made by hands eternal in the heavens (3772).
[2] Indeed for in this, we groan, "greatly desiring to put on (1902-*ependuomai*)[53] the (3613-*oiketerion*)[54] habitation of us" (*ex*) *from out of* heaven,
[3] if indeed ~~being clothed~~ *entering into* (1746-*enduo*)[55] not naked we shall be found.
[4] For indeed "we groan, the ones being in the tabernacle (4636-temporary tent) being burdened", inasmuch as we do not wish to

---

[51] Parallel New Testament in Greek and English; Zondervan Corporation; 1975.
[52] '*Oikodome*-3614' is a combination of two words: *oikos*-house + *doma*-rooftop (or house-covering) and can be figuratively used to describe Heaven as our spiritual covering. *Oikodome* denotes "a building, or edification, both literal (Matt. 24:1; Mk. 13:1-2) and figuratively (Rom. 14:19, 15:2); and it is also used of the believer's resurrection body (2 Cor. 5:1)." Strong's Concordance. This statement by Strong's is problematic since "the resurrection of the dead" which occurs 14 times by Jesus and the Apostles makes no mention of the body; the soul is raised in resurrection, not the body!
[53] (1902-*ependuomai*-2x) from 1909 (epi- is a **_superimposition_**, over, upon) and 1746 (enduo-to enter into, get into) with the idea of slipping into and superimposing over/ upon a new outer garment or clothing (i.e. body).
[54] (3613-*oiketerion*) is a very interesting word; it is a combination of two words (*oiketer*- "an inhabitant" + *oikos*- "a dwelling") which means more than just a habitation, residence or house… **it implies the inhabitant and the habitation are – one and the same.** The person and the dwelling "co-habit" the same space and place… in oneness. Translated as "residence, habitation," this word has escaped notice as the key to interpret this scripture, which Paul uses quite strategically. This word is mentioned only one other time, in Jude 6, to describe the heavenly habitation and residence of angels that some angels deserted, which we know - is Heaven, yet Paul is inferring man's habitation-residence for the host of earth (men) is – earth, for he makes no other claims whatsoever. Likewise, the angels who abandoned their "heavenly habitation" await judgment, and likewise so also men will await judgment when all will stand – and be present before – the judgment seat of Christ (v.10).
[55] (1746-*enduo*) "to sink into, to enter into, to get into." Strong's Concordance.

put off but to put on *over* (*ekduo*-1562 but to *ependuomai*-1902) [56], in order that "the mortal may be swallowed up by the life."
⁵ Now the [one] having wrought (2716)[57] us for this very thing [is] God, the [one] having given to us the earnest (728)[58] of the Spirit.
⁶ being ~~of good cheer~~ (2292-confident) therefore always and knowing 'being at home' (1736-*endemeo*)[59] in the body (4983)[60] 'we are away from home' (1553-*ekdemeo*)[61] *from* (ἀπὸ-575-*apo*-away from something near) the Lord;

---

[56] (1562-*ekduo*) to sink out of, strip, take off from, unclothe; figuratively, of putting off the body at death (the believer's state of being unclothed does not refer to the body in the grave but to the spirit, which awaits the "body of glory" at the resurrection." Strong's Concordance.

[57] (2716-*katergazomai*) - worked or toiled to accomplish; (past tense) finish. Strong's Concordance.

[58] Initial deposit and pledged promise, but forfeited if the purchase agreement has not been completed; 2 Cor. 1:22.

[59] (1736-*endemeo*) "to be in one's own country; i.e. home; "to be among one's people" and "one who is in his own place or land." And since we are the "host of earth" then where might you expect "our own place" be?

[60] (4983-*soma*) is "the body as a whole, an instrument of life" whereas "the 'body' is not the man for he can exist apart from his 'body' (2 Cor. 12:2-3)." Strong's Concordance.

[61] (1)Strong's lists this word as (553), but this is a typographical error of small significance, seeing as the correct word is (1553- *ekdemeo*, which occurs only 3x in verses 6, 8, and 9 – translated: be absent) -'*ek*' (from, out of) and '*demos*' (people) and means "to emigrate, to be away from people to go abroad, depart, be absent" in reference to "departing from the body as the earthly abode of the spirit." [Vine's gives regard only to the spirit in his explanation of this scripture and does not include "the soul." The home of "spirits" is heaven, to be sure, and if heaven is where our spirit will go, then what eternal "home" will our soul dwell in?].   (2) Regarding v.6, Vine's mentions "of being here in the body and absent from the Lord" is a standard interpretation, but this is difficult to understand since it does not matter where we are or where we go, as we cannot escape His presence (Psa. 139:8); and since Christ dwells in us (2 Cor. 6:16; Eph. 3:17; Col. 1:27) and we are in Christ (Rom. 8:1; 2 Cor. 1:21; Gal. 3:28), our soul is never abandoned nor leaves the presence of the Lord, "For He Himself has said, "***I will never leave you nor forsake you***"" (Heb. 13:3);

    (3) in v.8 "of being absent from the body and present with the Lord" is rightly translated, but there is no indication of "where" this is; and   (4) v.9 to be ambitious in pleasing the Lord regardless of whether we are at home in the body or away from the body – but being away from the body does not imply "in

⁷ for through faith, we walk, not through appearances; —
⁸ We are ~~of good cheer~~ (2292-confident) then and think it good rather 'to go away from home' (1553-*ekdemeo*) (*ek*) *out of* the body and 'to ~~come~~ being home' (1736-*endemeo*)⁶² *to* (4314)⁶³ the Lord·
⁹ Wherefore also we are ambitious (5389), whether 'being at home' (1736-*endemeo*) or 'being away from home' (1553-*ekdemeo*), to be well-pleasing to him.
¹⁰ – for "it behooves all us to be manifested" before the tribunal of Christ, in order that "each one may receive" the things through the body according to what things be practiced, either good or worthless.

Three points:

1) Paul is very specific about his word choices and several occur only within this particular passage. Placing this passage within the larger context of the promised resurrection, may we consider the following interpretation in keeping with the original terms implied by Paul to describe what happens to "the body" and what happens in "the resurrection," but not both terms together, as both Jesus and the Apostles preached the resurrection of the dead (not the resurrection of the body).

Heaven" with the Lord, yet it does imply being "present before Him" at a future time, which in this case is the tribunal (judgment) of Christ.

⁶² Note: in each verse, *endemeo* is contrasted with *ekdemeo* regarding "our earthen home" – **except** – in verse 8 where the word undergoes an alteration from "being at home" to "coming home" perhaps to support a heaven-home doctrine. The Greek text utilized by many translations, including the RSV, ASV and most arguably the NIV, "was an eclectic one" based upon the Nestle's Greek (1898) by taking textual agreement from two of three prior works; Zondervan Parallel New Testament in Greek and English, 1975; Introduction, p. ix, xix.

⁶³ '*Pros*-4314' is not the typical word for "*to* or into ('*eis*-1519' indicating the point reached or entered – of place, time or purpose) '*pros*' indicates motion. '*Pros*' is "a strengthened form of 4253 (*pro* – for, in front of, prior to (superior) – before, above) is a preposition of direction; forward to, i.e. toward; usually with the accusative case, the place, time, occasion, or respect, which is the destination of the relation." Strong's Concordance.

2) We must also carefully consider the smallest of words *"ek, en, ex"* as *"from, in, out of"* to help unlock the mystery of the eternal habitation we receive "from God, as coming (*ex*) from out of Heaven" which is superimposed upon us.

3) Paul's knows perfectly well that "Christ in us" is the hope of glory. Though our body must die, "what we are that remains, i.e. our soul" can never leave the Lord's presence, as He Himself promised: "the Holy Spirit will abide with you forever" (John 14:16) and "I will never leave you or forsake you" (Heb. 13:3). Once the Spirit abides in your heart through the new birth, you are already living in eternity – right now – and the earthen body is of little consequence.

New-earth theology (proposed)[64]

1 For we know that if our earthly temporary house-body is destroyed, we have a covering (it) (*ek*) *from* God, a spiritual house-body not made with hands, eternal (*en*) *in* the heavens.
2 For in this we groan, earnestly desiring (it) superimposed upon our being as "our future habitation-residence" which comes to us (*ex*) *from out of* heaven,
3 so that *entering into* (it) we shall not be found naked.[65]
4 For indeed we groan[66] within this burdened temporary body, inasmuch as we do not wish *to slip out of but to superimpose on*[67] (it) in order that mortality may be swallowed up by the life.
5 Now the one having prepared *for* us this very thing is God, who has given us the earnest of the Spirit as a guarantee.[68]

---

[64] This is proposed, since the author is not a Biblical scholar nor trained in rendering Greek translations, so some latitude according to grace is appreciated.
[65] Naked and ashamed, as in the Garden of Eden (Gen. 3:7; Rev. 3:17, 18).
[66] All creation groans for the glory to be revealed in man and in creation; Rom. 8:18-23.
[67] "To put on" is a term Paul used before: *to put on the new man*, Eph. 4:24; Col. 3:10; to put on Christ, Gal. 3:27; Rom. 13:14; i.e. our new (resurrection) house will be "put on over" us as new-earth men in resurrection glory.
[68] Nearly identical phraseology as 2 Cor. 1:22.

6 Being confident always, and knowing that 'being at home' in the body – 'we are absent' from the Lord;[69]
7 for we walk by faith, not by appearances.
8 We are confident then and think it good rather 'to be absent' from this body and be present **before** the Lord.
9 Wherefore also we are confident, whether 'being at home' or 'being absent,' we are to be well-pleasing to him.
10 For it behooves us all, since we will all stand as manifest resurrected ones **before** the tribunal (judgment seat) of Christ, in order that each one may receive the things through the body according to what things he practiced, either good or bad.

Paul and the other Apostles used various terms to compare and contrast the dual realities we live in, such as: present and absent, clothed and naked, spirit and flesh, good and bad, living and dead, corruptible and incorruption, temporary and eternal – with the whole point of teaching us the difference between the earthly and heavenly paradigms – one physical and the other spiritual (1 Cor. 15:53, 54). Heaven as an eternal destination is not even on their radar screen; to them, *the resurrection of the dead* was sufficient.[70]

> "But someone will say, "How are the dead raised up? And with what body do they come?" [36] Foolish one..." (1 Cor. 15:35, 36).

How are the dead raised? This is the question we should be asking (not what body do we get). We are raised up just as Christ Jesus was raised... according to glory. "Glory is raised in the resurrection, just as Christ was also raised in glory and in power (Rom. 6:4; 1 Pet. 1:21), and likewise, the souls of men – through

---

[69] See Footnote for verse 6 (2). How can we be away from the Lord if we cannot escape His presence (Psa. 139:8). This verse remains problematic for the author, as well as other commentators, as to the precise meaning implied by Paul. However, if the term "we are away – we are absent" is perceived as "we are sojourners" sent from heaven to earth, then this fits nicely into the resurrection doctrine of Paul's gospel.

[70] The resurrection, as noted in the scriptures and the original Nicene Creed, says "the resurrection of the dead." Not once is the term "resurrection of the body" mentioned except in later creeds and commentaries.

faith in Christ – will also 'be raised in glory and in power.' If God's glory is attached to it, then it will be raised and saved; if not, then it will be cast into fire and burned."[71]

The soul is resurrected, not the body... nor the spirit!

We are just as concerned as first century converts (and perhaps more so) in knowing what happens to the body in regard to the resurrection... yet this temporary body creates quite a distraction from what we should be focused on: the salvation of our soul! When the trumpet sounds, the ensuing judgment and resurrection shall determine where you go next! Since you are in Christ, the garment of salvation shall be your covering, yet those apart from salvation will be raised naked and ashamed into the resurrection of condemnation.

We should be more focused on what happens to our soul – rather than our body or our eternal destination!

Christ made His home in our heart – and with Christ we have an eternal spiritual home "in Him." Meditate on that! Regardless of wherever we go in this life or the hereafter, and regardless of wherever Christ is, *if* Christ abides in you and you abide in Him, then we are, therefore, never homeless apart from Him – and eternally able to enter into His peace and rest... wherever He is. Through a personal relationship with Jesus, grounded by faith, regardless of here, there, or in the air, we will be with Him and we will see Him as He truly is.

> "Beloved, now we are children of God; and it has not yet been revealed what we shall be, *but we know that **when** He is revealed*, we shall be like Him, for we shall see Him as He is" (1 John 3:2).

---

[71] Excerpt copied from "Commission" section titled "Resurrection Clarification."

"And in that day there shall be a Root of Jesse, Who shall stand as a banner to the people; For the Gentiles shall seek Him, and His resting place shall be glorious." (Isa. 11:10).

The kingdom age has begun. Go in name of Jesus… and let heaven out.

Grace and peace.

It's all about Jesus – and God gets the glory!

Amen.

6) Where Do We Go From Here?

> "I go to prepare a [*topos*] place for you" (John 14:2).

The '*topos*' place that Jesus is preparing for us – is the garden you are cultivating in your heart even now!

Hades and Death

Much of our misunderstanding regarding where we go after our body dies is born out of a "Heaven-only" doctrine as our eternal destination; however, there are two other places in God's kingdom that are mentioned within numerous scriptures that cast a different picture on where we might go and Who holds the keys of Hades *and* of Death:

> "I am He who lives, and was dead, and behold, I am alive forevermore. Amen. And I have the keys of Hades and of Death" (Rev. 1:18).

Jesus is speaking these words to the Apostle John as he is having a heavenly vision while upon the island of Patmos. This is the first of seven encounters John has with "One like the Son of Man," who clearly presents Himself in this moment as Jesus Christ: the Ancient of Days.

Most of us have been taught that Hell and Hades are the same place, but they are not. And most Bibles translate the word Hades (G86-*hades*) as Hell (G1067-*gehenna*), especially the KJV; however, Hades and Hell are very different places, and Hades and Death are separate places as well because they each have their own key(s).

So, let me ask you this: since Jesus talked about Hades as much as He talked about Hell, then why is nothing ever said from the pulpit regarding Hades? And if there are only two places where men go after they die (i.e. Heaven and Hell), as we have been taught by the church, then why are these two places (Hades and Death) mentioned by Jesus at all?

Hades (G86) occurs 11 times in the scriptures, and is a combination of two words: '*a*' (G1-not) and '*oida*' (G1492-seen) and is regarded as "the unseen abode of the dead; the place of departed souls; a temporary destination."[72] To say that I was unexpectedly surprised to learn '*oida*' (meaning: to see, perceive, understand, comprehend, know experientially) is a root word for Hades is an understatement if there ever was one. Hades is "the not seen place" or perhaps "the place of not understanding."

The Hebrew equivalent for Hades is *Sheol* (H7585), which has its' root from (H7592-*sha'el*) and means: "to inquire; to request, to demand." Sheol is regarded as: "the abode of the dead, the place of degradation; as far as the world is concerned, they have perished, yet they are still in a state of existence"[73] from God's perspective. Sheol, then, is "the ultimate resting place of all mankind"[74] (Gen. 37:35) for a season while we await the judgment according to our deeds.

Hell (G1067-*gehenna*) occurs 11 times, and is regarded as "the place (or state of) everlasting punishment."[75] It is interesting to note that all occurrences in the New Testament for Hell were uttered by Jesus – except one (2 Pet. 2:4) – and this occurrence refers to "*tartaros*" (G5020).

Death is referred to as a place less frequently than these other places in God's kingdom, which is regarded as a destination for souls in rebellion and disobedience to Jesus the Lord and, therefore, are already spiritually "dead in death" – being eternally separated from God.

So then, when we die, our body leaves us (our soul) to disintegrate

---

[72] Strong's Concordance.
[73] IBID.
[74] IBID.
[75] IBID.

and return once again where it came from: the earth. At this point, our soul is either "in Christ" waiting in Hades/Sheol or is dwelling in nakedness in Death. All souls will wait for the judgment, the resurrection, and the redemption; some will be resurrected into life eternal and others resurrected to condemnation. If you are "in Christ" and, having been clothed with Christ (Rom. 13:14; Gal. 3:27; Eph. 4:20-24; Isa. 61:10), you will receive a new resurrection body in the regeneration, which will be superimposed upon you as having come down "from out of Heaven."

There are three scriptures that will help us understand this concept of Hades in detail:

> "The sea gave up the dead who were in it, and Death and Hades delivered up the dead who were in them. And they were judged, each one according to his works" (Rev. 20:13).

> "For as the Father has life in Himself, so He has granted the Son to have life in Himself, [27] and has given Him authority to execute judgment also, because He is the Son of Man. [28] Do not marvel at this; for the hour is coming in which all who are in the graves will hear His voice [29] and come forth— those who have done good, to the resurrection of life, and those who have done evil, to the resurrection of condemnation" (John 5:26-29; see the footnote regarding "graves"[76]).

> "Then Death and Hades were cast into the lake of fire. This is the second death. [15] And anyone not found written in the Book of Life was cast into the

---

[76] Grave (*mnemeion*-3419) means, "a remembrance" and primarily denotes "a memorial" as anything done (like a monument) "to preserve the memory of things or persons." Strong's Concordance. The remembrance of "who" we are and what we've done remains with us and will be remembered by God in the '*mnemeion.*'

lake of fire" (Rev. 20:14, 15).

Hades, then, is one of three *temporary* places that holds "the dead" until the judgment of Christ, yet Hell is a *permanent* place of eternal torment. On the Day of Christ, three places (Death, Hades, and the sea) will give up the dead for judgment; those living apart from faith and are not saved "out of" Death, whose names are not written in the Book of Life, will remain in that place which is then cast into the Lake of Fire where they experience the second death… and eternal torment. And those waiting in Hades and the sea who are "in Christ" will be raised and judged in resurrection whereby the good will have a new body superimposed upon them (the resurrection of life), but the unjust, wicked and unright ones will be cast into Outer Darkness (the resurrection of condemnation)… where there will be weeping and gnashing of teeth. Is this beginning to make sense, now?

For many of us, our greatest fear and nightmare is being seen naked and ashamed, but today – our society flaunts it and unregenerate man's spirit is desensitized to it. Consider this point: three of man's greatest fears – falling, fire and nakedness – are related to eternal condemnation in Hell, and yet, eternal torment and torture is still not enough to change their mind.

Thus far, we have talked about Hades and Death, yet there are at least fourteen specific places within the kingdom of God that are mentioned in the scriptures, and Jesus alludes to many of them; so, why isn't the church teaching us the whole truth about the kingdom of God? Pardon my skepticism, but it is because (just like selling indulgences) you can still make money by selling Heaven to people that refuse to listen to the voice of the Spirit.

Places With Purpose

As I was meditating upon these things, the Holy Spirit brought one word to me: "places." It seems there are various places within the kingdom of God, and these places have specific purposes. There are three permanent realms in the kingdom of God (Heaven, Earth and Hell) and within these realms are temporary places for various persons according to things done upon the Earth.

Heaven: the presence of God:
- God's throne (Isa. 66:1)
- A place for worship before the throne with living creatures, elders, angels and others
- A temporary place under the altar for martyred saints (Rev. 6:9; 20:4)
- The New Jerusalem that comes down 'from out of' heaven in the regeneration (Heb. 11:16; Rev. 21)
- Jesus used the term "the kingdom of the heavens" (plural) and "heavens" twice (Matt. 24:29; Luke 12:33) to describe multiple aspects of and/or places in His kingdom
- Heavenly places, the interface between Heaven and Earth (Eph. 1:3; 2:6)

Earth: man's eternal residence:
- The visible realm; the physical reality of earth we can tangibly see and experience
- Hades: the unseen temporary realm of departed souls (Rev. 1:18; 20:13) that many believe is somewhere within "the heart of the earth" (Num. 16:32). [77] The Jewish term "Sheol" (Psa. 16:10) corresponds to Hades (Acts 2:27) within complementary texts, and possibly "Abraham's bosom" (Luke 16:22, 23)
- Death: another unseen temporary realm for unregenerate dead (Rev. 1:18; 20:13) as the resting place for those who have judged themselves unworthy of judgment by unbelief
- The sea: a physical reality in the visible realm that also temporarily holds the dead (which ceases to exist in the regeneration; Rev. 20:13; 21:1)
- Paradise, the Garden of God, Eden – that remains hidden behind the veil that will be restored in the regeneration at the culmination of all ages

---

[77] Willmington's Guide to the Bible, p.683, section B.

- Heavenly places, the interface between Earth and Hell (the unseen realm of principalities, powers, demons, devils and evil spirits that wage war against mankind and the body of Christ – His church; Eph. 3:10; 6:12)

Hell: the absence of God (with many places reserved for judgment and eternal torment):
- *Gehenna* (Hell) – the place for the second death after judgment (Rev. 2:11; 20:6, 15)
- The bottomless pit – a temporary place to hold "the dragon, that serpent of old, who is *the* Devil and Satan, and bound him for a thousand years" (Rev. 9:1; 20:1-3) that may also be "the abyss" to imprison demons awaiting judgment (Luke 8:31)
- The Pit – may be another reference for the abyss (Psa. 30:3; 49:9; 143:7)
- The Lake of Fire – a special place reserved for Satan (the devil), the beast and false prophet (Rev. 19:20; 20:10); in final judgment, Death and Hades are cast into this lake, as well as anyone not found written in the Book of Life (Rev. 20:14, 15)
- The Furnace of Fire – for those persons engaged in lawlessness as an offense to the kingdom of heaven (Matt. 13:41-42; 49-50) where there is wailing and gnashing of teeth
- *Tartaros* (5020- translated as Hell; 2 Pet. 2:4; Jude 6), "the deepest abyss of Hades," [78] a special place for fallen angels who left their proper domain, interfered with God's plan of creation and redemption for mankind (and the earth), and sinned against the daughters of men (Gen. 6:2)
- Outer Darkness – the place reserved for hypocrites, wicked, lazy, abominable and unprofitable servants, and unfaithful stewards where eternal torment following judgment occurs (Matt. 8:12; 22:13; 25:30; Jude 13; it is possible this place may be an element of earth, yet not as a place where joy or

---

[78] Strong's

peace resides, which may explain why the wall around the Holy City is 240' tall)

There are specific places in the kingdom of God for specific persons according to deeds done upon earth; some according to faithful obedience – some according to disobedience and some according to unbelief. And there are specific places in Hell for specific persons as characterized by their crimes, as well as varying degrees of torment, including "his own place" for Judas Iscariot who betrayed Jesus (Acts 1:25).

This next point is very important because – we associate the statement by Jesus "I go to prepare a place for you" as being Heaven, and yet… Judas was also present when these words were spoken to the disciples, so let Jesus decide which '*topos*' place you will be going to. Now then, within the context of these various places which have been identified in the scriptures, there are many places in the kingdom of God – each with specific purpose for specific people according to their deeds done upon the earth.

These citations may also help us understand the kingdom of God as it relates to "in My Father's house (*oikia*) are many *rooms*" (*mone*-3488, meaning: a staying, residence, dwelling place; [79] John 14:2; 23). Perhaps a better translation is: "In My Father's house are many places." This is why I refer to Earth as the sanctification room, Hades as the courtroom, Death as the rebellion room, and Heaven as God's throne room. Let me explain…

Death

At the onset of this book or the Image Bearer series, I was not given understanding by the Lord regarding the place called Death, but twelve months after this original document was finished, this understanding came to me by the Spirit:

---

[79] IBID.

- To live and be alive is not the same as "life" [80]
- To die and be dead is not the same as "death"
- Jesus is the Life (John 14:6); the life we live is Christ's life that He breathed into us
- When we die, the spirit and the life that were given to us by God (to assist this body of flesh) will return to Him who gave it to us (Eccl. 12:7), as they belong to Him (1 Cor. 6:20), then the body returns to the earth, and our soul waits in Hades or Death
- At the judgment of our soul, we are raised up and made alive again to stand before Jesus, and to "come forth— those who have done good, to the resurrection of life, and those who have done evil, to the resurrection of condemnation" (John 5:29)…
  - and those who are found in Christ who have been **preserved** by Christ and "known by Him" will experience "the Resurrection and the Life" (i.e. Christ Himself; John 11:25) from out of Hades to receive glorified bodies in the Paradise of God
  - but those who are not clothed in Christ are **reserved** for condemnation

The only way we can comprehend the meaning of these spiritual words is by being born anew by the Holy Spirit. Webster's Dictionary only defines words from man's perspective, not God's.

Therefore, "Death" is the place where unregenerate souls who stand in rebellion against Jesus, who refused to acknowledge Him as Lord and repent – will wait in conscious nakedness for judgment and eternal torment. At the judgment, these rebellious souls will not be raised "out of" Death whereby all who remain in Death are cast into the Lake of Fire, forever separated from God, where everlasting torture of their eternal soul happens always and forever – in Hell.

---

[80] "Eternal life stresses the quality of life; everlasting life stresses its duration." Strong's, '*aion*'-G165 (1e).

> Jesus said: "Most assuredly, I say to you, he who hears My word and believes in Him who sent Me has everlasting life, and shall not come into judgment, but has passed from death into life" (John 5:24).
>
> "Most assuredly, I say to you, if anyone keeps My word he shall never see death" (John 8:51).
>
> "We know that we have passed from death to life, because we love the brethren. He who does not love his brother abides in death" (1 John 3:14).

It is important for us to read the word "death" as a place *and* as a state of being (i.e. dead).

"As life never means mere existence, so "death," the opposite of life, never means nonexistence, but separation always." [81] "As spiritual life is conscious existence in communion with God, so spiritual death is conscious existence in separation from God." [82]

In contrast, those who have submitted their allegiance to Jesus as Lord and Master – as His disciples, having been saved by Him who is "the Life," are no longer in danger of entering into Death or Hell because they have passed from death to life; however, not all who enter into Hades are disciples… they have merely been "ushered, assembled" into the courtroom of Hades because they made a profession of faith in Jesus, but their works according to righteousness and faithful obedience (or lack thereof) have yet to be judged by Jesus.

Do you have the conscious awareness of God's presence in your life? Do you live your life with the conscious awareness that Jesus, the Lord of the universe, is dwelling within you? Are you aware that, because Christ is in you, your heavenly Father is also

---

[81] Word study on "die" (*apothnesko*-G599). Strong's Concordance.
[82] Word study on "death" (*thanatos*-G2288). Strong's Concordance

abiding in oneness within you and knows your thoughts, sees what you look at and hears every word and utterance you make? Are you taking your spiritual relationship with Jesus Christ for granted – that is, on your terms or are you living as His disciple on His terms? Jesus is LORD of lords!

> "For the LORD is our Judge, the LORD is our Lawgiver, the LORD is our King" (Isa. 33:22).

Test your faith and judge yourself to see if your eternal hope is based upon your faith in a religious denomination that may have been teaching you many things that are contrary to scripture (like everyone goes to Heaven) – or, by grace through faith, having been thoroughly persuaded and convinced, you have put on Christ and, therefore, having a love and trust personal discipleship relationship with the Lord Jesus, will be found "in Him" on the Day of Christ.

> "Nevertheless the solid foundation of God stands, having this seal: "The Lord knows those who are His," and, "Let everyone who names the name of Christ *depart from iniquity*." (2 Tim. 2:19).

Resurrection happens…

…and so does poor judgment.

What Happens in Hades

We can only infer what goes on in the unseen place called Hades by reading the scriptures, since no one having gone there has ever come back – nor is this permitted – because there is a great chasm between Hades and Death such that no one can go back and forth between them – nor do people go back and forth between these places and earth either, and yet, what is unseen by men (living on the earth) does not appear to be unseen in the spiritual realm. Perhaps the best understanding we have is based upon the words of Christ Himself, who created everything, and He alone knows the purpose for every place in the kingdom of God.

> "So it was that the beggar died, and was carried by the angels to Abraham's bosom. The rich man also died and was buried. ²³ And being in torments in Hades, he lifted up his eyes and saw Abraham afar off, and Lazarus in his bosom" (Luke 16:22, 23)

In my study of the many places in God's kingdom, Hades and Death are two places within the unseen realm of Earth where the souls of men wait for judgment and resurrection. Waiting does not necessarily imply an unconsciousness of the soul, which some claim is soul sleep; we are still alive from God's perspective and there remains a conscious awareness by the soul that continues to think and to feel emotion. Our spiritual heart and mind, as elements of our soul (our inner man), are still alive because our soul is eternal, and within this context… are very much alive *and* active with thoughts *and* feelings; however, I found no evidence that Hades or Death were places of torment like Hell, so this scripture spoken by Jesus has either become mistranslated over the years or else, as I have come to believe and prefer… every word spoken by Jesus *is to be taken quite literally.*

Is the word "Hades" accurate and is the word "torment" accurate? Yes, they are accurate translations; however, as I began to study the root meaning of "torment," the Holy Spirit brought fresh understanding *to me*… to alter my perspective regarding what torment means.

The word (*basanos*-391) translated "torment" implies, "through the notion of going to the bottom." This word means "touch-stone, which is a black siliceous stone used to test the purity of gold or silver by the color of the streak produced on it by rubbing it with either metal." [83] The application of this word implies gold and silver (the works of men) are being tested and questioned by the touch-stone to authenticate and verify the quality and character of the metals being tested. And this definition corresponds to the

---

[83] Word study on torment '*basanos*' (G931) only occurs three times, twice said by Jesus, Matt. 4:24, as well as 'tormentors' (G930) in Matt. 18:34.

Hebrew word Sheol meaning: "to inquire; to request, to demand."

Hades, then, "through the notion of going to the bottom" and Sheol, "the inquiry that demands a response" represent the same place where man waits, is raised for questioning, and therefore must give an answer (an accounting) for everything that we have said and done in regards to our life on Earth. This is not the place of judgment (at least not yet)… this place is like a courtroom, where a time of formal hearing and then a rigorous interrogation for every person occurs… and may also be regarded as prison (as a temporary holding place to wait for the formal hearing of your case).

And another important point as well: Heaven is not the courtroom or place of adjudication. Heaven is God's throne and Hades is the courtroom (or mudroom) for God's justice.

One additional point: **Hades is not 'purgatory'** which is taught (erringly) as being "the state" (not a place) "in which those suffer for a time who die guilty of venial sins, or without having satisfied for the punishment due to their sins."[84] The doctrine of purgatory is a works-based methodology of attaining heaven through "temporal punishment" that also teaches adherents of this doctrine to help other souls trapped in purgatory "by offering prayers, fasts, almsdeeds; by indulgences, and by having Masses said for them."[85] Purgatory is marketed (falsely) as the place where you get a second chance to earn salvation, or have others pray your way into heaven, or perform penance to pay away your sins, or pray away the sin of others to get them into heaven. ***Earth is our second chance to be sanctified!*** That doctrine diminishes Christ's trustworthiness to

---

[84] Baltimore Catechism (book 4), 1988, p. 320-321.
[85] IBID. It is interesting to note that the prayers and good works of the living are able to help the dead get out of purgatory (which is unscriptural), yet those in purgatory "cannot help themselves – by their prayers." This doctrine emphasizes praying for those who precede you in death, but if you are part of the last generation upon the earth, then there is no longer anyone left behind to pray you into heaven, and thus, the doctrine of purgatory has all the hallmark qualities of a ponzi scheme to reward those who join quickly before the bottom falls out.

forgive our sins, His faithfulness to save us by grace, His Preeminence as Lord of our life to Reign Supreme far beyond the most heinous sins we may have committed... and the power of the Holy Spirit to sanctify us to live "apart from sin." By advocating a reality that exists beyond Earth where sin is allowed to exist is, by definition: HELL!

Furthermore, this doctrine teaches "the slightest stain upon their souls" will prevent them from entering into God's presence, which is rooted upon the premise that sin is attached to the soul. Find even one scripture in the Bible to defend this opinion! Where does the Bible say "sin" resides? Man-centric opinions have wrestled with the doctrines of "original sin" and "sinful nature" for thousands of years, yet the idea that anything of this world, including sin, as being more powerful than the Holy Spirit's ability to sanctify us and help us resist temptation *and* avoid the near occasion to sin is inherently inconsistent with the gospel of grace and truth revealed to us by Christ Himself. We were created in the similitude of Jesus... and our true nature (i.e. our soul) was given a divine nature (i.e. our spirit; 2 Pet. 1:4) which was divinely infused into us as beings "created in His own image according to His own likeness" to become like Him in everything we think, say and do.

Sin (which is separation from God) resides in our members (i.e. the flesh; Rom. 7:23; see also Matt; 5:29; Rom. 6:13; 7:5), which was "predestined" for corruption (Gal. 6:8).

> "For You will not leave *my* soul in Hades, nor will You allow Your Holy One to see corruption" (Acts 2:27).[86]

This scripture is about you (*my* soul)... and about Jesus (the Holy One). God will not leave your soul in Hades... when you put your faith and trust in Jesus.

---

[86] This scripture, copied from Psalm 16:10, allows us to correlate the terms Sheol and Hades – as the same place.

So now, if your doctrines cannot answer these eleven questions, which can all be found in the scriptures (references are found within all the books I write), then perhaps you have been taught a less-than gospel which prevents you from perceiving your primary mission on earth – apart from sin.

1. Why is man upon the earth?
2. Where did man come from?
3. Where is it referenced in the scriptures that man *goes to* heaven?[87]
4. Where is it referenced in the scriptures that sin stays with the soul?
5. Where does sin reside in man?
6. Where does this flesh go when it dies?
7. Where does the soul go after the body experiences death?
8. Who judges the living and the dead?
9. Is everyone considered worthy of judgment?
10. At the Judgment, is the soul judged by sin or by righteousness?
11. How would you define grace?

"These questions are extremely complex and man has been wrestling with finding the answers for many millennia, but I tell you the answers are very simple… and some questions are irrelevant; however, until religious men submit their minds to gain understanding through the tutoring of the Holy Spirit to reveal truth to them, their opinions are merely another series of man-made doctrines to explain what happens to man after he dies without ever comprehending why man is on earth to begin with."[88] One thing is certain… we are not here to be punished or tormented by God, as nothing could be farther from the truth. We are here to be sanctified and proofed according to faith. Jesus did not come into the world to condemn us (John 3:17)… but to save us, and yet… it is our own actions that will bear witness either for or

---

[87] There are 692 references for heaven, but not one mention is found, even when the verb conjugation is changed.
[88] Introduction to a future book about sinful nature by the author, "Principle In Peril."

against us.

> "For the Son of Man did not come to destroy men's lives but to save them" (Luke 9:56)... "for the Son of Man has come to seek and to save that which was lost" (Luke 19:10).

The word "destroy" and "lost" are the same word '*apollumi*-622' meaning: "to destroy utterly."[89] Jesus came to save those who are already "utterly destroyed" whereby there is little left of us, other than our repentant soul, that we can even bring to the table of redemption seeking salvation. Our salvation is based upon grace – through faith in Christ Jesus – and grace alone!

What Is Torment

What is torment? Well, for starters, it is not always torture. Torment, in one regard, is a self-questioning process that men sometimes perform within their mind in order to judge their own conduct and affairs upon the earth. It requires both a daily moral inventory and a rigorous self examination to see whether we are living life according to faith in righteousness that is pleasing to Jesus – or not. In my own mind, I have many thoughts and remembrances of things in my pre-Christ past that I am ashamed of, and there are also many opportunities when I failed to produce works of righteousness for lack of faith or obedience, and thus, in all these... my own conscience either convicts me or defends me (but rarely the latter). By self-questioning, my conscience will either torment me or allow me, *through repentance*, to rest in the peace of God who dwells within me. In this regard, we ought to judge ourselves lest we come under judgment (God's).

> "For if we would judge ourselves, we would not be judged" (1 Cor. 11:31).

---

[89] Strong's Concordance.

Torment, as defined in the dictionary[90] is:

> verb (used with object)
> 1. to afflict with great bodily or mental suffering; pain: to be tormented with headaches; 2. to worry or annoy excessively: to torment one with questions; 3. to throw into commotion; stir up; disturb.
> noun
> 4. a state of great bodily or mental suffering; agony; misery; 5. something that causes great bodily or mental pain or suffering; 6. a source of much trouble, worry, or annoyance; 7. an instrument of torture, as the rack or the thumbscrew; 8. the infliction of torture by means of such an instrument or the torture so inflicted.

My definition of torment is: "Thinking things through in your mind without arriving at a peaceful resolution in your heart."

If we are being tormented in our soul, then there is only one life-giving way to silence the many voices that come against us to condemn us wherein we may find the peace of God: REPENT. Go to Jesus Christ, confess your sin, apologize to Jesus for the wrong that you've done, and ask for His forgiveness. Once you have been forgiven, then move on... because "As far as the east is from the west, so far has He removed our transgressions from us" (Psa. 103:12).

Here, yet, is another important fact: a touch-stone does not test wood, straw or stubble – only metal; "tares" are gathered by angels and taken to the place called Death where they are being *reserved* for condemnation:

> "The enemy who sowed them is the devil, the harvest is the end of the age, and the reapers are the angels" (Matt. 13:39).

Can you imagine what is happening in Hades, the unseen place

---

[90] Source: Dictionary.com.

where believers in Christ go to wait until the judgment? A touchstone is only used to test the character and quality of metals (mankind) who have been *preserved* for salvation *from* condemnation to determine authenticity, which we can see as the gathering of two types of end-time harvest: to gather away those who remain rebellious upon the earth, and another one to gather others as fruit of the harvest (Rev. 14: 15, 18), which we see happening in the following message by Jesus:

> "All the *nations* will be gathered before Him, and He will separate them one from another, as a shepherd divides *his* sheep from the goats. [33] And He will set the sheep on His right hand, but the goats on the left. [34] Then the King will say to those on His right hand, 'Come, you blessed of My Father, inherit the kingdom prepared for you from the foundation of the world: [35] for I was hungry and you gave Me food; I was thirsty and you gave Me drink; I was a stranger and you took Me in; [36] I *was* naked and you clothed Me; I was sick and you visited Me; I was in prison and you came to Me" (Matt. 25:32-36).

This gathering of people (*ethnos*-G1484/people of the same nature, genus, culture – *nation*) represents those people who were not reaped by angels in the first harvest (by separating tares from wheat)… because wheat people have been marked as having the same culture (believing in Jesus) and were sealed for salvation. The reason theologians interpret sheep and goats as saved and unregenerate, in the same way they make a distinction between wheat and tares, is because they erringly preach a "Heaven-only" destination whereby sheep go to Heaven and goats go to Hell. Jesus, however, used the term "everlasting punishment" a term which occurs only once.

Well, what does Jesus mean by sheep and goats? Jesus is the Shepherd of "His sheep" who hear His voice and follow Him (John 10:27) and tares are the offspring of their father – Satan, the Devil, who are gathered away by reapers (angels), but what are "the goats" and who do they represent? The term "goat" that Jesus used is *'eriphos'* (G2056) and means: a kid, the offspring of goats; (i.e. a baby goat; see Luke 15:29). Allow me to express an opinion: Jesus is separating "His sheep" from "the kids" that were invited to have a covenantal relationship with Him, but they refused "to be transformed by the renewing of their mind" and they refused sanctification by the Holy Spirit, and thus, they were never converted (transformed) from kids into sheep. These kids never matured; they preferred to be the offspring of goats rather than the offspring of God… simply because they complacently preferred milk-toast theology within a watered-down gospel rather than eating the meat of Christ's gospel with the ever-present guidance of the Holy Spirit dwelling in them.

What ethnos people group, club or culture have you embraced that is more meaningful to you than the culture of Christ and becoming His disciple? (There are many clubs and fraternal organizations that gather together to accomplish many good things that seem to be aligned with the gospel of Christ, but in pretense only is the name Jesus mentioned.)

At this point, the nations have been gathered together and the court of God's justice is collecting evidence from us while being questioned in God's courtroom regarding everything we said and did – and this is being performed in the presence of many witnesses (an assembly) – whereby the Lord, who always rules in justice, will render a verdict (for or against us) based upon our testimony – and the basis of two or more witnesses.

When the Lord asks us to give an account…what will we say? How will we respond? Were we too busy? Were we too focused on our plans and our agenda? Were we so blind building our own kingdom? Were we too busy having fun with our self-obsessed lives that we refused to see our brothers and sisters in need? Were you too content being a goat to become a disciple? What if Jesus needs to only ask us four questions:

1. Did you believe Me? Then why didn't you do what I told you to do?
2. Did you learn to Love? Did you live according to My commandment: "Love one another as I have loved you."
3. Did you hear My voice and obey My word? (John 10:27)
4. Did you have any care for your brothers, sisters and strangers in the world? (Matt. 28:40)

Perhaps we will be asked only one question:

> What did you do to bring glory to My name
> with the gifts I gave you?

Jesus has blessed us with every spiritual gift, including life itself, but what do we have to show for it? By His great mercy, Jesus has forgiven us a great debt, but – have we forgiven others with the same forgiveness and mercy wrought by love that He endured for us upon the cross?

> "Then his master, after he had called him, said to him, 'You wicked servant! I forgave you all that debt because you begged me. [33] Should you not also have had compassion on your fellow servant, just as I had pity on you?' [34] And his master was angry, and delivered him to the torturers [tormentors-*basanistas*-930] until he should pay all that was due to him. [35] "So My heavenly Father also will do to you if each of you, from his heart, does not forgive his brother his trespasses" (Matt. 18:32-35).

This is an interesting statement by Jesus that seems to indicate there is a place within God's kingdom where wicked, reluctant and unfaithful servants go to be tormented until they pay all that is owed. Well, when this debt is paid, then what happens next? How is the debt paid? This is just my understanding, so treat it accordingly: these people will never be able to overcome the enormous debt they owe Christ Jesus for their unfaithfulness to Him – and their disobedience to His commands! They are sent there to be tormented, yet never with any hope of leaving.

According to the principle of sowing and reaping, we will reap unto ourselves in the courtroom of Hades whatever we have sown in this life and done unto others:

- by the measure we show forgiveness to others is the same measure God will forgive us
- by the measure we show mercy to others is the same measure God will be merciful to us
- by the measure we show grace to others is the same measure God will bestow favor on us
- by the measure we have judged others is the same measure God will judge us

"Judge not, that you be not judged. [2] For with what judgment you judge, you will be judged; and with the measure you use, it will be measured back to you" (Matt. 7:1).

"Judge not, and you shall not be judged. Condemn not, and you shall not be condemned. Forgive, and you will be forgiven" (Luke 6:37).

The litmus test on earth that determines our willing obedience to walk in the truth that Jesus taught us and to operate (live life) according to "kingdom of God" principles is best summarized in the Beatitudes; the meek shall inherit the earth because they placed Jesus foremost (preeminent) in their heart and esteemed their neighbor ahead of themselves.

- Did you love your neighbor?
- Did you honor your neighbor?
- Did you honor your parents?
- Did you reverence one another with holy affection?
- Did you commit yourself to the well-being of others?
- Did you have a care for anyone other than yourself?

- Did you think the Ten Commandments were just really good suggestions?

Now, then, let me ask you this: if we have been saved and have also been forgiven much, by grace through faith, then why are we even being questioned in Hades? Aren't we automatically granted eternal life in Heaven based upon God's promises which can never be countermanded? And this is why the church does not teach us about Hades... because our initial salvation is a "once saved always saved" guarantee by justification that keeps us out of Death and Hell by Jesus our Savior, *but* the second part of our salvation – being raised up out of Hades into "the Paradise of God" – is conditional by Jesus based upon "if" we regarded Him as Lord and Master and, through justification... obeyed His commands. Read the Gospel of John, chapter 15, to get a complete sense what Jesus is teaching us.

- "Every branch in Me that does not bear fruit He [the Father] takes away; and every *branch* that bears fruit He prunes, that it may bear more fruit" (John 15:2)
- *"If anyone does not abide in Me*, he is cast out as a branch and is withered; and they gather them and throw *them* into the fire, and they are burned (v.6)
- *"If you keep My commandments, you will abide in My love*, just as I have kept My Father's commandments and abide in His love" (v.10)
- "This is My commandment, that you love one another as I have loved you" (v.12)
- *"You are My friends if you do whatever I command you"* (v.14)

Hades is the courtroom where all souls according to faith in God through Christ Jesus will stand before Jesus our Judge... and everyone must give an account for what they did with His talents. Those who are in Hades are there because they have called upon the Lord for salvation and Christ's righteousness has been imputed to them – in whom there is no longer the condemnation that separates them from God (John 3:19). In essence, they have been saved (delivered from Death) that is the result of sin (not believing Jesus is Lord and repenting), but those brothers who called upon His name, yet continue in sin, have not been saved from future judgment (read Rom. 6:16; 1 John 5:16, 17).

Those in whom sin remains (because they have not declared Jesus Lord) are never given an opportunity to see the courtroom of Hades; they have already "judged themselves" unworthy of judgment by their own faithlessness, and by their own words they are still *dead* in trespasses and "in sin" – whereby they (being tares) will be gathered by angels to wait in the place of no return called "Death" – a place reserved for punishment.

It is interesting to note that two parables by Jesus speak to our preparation on earth – which is analogous to the courtroom of Hades which is also in the earth (read Matthew 25). Ten virgins were "invited" to the wedding of the bridegroom, but only five had their oil lamps prepared with "oil in them." And likewise, three "servants" were given talents (spiritual endowments) with which to serve their Master; the servant with five talents made five more, the servant with two made two more, but the servant with one talent simply hid his in the soil… which was never used to benefit anyone or produce anything good in the kingdom of God (it wasn't even invested wisely in a bank to earn interest). These parables are not talking about oil or money, but rather, the gifts of God (spiritual endowments; grace gifts – i.e. the attributes of God's character given to us and manifested by us in service to Him) that we were given us to expand the kingdom of heaven upon the earth, in faithful service to Jesus – and to love (take care of) one another. The talents earned by these servants will come in handy in the resurrection – to purchase gold and white garments from the Lord (Rev. 3:18) – which will be discussed a little later.

"Did you love your brother?" Are you the sole beneficiary of God's talents that He gave you?

We may be asked only one question: did you obey My commandment to love as I loved you?

> "Assuredly, I say to you, inasmuch as you did it to one of the least of these My brethren, you did it to Me" (Matt. 25:40).

To the five foolish virgins, the Lord says to them, "Assuredly, I say to you, I do not know you" – and likewise, the wicked, lazy and unprofitable servant who buried his talent was "cast into the *outer darkness* where there will be weeping and gnashing of teeth" (Matt. 25:12, 30). In both instances, the Master invited these individuals into His presence whereby they were questioned and told to give an account for their actions, much like similar individuals who professed they knew the Lord, but truly didn't reverence Him in their heart...

> "Not everyone who says to Me, 'Lord, Lord,' shall enter the kingdom of heaven, but he who does the will of My Father in heaven. [22] Many will say to Me in that day, 'Lord, Lord, have we not prophesied in Your name, cast out demons in Your name, and done many wonders in Your name?' [23] And then I will declare to them, 'I never knew you; depart from Me, you who practice lawlessness!'" (Matt. 7:22, 23).

> "The master of that servant will come on a day when he is not looking for him and at an hour that he is not aware of, [51] and will cut him in two and appoint him his portion with the hypocrites. There shall be weeping and gnashing of teeth" (Matt. 24:50, 51).

The point is this: even though we have declared Jesus our Savior (and saved from Death), we will be judged by Jesus our Lord and Master in Hades regarding our works of obedience unto Him. Five foolish virgins were refused admittance into the wedding feast and the wicked servant was cast "into outer darkness." So, where do you suppose "outer darkness" is located where these servants will experience "weeping and gnashing of teeth"? Well, that really doesn't matter, but what does matter is this: they are weeping and gnashing their teeth (in torment) because they forfeited their opportunity to spend eternity in Paradise with Jesus. They could have been obedient sheep... but they preferred being a goat. And this is my biggest issue with sheep merchants who keep selling the promise of Heaven (which we were never promised) in order to placate our fears whereby many have adopted a false gospel born out of lukewarm, unrighteous mediocrity and self-righteous, religious performance... because these merchants are sentencing multitudes upon multitudes to torment with a false expectation of life eternal in Heaven – without presenting all the facts about the reality of Hades! Anathema!

Therefore, it is critically important to comprehend this point: if a person claims to be redeemed but is not "raised up" out of Hades by Jesus, and thus, not being found in the Book of Life, then they will either be cast into Outer Darkness where there will be weeping and gnashing of teeth (Matt. 8:12; 22:13; 25:30), which may also be "the furnace of fire" (Matt. 13:42), or they will remain in Hades to be cast into "the lake of fire" in Hell (Rev. 20:14, 15).

Has your name been erased from the Book of Life?

Sons of the kingdom... it should never come to this!!! Why settle for mediocrity when the Lord has blessed us with every good and perfect gift from above, as well as having been created with a divine nature as *elohims* in the likeness of our Creator and *Elohim*, Jesus Christ? You are the '*ekklesia*' – the ones called out from darkness to be the light of the world. Why have you compromised your lamps to lose oil and become dim – and clung to your old wineskins so as to get by with just enough patches of truth to escape Hell... only to be cast into Outer Darkness? Saints of God – you were redeemed for more than this!

If the fear of the Lord has come upon you at this point regarding your eternal destiny, then ask Jesus what you must do concerning your salvation. Ask Jesus – and stop running to pastors and priests for their opinion who keep teaching about Heaven only. Ask Jesus – and listen intently for His reply. Feigned ambivalence is not an excuse anymore because the truth about many places in the kingdom of God has been made known to you, but even now... the choice is yours.

> "But I will show you whom you should fear: Fear Him who, after He has killed, has power to cast into hell; yes, I say to you, fear Him!' (Luke 12:5).

> "And do not fear those who kill the body but cannot kill the soul. But rather fear Him who is able to destroy both soul and body in hell (Matt. 10:28).

Why do we hold the Lord's promises in contempt? Even if we have been invited into the wedding feast, do we arrogantly think Jesus will keep His promises to us if we broke and disregarded our covenantal agreement with Him?

> "But when the king came in to see the guests, he saw a man there who did not have on a wedding garment. [12] So he said to him, 'Friend, how did you come in here without a wedding garment?' And he was speechless. [13] Then the king said to the servants, 'Bind him hand and foot, take him away, *and cast him into outer darkness*; there will be weeping and gnashing of teeth.'[14] "***For many are called, but few are chosen***" (Matt. 22:11-14).

The wedding garment that Jesus mentions is not something that we bring with us to the wedding feast. The word "garment" is **'*enduma*'** (G1742); this is glory clothing (raiment, like that of angels; Matt. 28:3) the robe of righteousness that we receive in the resurrection that comes down to us "from out of" Heaven and is superimposed upon us (or perhaps we enter into) that Paul mentions in 2 Cor. 5:3. This wedding garment is a robe of righteousness – for deeds of righteousness done in His name. What does your wedding garment look like?

How this person was able to be present is a curious thing, indeed, but more importantly… the aftermath of being discovered without the robe of righteousness is the true lesson of this parable because this person was invited at one point to live according to righteousness and truth, but now we see this person being ejected and going to the place where all wicked, lazy, unjust stewards, unprofitable servants and hypocrites go on account of unrightness: Outer Darkness.

Consider, now, all the parables and teachings by Jesus… to firstly remove the tares from the wheat, and secondly… to "separate" various unclean things that are mixed in among the clean:

- To gather out those things that offend
- To gather out those who practice lawlessness
- To separate those evildoers that do wickedness and do things that defile
- The dragnet to separate the wicked from among the just

As you read these end-of-the-age accounts, keep in mind… the righteous are not removed, nor are they taken up from earth. Contrarily, it is the other way around.

> "Therefore as the tares are gathered and burned in the fire, so it will be at the end of this age; [41] the Son of Man will send out His angels, and *they will gather out of His kingdom all things that offend, and those who practice lawlessness,* [42] and will cast them into the furnace of fire. There will be wailing and gnashing of teeth. [43] **Then** the righteous will shine forth as the sun in the kingdom of their Father. He who has ears to hear, let him hear! (Matt. 13:40-43; these are three events; the author added a semi-colon at the end of v. 40 in keeping with the original text).

Angels are reapers (v.40), they gather tares (semi-colon); then angels gather those things that offend, then the righteous shine.

Three different words translated "gather" are used in Matthew's Gospel:

- '*Sullego*-4816' – to gather in order to remove; take away (used negatively in most instances, but favorably (below; v.48) to gather good souls away from the sea that is destined to be cast into the lake of fire; Rev. 20:14, 15)
- '*Sunago*-4863' – to collect or gather together (hospitably); the good wheat (v.13:30)
- '*Episunago*-1996' – to gather up together (in the same place); the elect (Matt. 24:31)

> "Again, the kingdom of heaven is like a dragnet that was cast into the sea and gathered some of every kind, [48] which, when it was full, they drew to shore; and they sat down and gathered the good into vessels, but threw the bad away. [49] So it will be at the end of the age. *The angels will come forth, separate the wicked from among the just,* [50] and cast them into the furnace of fire. There will be wailing and gnashing of teeth" (Matt. 13:47-51).

Two accounts are recorded (nearly back-to-back) in which the wicked are separated from the just; the first account describes souls living on the earth, and the second account describes the souls of the dead in the sea. The righteous do not rise up and leave the earth... the righteous remain! And the good in the sea will be gathered from the sea and '*episunago*' joined together "with" the righteous (the elect)... in the same place: the New Earth. And as the account in Matthew 24:31 indicates... this gathering together will be done "after" the great tribulation!

> "A man is not established by wickedness, but the root of the righteous cannot be moved" (Prov. 12:3).

If, however, when we die, there are only two options for our eternal destination (as in Heaven or Hell), which numerous denominations have been teaching for centuries, then the scriptures seem to indicate all that any person must do to inherit eternal life is to confess with our mouth that Jesus is Lord, yet this doctrine omits the most important part... live according to "righteousness which is according to faith" (Heb. 11:7). Faith must operate according to righteousness!

> "They profess to know God, but in works they deny *Him,* being abominable, disobedient, and disqualified for every good work" (Titus 1:16).

Outer Darkness is the place these persons will be cast into. So, now, consider these questions:

- What happens to this person if their life does not produce the fruit of righteousness that glorifies the Father?
- What if they talk about knowing Jesus as having belief in a doctrine without having a personal relationship with Him?
- What if they profess Jesus as their Savior but refuse to declare Him their Lord and Master – to do all that He commands?
- What if a person claims to believe in Jesus but continues to walk in rebellion and does those things deserving "Death" (fornication, adultery, drunkenness, etc; Gal. 5:19-21)?
- What if they declare Jesus Lord but refuse to listen to His voice (John 10:27)?
- What if they refuse to take up the cross that Jesus has apportioned to them?

> "*If* anyone desires to come after Me, let him deny himself, and take up his cross, and follow Me" (Matt. 16:24).

> "Now the works of the flesh are evident, which are: adultery, fornication, uncleanness, lewdness, [20] idolatry, sorcery, hatred, contentions, jealousies, outbursts of wrath, selfish ambitions, dissensions, heresies, [21] envy, murders, drunkenness, revelries,

and the like; of which I tell you beforehand, just as I also told you in time past, that those who practice such things will not inherit the kingdom of God" (Gal. 5:19-21); add to this list what Jesus said: "evil thoughts, murders, adulteries, fornications, thefts, false witness, blasphemies" (Matt. 15:19).

Do any of these people (above) living apart from righteousness and sanctification in the truth have a right to be saved and enter into God's holy presence? "Once saved always saved" applies to our initial salvation from the place called "Death" whereby the sanctification process begins; however, we can reject the sanctification process at any time… and forfeit the promise of life eternal in Paradise. Our works will be judged in a courtroom in Hades by Jesus Christ – in equal measure to the manner in which we loved the Lord – to the truth we believed – and offered grace and forgiveness to one another. Jesus created us as "gateways of grace" that we should release His grace upon the earth, dispel the darkness with the light of truth… and shift the atmosphere on this planet with the attributes of God's grace and love freely dispensed to others.

The promise of life eternal is conditional… if… we remain in the truth and endure faithfully to the end. Maintaining intimacy with Jesus… is paramount!

Some of our brothers and sisters have abandoned the faith. There are many reasons why this happens, but I am of the opinion that God failed to meet "their" need, as something He was required to do – in their best interest – while they remained as lord upon the throne of their heart. God did not meet their expectations. Hum? This turning away was the result of God's testing to see if they would get off their throne and endure despite all the precious promises that worldly men said they were entitled to. Sadly, we have all heard the entitlement message from the pulpit of man, but it is still our responsibility to search the scriptures to see if what they promised us – is according to the truth. Nearly all of the promises in the scriptures are "if-then" conditional upon our obedience to the truth. Live according to the truth. If you want to walk out of God's hand, then that's your choice – albeit a very foolish one.

The spiritual life we have in Christ is a broad spectrum of faith having basic truth with childlike faith on one end and miraculous gifts with *dunamis* power at the other end. Ask Jesus how He wants you to live your life rather than the preacher; ask Him what your place and position in life is and seek Him for every major life decision. If you are a widow, the Apostle Paul said to remain as a widow, but if you are a widow, then remain a widow with spiritual life according to the truth – and resist the temptation to seek worldly pleasures… thus incurring the Lord's condemnation.

> "Now she who is really a widow, and left alone, trusts in God and continues in supplications and prayers night and day. [6] ***But she who lives in pleasure is dead while she lives***." [Paul continues]… [12] "having condemnation because they have cast off their first faith" (1 Tim. 5:5-6, 12).

Even though this older widow had spiritual life, the scriptures regard her as "being dead" '*thnesko*-2348' (as one having forfeited spiritual life). Salvation is a gift, not an entitlement!

The Apostle Paul taught us we may be saved, as one passing through the fire, even though our works are burned (1 Cor. 3:15); he understood the Lord's gifts and commandments are irrevocable, but His promises are conditional.

> "And you, who once were alienated and enemies in your mind by wicked works, yet now He has reconciled [22] in the body of His flesh through death, to present you holy, and blameless, and above reproach in His sight— [23] ***if indeed you continue in the faith***, grounded and steadfast, and are not moved away from the hope of the gospel which you heard" (Col. 1:21-23).

> "Moreover, brethren, I declare to you the gospel which I preached to you, which also you received and in which you stand, ² by which also you are saved, *if you hold fast that word* which I preached to you—unless you believed in vain" (1 Cor. 15:2; see also Rom. 11:19-22).

The writer of Hebrews makes similar statements regarding the conditional "if-then" of faith:

- " ⁶ but Christ as a Son over His own house, whose house we are *if we hold fast* the confidence and the rejoicing of the hope firm to the end" (Heb. 3:6)
- "For we have become partakers of Christ *if we hold the beginning of our confidence steadfast to the end*" (Heb. 3:14)
- "But **if** you are without chastening, of which all have become partakers, **then** you are illegitimate and not sons" (Heb. 12:8)

The sickle of God's truth makes no mistakes – and without partiality – makes no distinction! The Lord's sickle does not operate according to human standards or perceptions, but according to the standards of God Almighty; righteousness and truth *is* the sword in His hand. Our eternal salvation is conditional based upon our obedient response to our "if-then" covenant with Him!

> "Then he said to his servants, 'The wedding is ready, but those who were invited were not worthy" (Matt. 22:8).

We were invited by Jesus to enter into a covenant with Him, but this does not mean everyone who was invited has accepted the invitation nor does it mean you are entitled to enter into the kingdom of God because you merely accepted it. Nearly all the parables by Jesus teach us about aligning ourselves to God's truth:

apart from the Spirit of God, the truth is not operational in us, so we must attach ourselves to Truth – with understanding – that produces righteousness! If you are not doing the will of God and are not pursuing righteousness in truth, when what right do you have to gain entrance into a place of grace and holiness that is being prepared by Jesus for His faithful saints if, by continuing to walk in disobedience, you *shall* be disqualified?

God does not compromise His truth, His laws or His integrity – to accommodate our sinfulness. And thus, our life shall serve as our own testimony as either a witness for us – or against us.

> "And he said to him, 'Out of your own mouth I will judge you, you wicked servant. You knew that I was an austere man, collecting what I did not deposit and reaping what I did not sow" (Luke 19:22).

> "Every tree that does not bear good fruit is cut down and thrown into the fire. [20] Therefore by their fruits you will know them" (Matt. 7:19, 20).

Gates, Doors and The Entrance

Pay careful attention to this very important message by Jesus (in NKJV and Greek):

> "Then one said to Him, "Lord, are there few who are saved?" And He said to them, [24] "***Strive to enter through the narrow*** ~~***gate***~~ ***door***, for many, I say to you, will seek to enter and will not be able" (Luke 13:23, 24; ~~change~~ made by author).

> "Ἀγωνίζεσθε (*agonizomai*-G75; struggle) εἰσελθεῖν (G1525; to enter) διὰ (*dia*-G1223; through) τῆς (the) στενῆς (*stenos*-G4728; narrow, from obstacles standing close about) θύρας (*thura*-G2374; door)" (Luke 13:24).

The word "strive" *'agonizomai'* – means "to struggle; Engl. agonize" and comes from the root word *'agon'* (G73) that is translated "contest" (as in, "Fight (*agonizomai*) the good fight (*agon*-contest) of faith" (1 Tim. 6:12). The agonizing struggle to stay the course from all the obstacles that are standing close about which create physical pain and emotional torment prevents many from entering through "the door" to life eternal with Christ. Now look at a similar verse and see how the terms differentiate for these openings (gate vs. door).

> "Enter by the narrow [G4728-στενῆς- *stenos*] gate [G4439-πύλης-*pule*]; for wide *is* the gate [*pule*] and broad *is* the way that leads to destruction, and there are many who go in by it. Because narrow [*stenos*] *is* the gate [*pule*] and difficult [*thlibo*-G2346; afflict, suffer tribulation; 1 Thess. 3:4] *is* the way which leads to life, ***and there are few who find it***" (Matt. 7:13, 14).

The gate is narrow, yet difficult is the way which leads to the door… and thus, few find it.

Herein lies a dilemma: Strong's properly designates the word 'gate' in Matt. 7:13-14 as (G4439-πύλη- *pule*-gate) but improperly designates 'gate' in Luke 13:24 (as G4439) when it is actually (G2374-θύρας- *thura*-door). These are very different words, so why is this important? Because the Greek language uses very specific words to convey very specific meanings (there are eight words for wash, eight for doubt, four for love and seventeen for understand); and thus, *'pule'* (G4439) is a gate that many people use, yet *'thura'* (G2374) is a door, portal or entrance that, in this instance, few will enter through! *'Thura'* is the same term used to describe Jesus Himself… "He that enters by the *'thura' door* is the shepherd" and "I am the *'Thura' Door*" (John 10:2, 9; see also Rev. 3:8, 20).

The larger context of Christ's statements now seems to indicate... these scriptures describe two different ways with two different entrances, wherein you are a gate(way) – and Jesus is the Door.

Few will find the narrow gate, and fewer still will agonize long enough to enter through the narrow door.

Jesus said, "I am the *way*" (*hodos*-3598- way; as a means of access) whereby Jesus represents both the access (way) and the entrance (door) *through whom* we enter into salvation. Jesus is the only way to gain access to the Father which is accomplished... *through* Christ alone! (John 14:6) But you have an access way and an entrance gate as well. Let me explain it this way:

- men are gateways that can provide or restrict access – to or from – heavenly things
- our struggle to find the narrow gate (*pule*) and thus enter through the narrow door (Christ) is made difficult because a "crowd of trouble" and the cares of this world are standing in the way, as in family traditions, peer pressure, bad theology and teachings by '*allos*' *others* of a similar way (John 10:1) and few are those that find it (the truth) because they are being afflicted with difficulty, encounter trouble and suffer persecution by others that resist Godly change that requires all men to live according to the truth
- our struggle to gain entrance to the Door (thura) called Jesus is guarded by the Doorkeeper (the Spirit of truth) whose sanctification process to change us through the renewing of our mind is a process made very narrow by trials, testing and proofing of our soul, which everyone encounters, but few overcome
- and our struggle is made even more complicated by tribulation – by Satan, by principalities and powers, and by the spirit of antichrist that rule the kingdom of darkness (this world) with impunity against those who seek to be aligned with Jesus Christ

This way of Christ is difficult. Period! And few enter in! The agonizing struggle to find the *'pule'* gate (made narrow and obstructed by others) that leads to Door of Christ and life eternal is fraught with great adversity, affliction, tribulation, and persecution ***from without*** – and the *'thura'* entranceway through sanctification to be radically changed and transformed by the Holy Spirit ***from within*** … is why many are called – but few are willing to endure the testing and proofing of their soul and win the prize (salvation in Paradise) through perseverance!

And this is precisely why few ever find the Lord's salvation! Jesus taught us in the Parable of the Sower: the seed that grows upright and bears the fruit of righteousness does so in midst of much adversity (from without and within), including rocky ground (your own unbelief and lack of understanding), bad wayside theology, and thorns that thwart your growth in Christ. Truly, these enormous difficulties are virtually insurmountable (now get this) *apart from the Spirit*!

There are a great many things that work against being a disciple of Jesus; however, blessed are those who endure, persevere and remain steadfast in faithful obedience to Christ unto the end… and overcome… for great will their reward be!

Remain steadfast. Endure. Continue to seek and press in. Grab hold of the truth… and hang on!

> "Many are the afflictions of the righteous, but the LORD delivers him out of them all" (Psa. 34:19).

> "For our light affliction, which is but for a moment, is working for us a far more exceeding and eternal weight of glory" (2 Cor. 4:17).

> "These things I have spoken to you, that in Me you may have peace. In the world you will have tribulation; but be of good cheer, I have overcome the world" (John 16:33).

If you haven't been afflicted, then you haven't been affected... and are probably on the wrong pathway (which leads to destruction).

The Message translation says it like this: "A bystander said, "Master, will only a few be saved?" He said, "Whether few or many is none of your business. Put your mind on your life with God. The way to life—to God!—is vigorous [*I prefer rigorous*] and requires your total attention. A lot of you are going to assume that you'll sit down to God's salvation banquet just because you've been hanging around the neighborhood all your lives. Well, one day you're going to be banging on the door, wanting to get in, but you'll find the door locked and the Master saying, 'Sorry, you're not on my guest list.'" (Matt. 7:14)

The agonizing struggle to enter Paradise is much like a contest wherein many compete, but few win the prize. Many are called (invited into the Lord's covenant) but few are chosen (given entrance based upon the robe of righteousness). Yet we have a Paraclete, the Holy Spirit, who is dwelling alongside us to help us on this sojourn to gain entrance, who Himself is the Doorkeeper (θυρωρὸς *thuroros*-G2377; porter KJV) and guards the entrance (θύρας *thura*) to the Door (Thura-Jesus Christ; John 10:3)... but few are willing to yield to the Holy Spirit's guidance and transformational renewing of their mind to manifest "Christ in you" on the earth.

Agony now or torment forever – the choice is yours. Either we agonize through faith in this life, being steadfast in truth to faithfully endure even in the midst of much adversity, or we shall experience torment in outer darkness for all eternity with much weeping and gnashing of teeth. There really are two destinations after death once you profess Jesus as Lord, but Heaven isn't one of them (unless you've been martyred); either you will gain entrance into Paradise as one who is raised up out of Hades – or you will be cast into Outer Darkness where there will be weeping and gnashing of teeth (torment). Two places... yet the choice is yours!

When I was a teen, I heard the truth of the gospel from a marvelous "hell, fire and brimstone" preacher in the Order of St. Francis – and it altered my reality immensely, that is, until one day after Mass I overheard rancor gossip by bitty old ladies moments after hearing the truth of Jesus Christ proclaimed; it fractured the foundation of my faith – and I walked away from Jesus and into the darkness for many years. These ladies created an "obstacle standing close about" that caused my faith to waiver. Listen up! ***IF*** you profess Jesus as your Lord and your God, ***THEN*** do that He commands… or stop calling yourself a Christian by pretending to be a follower of Christ that becomes an obstruction to others. So I ask: do you claim to be a son or daughter of the kingdom yet live like a hypocrite? ***Outer Darkness is a place reserved for hypocrites!***

> "But the *sons of the kingdom* will be cast out into ***outer darkness***. There will be weeping and gnashing of teeth" (Matt. 8:12).

Through faith in Christ, you are a son or daughter of the kingdom who has been invited by the King to the banquet feast, but if you are not clothed in Christ's righteousness, then you have not accepted the invitation of Jesus "according to the terms of His covenant" with you… and thus… Outer Darkness awaits.

Clothed In Christ

Jesus came to save us from the judgment that He, as the Judge of this world, will implement on the Day of Christ. Jesus desires that we live according to faith in Him, obey His commands and walk according to the Spirit in order to produce works of righteousness whereby He can save us and *also* reward us in the hereafter…

> "… ***and be found in Him***, not having my own righteousness, which is from the law, but that which is through faith in Christ, the righteousness which is from God by faith" (Phil. 3:9).

> "I will greatly rejoice in the Lord, my soul shall be joyful in my God; **_for He has clothed me with the garments of salvation, He has covered me with the robe of righteousness_**, as a bridegroom decks himself with ornaments, and as a bride adorns herself with her jewels" (Isa. 61:10)

So now, let's recall the Lord's first expression regarding His mission of salvation on earth:

> "The Spirit of the Lord GOD *is* upon Me, because *the LORD has anointed Me to preach good tidings to the poor*; He has sent Me to heal the brokenhearted, to proclaim liberty to the captives, and the opening of the prison to those who are bound; ² to proclaim the acceptable year of the LORD, and the day of vengeance of our God; to comfort all who mourn, ³ to console those who mourn in Zion, to give them beauty for ashes, the oil of joy for mourning, *the garment of praise for the spirit of heaviness; that they may be called trees of righteousness*, the planting of the LORD, that He may be glorified" (Isa. 16:1-3).

In order to more fully comprehend what happens to us when we die, we need to see our physical body as a "garment" that has been placed upon us (i.e. formed over our soul). When we die, this earthly garment (also called an earthen vessel, the body of flesh) will leave our soul and return to the earth, but this is only one of three types of clothing mentioned in the scriptures: physical, spiritual and eternal. Consider spiritual clothing in the following verses:

> "He who overcomes shall be clothed in white garments, and I *will not blot out* his name from the Book of Life" (Rev. 3:5).

> "I counsel you to buy from Me gold refined in the fire, that you may be rich; and white garments, that

you may be clothed, that the shame of your
nakedness may not be revealed; and anoint your
eyes with eye salve, that you may see" (Rev. 3:18).

The Lord is instructing us to live life in such a manner so as to have credit in our heavenly faith account in order to exchange our deeds of righteousness for white garments (of righteousness) in the hereafter. Righteousness, it seems, is the currency of Heaven that is not consumed in the fire. What manner of clothes will you be wearing (if any) for all eternity?

Recall, now, what we were taught about having "just enough" faith in order to enter into eternal life, but not enough works to follow after us:

> "Now if anyone builds on this foundation with gold, silver, precious stones, wood, hay, straw, [13] each one's work will become clear; for the Day will declare it, because it will be revealed by fire; and the fire will test each one's work, of what sort it is. [14] If anyone's work which he has built on it endures, he will receive a reward. [15] ***If anyone's work is burned, he will suffer loss; but he himself will be saved, yet so as through fire***" (1 Cor. 3:12-15).

When the faithful in Christ come into the presence of the Lord's judgment fire, the Lord will be *with us* as our Protector and Deliverer…

> "When you pass through the waters, ***I will be with you***; and through the rivers, they shall not overflow you. When you walk through the fire, you shall not be burned, nor shall the flame scorch you" (Isa. 43:2).

Yet those who disregard the Lord Jesus will encounter His indignation with fire…

> "So the Light of Israel will be for a fire, and his Holy One for a flame; it will burn and devour His thorns and his briers in one day" (Isa. 10:17).
>
> "And anyone not found written in the Book of Life was cast into the lake of fire" (Rev. 20:15).
>
> "A fire devours before them, and behind them a flame burns; **the land is like the Garden of Eden before them**, and behind them a desolate wilderness; surely nothing shall escape them" (Joel 2:3).

The spiritual garment that we receive in the resurrection, which comes down to us "from out of heaven" will be commensurate with the works of righteousness we did in Christ's name that glorifies the Father. This garment is not based upon our "good works" in self-righteous human effort; rather, it is based upon obedient works of righteousness whereby God is given all the glory for the good you've done. Now then, are you taking credit for the good works you did on earth? If you are taking credit for them, then they cannot be credited into your faith account… and those earthly works will be burned, but you yourself will be saved (yet saved in nakedness as one barely escaping through the fire).

Why do we spend so much time, effort and money accumulating "stuff" on earth that must be left behind, but spend so little time concerning ourselves with works of righteousness which will be needed to purchase gold and acquire clothes in the resurrection? What type of garment do you think you will wear for all eternity if your life were required of you right now?

> "If your hand causes you to sin, cut it off. It is better for you to *enter into life* maimed, rather than having two hands, to go to hell, into the fire that shall never be quenched" (Mark 9:43).
>
> "… but others save with fear, pulling them out of the fire, hating even the garment defiled by the

flesh" (Jude 23).

So, then, there are three aspects of salvation and two aspects of redemption:

1. We were saved (by Christ's atonement for our sin upon the cross on Calvary)
2. We are being saved (through sanctification in God's truth by the Holy Spirit)
3. We will be saved (in the judgment and resurrection where all men must give an account)
   a) from Death into Hades – our first redemption, steadfast and true, through faith
   b) from Hades into Paradise – our second redemption, in righteousness, to exchange our righteousness and obedience (to Jesus) for heavenly garments and true riches

And this is why we are instructed to work out your own salvation with fear and trembling… in order to be raised out of Hades and into the Lord's redemption for His beloved into the Paradise of God. The Lord's regeneration *'palingenesia,'* literally means: genesis again. We are entering into Life, anew again, into the Garden of Eden – which is the Garden of God.

> "Therefore, my beloved, as you have always obeyed, not as in my presence only, but now much more in my absence, work out ***your own*** salvation with fear and trembling; [13] *for it is God who works in you* both to will and to do for His good pleasure" (Phil. 2:12, 13).

Is Jesus your redeemer and your redemption? Are you His beloved? Now that you know Who will be waiting for you on the other side, do you have any idea where you may be going if you died this very moment? And what would you *exchange* right now in this life to possess heavenly currency (righteousness through faith) and life eternal with Jesus in the hereafter?

> "For whoever desires to save his life will lose it, but whoever loses his life for My sake will find it. ²⁶ For what profit is it to a man if he gains the whole world, and loses his own soul? ***Or what will a man give in exchange for his soul?*** ²⁷ For the Son of Man will come in the glory of His Father with His angels, and then He will reward each according to his works" (Matt. 16:25-27).

The word "exchange" is '*antallagma*' (G465) and means "an equivalent or *ransom*; exchange"[91] that constitutes "the price at which the exchange is effected." Jesus only used this term once, in regard to our soul, and we need to perceive this term used as the second part of the exchange (3b) that occurs in Hades – which Christ instituted by His initial ransom (3a) by His sacrificial death so that we may escape Death. So, what are you willing to exchange with Jesus for your soul?

> "For even the Son of Man did not come to be served, but to serve, and to give His life a ***ransom*** for many" (Mark 10:45; see also 1 Tim. 2:6).

> "I will *ransom* them from the power of the grave; I will redeem them from death. O Death, I will be your plagues! O Grave, I will be your destruction! Pity is hidden from My eyes" (Hosea 13:14).

What are you storing up that you will you be able to give Jesus in *exchange* for your soul?" Will sin be a noose around your neck or will righteousness be a garland around your soul?

On the Day of Christ, "Pity is hidden from My eyes, says the Lord." Jesus will judge without partiality or favoritism; Jesus is *Jehovah Tsidkenu*, the *LORD OUR RIGHTEOUSNESS*, and He will sit upon His throne and govern in righteousness and truth. What are you willing to sacrifice in this life in order to ransom your soul? Are you willing to present yourself as a living sacrifice

---

[91] Strong's Concordance.

that is holy and acceptable to God... which is your reasonable service (Rom. 12:1)? Will you be prepared on that Day to even speak one word in your favor in order to ransom your soul?

On account of God's great mercy, Jesus created a way of escape out of Death – by grace through faith, but this way only escapes Death; the only way that you may escape from being cast into Outer Darkness where there will be weeping and gnashing of teeth before everything in Hades is cast into the lake of fire is by paying your ransom *in righteousness currency* to save your soul. What will you be able to give Jesus in *exchange* for your soul?"

Walk in the Way of Christ Jesus! Jesus is the Way! Follow Jesus, hear His voice and do what He tells you!

> "Enter by the narrow gate; for wide is the gate and broad is the way that leads to destruction, and there are many who go in by it. Because narrow *is* the gate and difficult *is* the way which leads to life, and there are few who find it" (Matt. 7:13, 14).

The person that sets the prisoner free... is yourself... according to righteousness in Christ.

Can anyone else set you free from sin? No! Because sin is "separation from God" that only you can resolve with Him and Him alone, but some traditions teach a contradictory doctrine.

- There is the sin of unbelief, which is rebellion, that leads to death into Death
- There is repetitive sin, which is disobedience (iniquity), that leads to destruction into Outer Darkness (If you believed Me, then why didn't you do what I told you?)
- There is occasional sin, which leads to conviction by the Holy Spirit, unto repentance, conversion and sanctification to be holy as your heavenly Father is holy; it is forgivable sin wherein obedient believers are rewarded with Life

Eternal in Paradise... as well as true riches according to righteousness

Jesus established a new earth reality where the sin of the world has been "taken away," including our sin which He bore upon Calvary's cross – once – and for all. No other secondary sacrificial offering shall ever be required for sin ever again. Ever!!! Our Sin Bearer took all the sin away that results in man's separation from God and He has commanded us to abide with Him and obey His commands; however, on account of free will – we can continue to walk in the manner of the old man in the old world according to the old covenant. But if you want to live according to this new earth paradigm, which is according to grace, then it begins by declaring your allegiance to Jesus as your Lord and Master to become His disciple.

Carried By Angels

Indeed, we will either go to Hades or Death after we die, but how will we get there? Once again, I refer to the teaching by Jesus about the beggar and Lazarus (not Christ's friend).

> "So it was that the beggar died, and was carried by the angels to Abraham's bosom. The rich man also died and was buried" (Luke 16:22).

Angels, it seems, are sent by Jesus to carry us to our after-life destination. Consider all the messages by Jesus regarding angels who gather us and carry us to our destination:

> "The Son of Man will send out His angels, and they will gather out of His kingdom all things that offend, and those who practice lawlessness" (Matt. 13:41).

> "So it will be at the end of the age. The angels will come forth, separate the wicked from among the just" (Matt. 13:49).

> "And He will send His angels with a great sound of a trumpet, and they will gather together His elect from the four winds, from one end of heaven to the other" (Matt. 24:31; Mark 13:27).

There has been much speculation by church preachers and teachers regarding who "His elect" are, as if some have been predestined or predetermined for salvation, but now we know that this is no longer the case because all are predestined for salvation, but not all become His elect…

> "Behold! My Servant whom I uphold, **My Elect One** *in whom* My soul delights! I have put My Spirit upon Him; He will bring forth justice to the Gentiles" (Isa. 42:1).

Jesus is "My Elect One" – the Christ of God, and "His elect" represent those who hear His voice, become His disciple, are sanctified by the Holy Spirit and dedicate their life in service to Jesus, as living sacrifices… to manifest Christ Jesus in the earth in order to save many souls alive.

"And the gates (*pule*) of Hades shall not prevail against" Jesus Christ's church, the Bride, His '*ekklesia*' called out ones that He gathers together… as His elect! (Matt. 16:18)

> "O Death, where *is* your sting? O Hades, where *is* your victory?" (1 Cor. 15:55)

"This life is just a shadow and foretaste of life eternal on earth, but our doctrines do not even teach us how to prepare for life beyond our initial salvation from Death to life (into Hades) – or our just reward from Hades into life eternal in Paradise. If you are not preparing for life eternal in Paradise right here and now, then what on earth are you doing?

> "… by so much more Jesus has become a surety of a better covenant" (Heb. 7:22).

"Once saved always saved" through faith in Christ is the initial promise (step one: our surety) of salvation *from Death* (the place for those unworthy of judgment) *to life* (the place for those worthy to receive judgment and recompense); however, if you refuse to "hear His voice" for the sanctification of your faith (which constitutes a full faith conversion to turn away from this world to obediently follow Christ) is compromised by disobedience, then life eternal (step two: the guarantee by the Spirit) can be forfeited by you and your eternity now resides in outer darkness. Life eternal is the Paradise of God for good and faithful stewards, not lukewarm complacent unsanctified mediocre goats.

"The Old Covenant existed with many promises, yet Jesus instituted a New Covenant with better promises that are guaranteed by Him as the surety (initial earnest payment and redemption) of this better covenant… *and…* He sent forth His Spirit to also serve as a guarantee for this covenant for those who profess discipleship obedience to Christ whereby they will receive the promise of resurrection into life eternal… by the Spirit. The word "surety" (*egguos*-1450) represents something a bondsman (in this case, Christ) pledges as "bail who personally answers for anyone, whether with his life or with his property."[92] Jesus offered Himself as a living sacrifice to post bail on your behalf to save you from Death, but now we must "work out our own salvation with fear and trembling" under the guidance and tutoring of the Holy Spirit to sanctify us and prepare us for works of righteousness… in the name of Jesus Christ."[93]

Jesus holds the keys of Hades and of Death, and He alone will judge everyone in righteousness.

Will you be counted worthy to receive the crown of life? Will you hear, "Well done, good and faithful servant. Enter into the joy prepared for you?" or will you hear weeping and gnashing of teeth in Outer Darkness? So I say to you, live according to the Spirit of

---

[92] Strong's Concordance.
[93] Excerpts from "Dominion" section titled "Stewards of Eternity."

life in Christ Jesus – and do so without any regrets! Live according to God's truth– and walk according to the Spirit … in spirit and in truth. Your life, even now, is being held in the balance.

Many are called – but few are chosen!

"But he who is joined to the Lord is one spirit with Him" (1 Cor. 6:17).

"If we live in the Spirit, let us also walk in the Spirit" (Gal. 5:25)

"Now the Lord is the Spirit; and where the Spirit of the Lord is, there is liberty" (2 Cor. 3:17).

It's all about Jesus – and God gets the glory!

Amen!

7. Judgment and Resurrection

This section talks about the resurrection of the dead. If you knew exactly what would happen to you after you died, would you want to know as much detail as possible… especially if you could initiate a course correction to improve your eternal outcome? If yes, then keep reading.

For starters, the term "resurrection of the body" is not found in the scriptures or in the Nicene Creed. Next up: the terms "resurrection of the dead" and "raised from the dead" are not synonymous. Thirdly: if you experience resurrection, do you automatically go to a better place? The short answer is: no. Upon close examination, we will place clarifying light between these terms as being two separate events, and contemplate several words to sort this out:

- '*Anastasis*-386' – resurrection; to make stand up again; *anastasis* stresses the final state of the one raised[94]
- '*Anistemi*-450' – "to stand up, or make to stand up;" raise him up (John 6:39, 40, 44, 54) pertains to rising up at the judgment on the last day; and is a term Jesus used of Himself rising the third day (Matt. 20:19)
- '*Egeiro*-1453' – to awaken; arise; rise up; to rouse from sleep (or figuratively from obscurity, inactivity, ruins, nonexistence); said of Jesus by Jesus (John 2:19; Luke 9:22), said of Jesus by chief priests and Pharisees (Matt. 27:63); said of the resurrection of believers; (from the root word '*ageiro*-58' denoting "to gather; a place of assembly") [95]
- '*Egersis*-1454' – said of Jesus (Matt. 27:53) stresses the invigoration of the one raised up

There are at least 24 scriptures that refer to "rise(n), raise(d)(ing), (a)rose – from the dead" and 17 scriptures that refer to the "resurrection (of/from) the dead."

---

[94] Strong's Concordance. The note on '*egersis*' is found in '*anastasis*-386.'
[95] IBID.

In the scriptures, there are nine specific instances when the dead were raised (other than Jesus), yet in all instances (with the possible exception of those raised up the moment when Jesus died and tombs were opened), every person that was raised up physically – died again at a later time. Being raised from the dead, in this regard, is much different than experiencing resurrection.

- The widow's son by Elijah (1 Kings 17:21-24)
- The Shunammite's son by Elisha (2 Kings 4:32-35)
- A warrior whose dead body was placed in Elisha's tomb (2 Kings 13:20, 21)
- Lazarus, the friend of Jesus (John 11:43, 44)
- The widow's son by Jesus (Luke 7:12-15)
- The daughter of Jairus by Jesus (Mark 5:35-43)
- Tabitha by Peter (Acts 9:36-43)
- Eutychus by Paul – after he fell out a third-floor window (Acts 20:9-12)
- A number of people at the moment of Christ's death (Matt. 27:51-52)

Our body is merely a temporary house or tabernacle for our soul and spirit, as well as being a temple for the Holy Spirit. Jesus referred to His human body as a temple (tabernacle) predicting He would "destroy it" and in three days raise [1453] it up (John 2:19). Jesus said, "No one takes it from Me, but I lay it down of Myself. I have power to lay it [My life] down, and I have power to take it again. This command I have received from My Father" (John 10:18). Even though Jesus was put to death, it is imperative to see that Jesus laid His life down of His own accord (i.e. no one took it from Him). In both instances, Jesus did not reference the resurrection, yet when Jesus was questioned by the Sadducees about the resurrection, He criticized them for not knowing the scriptures or the power of God:

> "Then some Sadducees, who say there is no resurrection [386], came to Him; and they asked Him, saying: [19] "Teacher, Moses wrote to us that if

a man's brother dies [599], and leaves *his* wife behind, and leaves no children, his brother should take his wife and raise up [1817] offspring for his brother. [20] Now there were seven brothers. The first took a wife; and dying [599], he left no offspring. [21] And the second took her, and he died [599]; nor did he leave any offspring. And the third likewise. [22] So the seven had her and left no offspring. Last of all the woman died [599] also. [23] Therefore, in the resurrection, when they rise, whose wife will she be? For all seven had her as wife." [24] Jesus answered and said to them, "Are you not therefore mistaken, because you do not know the Scriptures nor the power of God? [25] For when they rise [450] from the dead [3498], they neither marry nor are given in marriage, but are like angels in heaven. [26] But concerning the dead [3498], that they rise [1453], have you not read in the book of Moses, in the *burning* bush *passage,* how God spoke to him, saying, 'I *am* the God of Abraham, the God of Isaac, and the God of Jacob'? [27] He is not the God of the dead [3498], but the God of the living. You are therefore greatly mistaken" (Mark 12:18-27).[96]

Additional word diagnostics will be needed as we proceed:

- '*apothnesko*-599' – "to die off; the separation of the soul from the body, i.e. the natural death of humans; to be dead"
- '*nekros*-3498' – "the death of the body; the actual spiritual condition of unsaved men"[97]

It is important to note the <u>incorrect</u> sequence proposed by the Sadducees "in the resurrection [386], when they rise [450]" and the

---

[96] The comma between "dead [3498] - that they rise" (v.26) in numerous translations was added by commentators.

[97] All terms and corresponding meanings are referenced from Strong's Concordance.

correct sequence and terms taught by Jesus: "for when they rise [450]... that they rise [1453]" (below) without mentioning the resurrection – which will become clearer as we take many scriptures into account. The Sadducees were "greatly mistaken!" What you have been taught about the resurrection may also be greatly mistaken.

> "The men of Nineveh will rise up [450] in the judgment [2920] with this generation and condemn [2632] it, because they repented at the preaching of Jonah; and indeed a greater than Jonah *is* here. [42] The queen of the South will rise up [1453] in the judgment [2920] with this generation and condemn [2632] it, for she came from the ends of the earth to hear the wisdom of Solomon; and indeed a greater than Solomon *is* here" (Matt. 12:41, 42).

The resurrection is a four-step process. The <u>correct</u> sequence seems to be: 1453 (to awaken), 450 (to arise, stand up and assemble), 2920 (the judgment process), 2917 (the determination) which results in either – a 2632 judgment against you for the 386 resurrection of condemnation, or – you are counted worthy for the 386 resurrection of life.

A similar sequence is found in military assemblies. "Two types of commands used in PRT are preparatory commands and commands of execution. The preparatory command describes and specifies what is required. All preparatory commands are given with rising voice inflection. The command of execution calls into action what has been prescribed. The interval between the two commands should be long enough to permit the Soldier to understand the first one before the second one is given. When the PRT leader addresses the formation and is commanding movement or announcing the name of an exercise, he does so from the position of attention." [98]

---

[98] US Army PRT (Physical Readiness Training) Information; section titled: "Commands" from FM 7-22.

The call to attention (1453; awaken) initiates the execution command (450) to arise.

> "But all things that are exposed are made manifest by the light, for whatever makes manifest is light. ¹⁴ Therefore He says:
>
> "Awake [1453], you who sleep,
> Arise [450] from the dead,
> And Christ will give you light" (Eph. 5:13-14).

The rising up of all persons in Hades (in this moment for judgment) includes an assembly of believers known as the '*ekklesia*-1577' ('*ek*' out + '*kaleo*' to call) meaning: "the called out one's" which is also the Greek word translated "church." In this assembly are various powers, principalities and governances – including the Church under the governance of Jesus Christ – whereby all knees shall bow in His presence as He judges – not only nations and powers (regardless of whether they submitted to His authority or not) – but individual persons as well.

The Lord our God, Jesus Christ, is King of kings and Sovereign over ALL!

> "When the Son of Man comes in His glory, and all the holy angels with Him, then He will sit on the throne of His glory. ³² All the nations will be gathered before Him, and He will separate them one from another, as a shepherd divides *his* sheep from the goats. ³³ And He will set the sheep on His right hand, but the goats on the left (Matt. 25:31-33).

Imagine, if you can, the "rising up" of all nations, people groups, governances, kingdoms, principalities, dominions and powers which are then "assembled" together each according to their kind whereby Jesus judges on the throne of His glory. Who does He judge first? Is it not the House of God? Who, then, judges the nations of this world?

> "Do you not know that the saints will judge the world? And if the world will be judged by you, are you unworthy to judge the smallest matters? [3] Do you not know that we shall judge angels? How much more, things that pertain to this life?" (1 Cor. 6:2, 3)

Let me ask you: if the saints are in heaven, then how can we judge the world?

> "Thus says the Lord of hosts: 'If you will walk in My ways, and if you will keep My command, then you shall also judge My house, and likewise have charge of My courts; I will give you places to walk among these who stand here" (Zech. 3:7).

> "Let the nations be wakened, and come up to the Valley of Jehoshaphat; for there I will sit to judge all the surrounding nations. [13] Put in the sickle, for the harvest is ripe. Come, go down; for the winepress is full, the vats overflow—for their wickedness is great" (Joel 3:12, 13).

The saints will judge angels. The disciples of Jesus will also judge the twelve tribes of Israel…

> "So Jesus said to them, "Assuredly I say to you, that in the regeneration, when the Son of Man sits on the throne of His glory, you who have followed Me will also sit on twelve thrones, judging the twelve tribes of Israel" (Matt. 19:28; see Luke 22:30).

Perhaps you can see… the Church has an enormous responsibility in God's plan of judging the world, the redemption and the regeneration. So I ask: is this judgment activity happening in Heaven, which is God's throne, or is this happening in the place of adjudication – called Hades? But… if you are in Heaven, as our doctrines have taught us – then explain how you are also expected to judge the nations of the world in Hades?

Back on point. Our God is a God of the living, not the dead (3498). This is curious statement since all men must die, but as we've learned thus far, dead (in this regard) is spiritual death as being separated from God (and perhaps eternally in the place called "Death" if repentance has not occurred thus remaining in unbelief and rebellion against Him). Jesus is King of kings, Jesus is God, Jesus is Judge of the living and the dead, and He will judge everyone in righteousness (Acts 10:42).

> "And He commanded us to preach to the people, and to testify that it is He who was ordained by God to be *Judge* of the living and the dead" (Acts 10:42).

From a spiritual perspective, because of Adam's condition, we were all born into a family that is spiritually dead (3498) and destined for destruction – as dead men walking – many just don't know it yet. When Jesus told us He came "to seek and save the lost" (Luke 19:10), we think we were just a little lost when, in actuality, the word "lost" means: "utterly destroyed." We were more than just lost; we were destroyed beyond recognition and we desperately need a Savior, but the alternate reality of Satan within this worldly paradigm tells us we are doing just fine, when in fact – we are already destroyed and destined for destruction. Many unbelieving ones have been blinded from the truth (by sin) and do not sense the need of a Savior… not even when calamity falls upon them. The Parable of the Prodigal Son has much to teach us in this regard.

Through repentance, faith in Jesus, and (the imperative) conversion, we have passed "from death to life" whereby our relationship with God is restored – if – we remain in relationship with – and continue in faithful obedience to – Him.

> "But you are not in the flesh but in the Spirit, if indeed the Spirit of God dwells in you. Now if anyone does not have the Spirit of Christ, he is not His. [10] And if Christ *is* in you, **the body is dead**

because of sin, but the spirit is life because of righteousness" (Rom. 8:9, 10).[99]

Much of our confusion about the resurrection comes from reading commentaries on the bible. The same problem people had with the resurrection 2,000 years ago is the same problem we have today: we are overly concerned by what happens to the physical body.

Commentators created teachings about the resurrection of the body, and I will use this simple illustration: the scripture above is contrasting the spiritual difference when the Spirit of God dwells in you – or not; as being His or not His, that is: Christ's. If Christ is in you, the body is (spiritually) dead because of sin – BUT NOW – the spirit within you is life because of righteousness. The next verse, however, has been used by commentators to talk about the resurrection of the body, but that is not what the Apostle Paul is teaching us.

> " But if the Spirit of Him who raised Jesus from the dead dwells in you, He who raised Christ from the dead will also give life to your mortal bodies through His Spirit who dwells in you" (Rom. 8:11).

He will give life to (2227; quicken-KJV) your "mortal" bodies through His Spirit who is now dwelling in you. This scripture applies to your existing mortal body (the one you're in now), not to a resurrected immortal body as some doctrines teach (which would contradict 1 Cor. 15:53, 54), so you may "now" glorify God with your spirit in your quickened body (made anew by the Spirit in the new birth) which are His! This is how we are supposed to be living on earth once we have been born anew... glorifying God in our body and in our spirit ... which are God's.

---

[99] The author believes this is one instance when the word spirit (small 's') was accurately used: "but the spirit is life." An identical word is found in John 3:6: "born of the Spirit" could be "spirit" (small 's').

"For you were bought at a price; therefore glorify God in your body and in your spirit, which are God's" (1 Cor. 6:20).

A similar commentator error was introduced in 1 Cor. 15:42 (which we will examine later). In the new birth, you were given a new heart and a new spirit – and – a quickened body (Rom. 8:9-11)! You became "a new creation" through faith in Christ… and now the renewing of your mind is the final step in this transformation process resulting in regeneration, i.e. newness again! Formerly, your body kept you captive in sin, but now – you are to glorify God in a quickened mortal body. From this point forward, we must not surrender our body to sinful lusts and passions again so as to engage in those activities that formerly kept us captive to sin.

"The flesh counts for nothing" (John 6:63), so stop obsessing on it… which is one sign that people remain trapped in the world's system (they continue to gratify the flesh).

In order for this to make any sense, **we must perceive the soul of our person as a spiritual being (an entity) that can exist without a body.** A person can be dead in the body (yet alive in Christ and will experience resurrection with Him; Rom. 6:11; John 6:40) or alive in the body but remain dead (a condition of separation from God). Rising from the dead, in this regard (metaphorically) is an action initiated by faith that precedes a later action of resurrection from the dead – enabled by God's power. Thus, being dead is a temporary spiritual condition (initially) for all men. Since we were all born into the paradigm of sin, we are all "dead in trespasses and sin" whereby we can only be saved "from being dead and destined for Death" through repentance and thus, made alive again (quickened) through faith in Jesus Christ. In this regard, according to faith, the temporary place where our soul waits until the Day of Christ (the judgment and the resurrection) is either in Death (for unregenerate souls alienated from God) or in Hades (for regenerate souls saved through faith in Jesus). The "resurrection of the just" (Luke 14:14) and the redemption[100] has yet to occur.

If you are alive with the life of Christ in you when you die, then you will never "be dead" for "God is a God of the living [regenerate], not the dead [unregenerate]." Technically speaking, if you are walking with Christ… then you are already living eternally! What happens to your body from this time forward is immaterial, both literally and figuratively. If Jesus is dwelling in your heart, then Jesus will always abide with you wherever your soul goes. You are never separated from Him, nor will He ever leave you or forsake you. What happens, then, to the souls of the dead waiting in Death that are separated from God?

> "They are dead, they will not live; they are deceased, they will not rise. Therefore You have punished and destroyed them, and made all their memory to perish" (Isa. 26:14).

The dead (those spiritually separated from God) waiting in Death do not rise. Thus, there are two conditions for the dead: those in Death who never rise, and those in Hades who, being alive according to faith… will rise for judgment. Yes, even the faithful will be judged.

"What does the Lord require (*darash*) of you?" (Micah 6:8). "*Darash*-1875' means: "to seek, inquire, ask, require" and implies making an inquest by performing a rigorous examination of everything that was said and done, and with it "often has the idea of avenging an offense against God"[101] (see Gen. 9:5). Where is this inquiry and rigorous examination performed in the Day of Judgment?"[102]

---

[100] There is much wisdom in reading Jeremiah 32:6-15 as a type and shadow of life on earth as earthen vessels in prison and our future redemption to receive houses, fields and vineyards… in the New Earth.
[101] Strong's Concordance.
[102] Excerpt copied from "Commission" section titles "Resurrection Clarification."

For starters, it's not done in Heaven. It's done in a courtroom in or near Hades.

The dead will rise. Judgment happens. The resurrection follows. These are three separate and distinct events occurring within "the resurrection of the dead" process. The nine events listed above are non-resurrection events; these persons were physically raised from the dead, yet their body perished a second time.

The resurrection of the dead begins by rising up – for judgment. This does not mean, necessarily, that the judgment of us is going to be bad; it simply means… we must arise and we must be judged by Jesus. Doctrines that teach we will not be judged by claiming justification, grace or mercy seem to understand little what the terms "require" and "judgment" mean.

Being raised from the dead is a term applied to all persons who died on earth and are raised for judgment, which can be synonymous with condemnation and damnation. Let me explain:

The terms damnation, condemnation and judgment are often used interchangeably to imply roughly the same thing; ('*krisis*-2920' is the process of investigation, the act of distinguishing and separating (i.e. judging, a tribunal; 2 Cor. 5:10), and '*krima*-2917' is the decision, verdict or sentence to be imposed resulting from the investigation).[103] '*Krisis*' will result in '*krima*' – the resurrection of '*krisis*' condemnation (i.e. interrogation and judgment) will result in the pronouncement of '*krima*' the sentence of condemnation… as in "to be condemned'" (Luke 24:20)[104] or some other pronouncement.

> "For it behooves all us to be manifested before the tribunal of Christ, in order that "each one may receive" the things through the body according to

---

[103] Definitions from Strong's Concordance.
[104] IBID.

> what things be practiced, either good or worthless"
> (2 Cor. 5:10).

We will be judged for the things we did "through the body" whereby we will be sent to the appropriate '*topos*' place according to our deeds, either good or bad, worthy or worthless, righteous or wicked, just or unjust… for deeds done by us upon the earth.

> "And this is the condemnation [2920], that the light has come into the world, and men loved darkness rather than light, because their deeds were evil" (John 3:19).

Jesus came as the Light of the World to testify to the truth wherein this is the condemnation: His visitation is the '*krima*' judging process He will use in separating those seeking truth, trusting Him and loving Him – versus those in rebellion (apart from faith) who refuse to submit their allegiance to Jesus because they loved darkness rather than light. The dragnet of faith will gather all "in faith," and when it is pulled ashore, angels will "separate the wicked from among the just" (Matt. 13:47-49).

The problem we often experience with words is: the thought process of producing a decision to act – and the action – is nearly identical. The thought (decision) to love and the act of loving someone are essentially… the same word: love. The same is true with hate and judgment. Verbs effectuate the noun. The act of judging and the pronouncement of judgment are nearly indistinguishable, hence the confusion regarding the judgment and the ensuing judgment – or the condemnation and the ensuing condemnation into various eternal places – and even greater condemnation for some.

When Jesus referred to the resurrection of condemnation, this is the process of raising the dead so the judgment and interrogation process may begin – before judgment is pronounced.

"Do not marvel at this; for the hour is coming in which all[105] who are in the graves will hear His voice [28] and come forth [proceed-1607]—those who have done good, to the resurrection of life, and those who have done evil, to the resurrection of condemnation [2920; judgment; damnation-KJV]" (John 5:28, 29).

All will hear His voice – rise and proceed toward judgment – then resurrection! Jesus knows fully what we have done and what we deserve; if we have done evil, the process of judgment [2920; condemnation] where we stand as a witness for or against ourselves in the presence of many witnesses, will result either in a finding [2917] of guilt that results in a sentence… or perhaps acquittal. All of us have done some form of evil on earth and this process will judge it. Justice will be served! Jesus judges in righteousness! The Holy Spirit is an inner witness who also testifies for or against us, which should motivate us to work out our own salvation with fear and trembling (Phil. 2:12). If we have done evil, we will receive condemnation (2917); however, if you have taken lightly the responsibilities as a teacher of truth (James 3:1) or you "devoured widow's homes or for a pretense make long prayers. These will receive greater condemnation [2917]" (Mark 12:40). Our actions have eternal consequences.

It is important to note: through repentance and faith, our prior sins were forgiven and shall be remembered no more, but continuation in dead works and unrepentant sin (post salvation) will be judged and condemned. Justification from death happens once upon salvation to restore us to a right relationship with God; yet justification hereafter is continuous… and is associated with right conduct and walking in righteousness.[106]

---

[105] The exact meaning and translation of this word was not determined by the author; see (v.25) for a possible conflict.

[106] Strong's makes an excellent case contrasting these dual perspectives of Paul (as ungodly being justified by faith) and James (only the right-doer is justified); Strong's exposition on 'justify-1344.' In this regard, the former, being saved

Those passing through judgment as having done good (did justly, loved mercy, walked humbly, lived according to righteousness) will participate in the resurrection of life… where the just will enjoy one final step: a rewards banquet in the presence of their enemies, no less.

The resurrection, it seems, is far more complicated than we expected, partly because:

- Teachers have been teaching there are only two places we go after the resurrection (heaven or hell) when, in fact, there are many places for deeds done on earth
- Teachers erringly classify people according to these two places as sheep or goats; and
- Believers have claimed the mercies of God and justification by faith, yet failed to perceive the process of justification is continuous and the process of judgment is far more rigorous than we've been taught, nor do we rightly perceive the Lord as a Judge who judges by fire with a sword of justice in His hand (Isa. 66:16) whereby many will not be able to endure His indignation (Jer. 10:10)

Yet the writer of Hebrews seems to think resurrection is an elementary teaching, as is eternal judgment. Why is there such a big disconnect? Because, the early church talked about righteousness, holiness, purity, the fear of the Lord and being willing to die for Jesus on account of faith, but we've sugar-coated the Gospel of Jesus, diluted the truth and covered our sins with chocolate so that now – everyone – is served dessert as they enter through pearly gates.

> "Therefore, leaving the discussion of the elementary principles of Christ, let us go on to perfection, not laying again the foundation of repentance from dead works and of faith toward God, [2] of the doctrine of baptisms, of laying on of hands, of resurrection of

---

out of sin (John 16:9) and justified by faith, the latter, living apart from sin and upholding righteous conduct.

the dead, and of eternal judgment [2917]" (Heb. 6:1, 2).

Repentance from dead works... now there's a topic I've never heard preached! The "once saved, always saved" doctrine cannot co-exist with the principle of repentance from dead works. Consider the believing widow who resumed her life "in pleasure – is dead even while she lives" (1 Tim. 5:6). Consider, also, the dozens of "if-then" conditional statements for saving faith. Our covenantal promises with Jesus are valid – only if – we keep out end of the agreement!

These concepts of being raised from the dead into a tribunal for judgment were very intriguing and often ridiculed as "insane" ideas against the early church, much like they are today; however, the Gospel of Jesus is predicated upon these truths, as are these: the dead are raised, judgment happens, and the resurrection of the dead are truthful teachings. Let's examine the following scripture(s) to see how some of these terms are used:

> "So also is the resurrection [386] of the dead. ~~The body~~ It is sown in corruption, it is raised [1453] in incorruption" (1 Cor. 15:42; ~~stricken~~ words were added by commentators. The correct translation for σπείρεται "it is sown" (which also occurs three more times) was reintroduced by the author in v.42. "It" refers to the soul (as one type of glory) being raised in resurrection).[107]

> "Women received their dead [3498] ~~raised~~ [386] resurrected to life again. Others were tortured, not accepting deliverance, that they might obtain a better resurrection" (Heb. 11:35; the better resurrection can refer to the first resurrection of

---

[107] Excerpt copied from "Commission" section titled "Resurrection Clarification."

martyrs; Rev. 20:4; and/or/perhaps the resurrection of the just; Luke 14:14).

"Then, behold, the veil of the temple was torn in two from top to bottom; and the earth quaked, and the rocks were split, [52] and the graves were opened; and many bodies of the saints who had fallen asleep were raised [1453]; [53] and coming out of the graves after His *resurrection* [1454], they went into the holy city and appeared to many" (Matt. 27:51-53; a more accurate term would be "*He arose*;" 1453 is the act of rising, 1454 stresses the excitation and invigoration of the one being raised; 1454 occurs only once in scripture and applies only to Jesus).

Being raised from the dead is the initial step to begin the judgment process; the resurrection stresses the final outcome of those being judged.[108]

"Now if Christ is preached that He has been raised [1453] from the dead, how do some among you say that there is no resurrection [386] of the dead? [13] But if there is no resurrection [386] of the dead, then Christ is not risen [1453]. [14] And if Christ is not risen [1453], then our preaching *is* empty and your faith *is* also empty" (1 Cor. 15:12-14).

This is critically important to read and understand as many times as necessary: being raised from the dead (450), awakened and assembled (1453) is the initial step to begin the judgment process followed by the resurrection, which stresses the final outcome of those being judged. (See Eph. 5:14).

The same concerns 2,000 years ago are the same concerns saints have today. We know the dead are raised, but we likewise associate being raised as synonymous with resurrection – which it isn't! Inclusive – yes; synonymous – no. Being raised from the

---

[108] Strong's Concordance; exposition on 'anastasis-386-resurrection.'

dead is proof the resurrection will occur, yet for whatever reason our doctrines bypass any mention of judgment to focus on the resurrection during our after-life funerals and celebrations. Throughout my Christian life, I have professed a grace gospel that focuses on what God has done for me and on my behalf that rails against a salvation of works, but this teaching created a clarifying light in how I now operate from grace – from a justification position of grace through faith to begin my walk of grace – followed by a justification position of incentive-based rewards in the resurrection accomplished through me by His grace. Yielding to the Lord… yields much!

Our salvation is by grace; our continued works upon the earth is – grace in action.

Grace does not stop working once we are saved; grace becomes the operational force to produce newness in us – through truth, change and oneness – to imitate Christ. The radical truth about grace compels us to continuously grow in grace to operate according to our fullest potential – in Christ. If there is any aspect of your life where you can say, after reading the Acts of the Apostles, "my life" is inconsistent with their example, then I suggest one thing: convert! Live according to the truth. If you know you could be doing more for Christ – then start doing it (and you will be rewarded for doing so). Stop talking and do something. Stop preaching and start living it. Great is your reward in heaven; read (Matt. 5:12; Rev. 20:4) to learn what this means.

Why wait for the afterlife… when you can do it now? Live today like there's no tomorrow.[109]

So I ask again: if you knew exactly what would happen to you after you died, would you want to know as much detail as possible… especially if you could initiate a course correction to improve your eternal outcome in terms of location, incentive compensation, inheritance and positional placement in the New

---

[109] "Dream is if you'll live forever, live as if you'll die today." James Dean.

Earth? Do you prefer digging dirt planting potatoes for all eternity or do you prefer better? Do you prefer living in outer darkness where there is wailing and gnashing of teeth for hypocrites and all persons pretending to be Christian or do you want to start living according to the gospel of truth that Christ taught and change this world from darkness to light? Your destiny awaits!

Just enough to get by… may not be enough. Righteousness is the gold standard in God's kingdom.

> "But seek first the kingdom of God and His righteousness, and all these things shall be added to you" (Matt. 6:33).

Some who rise from the dead will experience the resurrection of condemnation, but all who rise from the dead with Jesus in the resurrection of life will enter into Paradise.

> "Most assuredly, I say to you, the hour is coming, and now is, when the dead will hear the voice of the Son of **Go**d; and those who hear will live" (John 5:25).

When the Lord calls out to those in Hades, I am of this opinion: the only ones who hear the voice of Jesus are those who learned what His voice sounded like on earth (John 10:27)… who have ears to hear and also sought to understand the message. Only those who hear and understand… shall live!

Strong's makes an excellent point in his exposition of '*zoopoieo*-2227' translated "quicken, make alive" in that "quicken means to enable to respond to His voice immediately. Once born again and indwelt by the Holy Spirit, one does not have to wait in order to respond. Response comes fully and instantaneously."[110] If you cannot hear the Voice of Jesus, then go back to the beginning of the Image Bearer series and read "Listen: How To Hear God's Voice – better."

---

[110] Strong's exposition of '*zoopoieo*-2227' translated "quicken, make alive."

> "My sheep hear My voice, and I know them, and
> they follow Me" (John 10:27).

Stop! Don't keep reading if you cannot hear His voice. Your salvation is predicated on it!

> "I have hope in God, which they themselves also
> accept, that there will be a resurrection of the dead,
> both of the just and the unjust" (Acts 24:15).

Being raised from the dead, at this point, are those persons in Hades who believed in Jesus... as sons of obedience who lived in a listening manner (the just, the sheep) and sons of disobedience (the unjust, the goats). As for the sons of rebellion in unbelief, they are dead; they do not rise; there is silence in Death.

> "And I saw the dead [3498], small and great,
> standing before God, and books were opened. And
> another book was opened, which is the Book of
> Life. And the dead [3498] were judged according to
> their works, by the things which were written in the
> books" (Rev. 20:12).

The resurrection which follows the rising of the dead and judgment, at this point, has two parts:

1. The resurrection of condemnation (for unjust, unfaithful, unworthy, hypocrites, unprofitable servants, unfaithful stewards, goats) to be cast into Outer Darkness
2. The resurrection of life along with reward and recompense (the resurrection of the just)

Pay careful attention to this message by the Spirit to the leader of the church in Sardis:

> "And to the angel of the church in Sardis write,
> 'These things says He who has the seven Spirits of
> God and the seven stars: "I know your works, *that*

> *you have a name that you are alive,* ***but you are dead***" (Rev. 3:1).

This church leader was teaching this congregation they have a name that they claim makes them alive… but they are dead. The Spirit continues with the Lord's message for this church:

> "Nevertheless, you have a few names even in Sardis who have not defiled their garments; and they shall walk with Me in white, for they are worthy. ⁵ He who overcomes shall be clothed in white garments, ***and I will not blot out his name from the Book of Life***; but I will confess his name before My Father and before His angels" (Rev. 3:4, 5).

Sardis is a dead church full of "dead awaiting Death" people, but there are some in this church who are counted worthy to be judged – whereby those who overcome shall be clothed in white garments. This is incredibly good news for multitudes of persons that seem stuck in dead churches without any spiritually-alive persons around them, so I encourage you to remain faithful and continue steadfast in loving adoration and devotion to Jesus, your High Priest, who will deliver you from the land of dead into the land of the redeemed. Amen! It also seems noteworthy that our faith journey begins with our name written in the Book of Life; however, some actions by us will result in our names being erased. Wisdom is needed to comprehend the point of this truth.

It is important for the author to recognize the Holy Spirit as the One guiding him through the scriptures to see the end from the beginning, as I have no formal training or prior teaching in this topic, nor have I received supernatural revelation through dreams and visions, nor have I visited the places being referenced. The author is merely a listener who writes what he hears.

> "Jesus said to him, "Let the dead bury their own dead, but you go and preach the kingdom of God" (Luke 9:60).

Likewise, I say to you... go and preach the Gospel of Truth and establish the kingdom of heaven on Earth. Go therefore, and make disciples of all nations... and proclaim the Good News.
Jesus died and arose from the grave. Jesus is alive. These facts are incontrovertible, and yet Jesus told us: "I am the Resurrection and the Life" (John 11:25). Jesus is both God and Christ and Messiah, so why would Jesus need to be resurrected when He IS the Resurrection? The short answer is: He didn't. The reason Jesus did the things He did was to prove to all of us that He is who He said He is – and – to teach what is going to happen to us. For example, He sanctified Himself to teach us we must also be sanctified. Jesus was raised from the dead and the resurrection is going to occur... and Jesus became the living proof this will occur!

> "But now Christ is risen from the dead, and has become the firstfruits of those who have fallen asleep. [21] For since by man came death, by Man also came the resurrection of the dead" (1 Cor. 15:20, 21).

Jesus raised (450) Himself on the Third Day, yet never once did Jesus indicate He would experience resurrection (which is the final state of the one raised after judgment, which Jesus never needed). Resurrection is associated with judgment, yet Jesus is the Resurrection and Jesus is the Judge. Therefore, Jesus was raised, but never resurrected – despite eight scriptures to the contrary (Acts 1:22; 2:31; 4:2, 33; Rom. 6:5; Phil. 3:10; 1 Pet. 1:3; 3:21). This teaching does not contradict scripture – it merely clarifies the teaching of being raised and the resurrection that follows.

Jesus is Lord. Jesus is the Life. Jesus is ALL that we hoped a loving God would be.

Man was encoded in his spiritual and natural DNA by God to arise and walk. Consider this analogy: young babies begin to crawl on their own, then they seek to stand upright and then toddle so they can walk, as something natural to man... and this is true for the spiritual man as well, as desiring to arise, stand upright and walk again in the resurrection (*anastasis* means literally: to stand again). In the resurrection, we are rising up and made to stand again, which is the true nature and character of the believer, but I wonder if disobedient saints might prefer lying down and refuse rising up even when the trumpet sounds and the Lord calls their name.

The Spirit guided me in this truth, so ask the Spirit to teach you what you must know and convict your heart if need be. Judgment happens… and the redemption of your soul is costly (Psa. 49:9).

It's all about Jesus – and God gets the glory! Amen!

8) The Earthly (Kingdom of) Heaven

> "May you be blessed by the LORD, Who made heaven and earth. [16] The heaven, even the heavens, are the LORD's; ***but the earth He has given to the children of men***" (Psa. 115:15, 16).

Let us now look at earth as "the kingdom of heaven" that Jesus, who is King of Heaven, redeemed and established – from a New Earth doctrine perspective, knowing foremost that we are image bearers and kingdom builders who were sent to exercise God's authority to have dominion over the worldly dominion of Satan, and to invade, take back and re-occupy stolen territory (earth) and advance Christ's kingdom with the power of the Holy Spirit operating within us to release the substance of heavenly things through us.

A great many books have been written about this subject and there are some wonderful teachings about living your life 'now' as a citizen of heaven with the reality of heaven operating presently within you as a follower and disciple of Jesus Christ. When we live as a new creation, as a born anew transformed individual who lives with a renewed mindset to "think like Jesus and live like Jesus – as one walking in the fullness of the Spirit," then please read every book that is available to understand this new life with Christ abiding in you and the Holy Spirit dwelling within you to empower you with delegated authority that was granted to you – to have dominion.

Think about the kingdom of heaven, not only as a heavenly place upon earth, but also as an event that is happening within your heart and soul every day to make an abode for the Father and Son to abide in.

- Think about being connected to the kingdom of God, like a branch on a vine, as seeds of truth sown upon the field of faith in your heart which take *root* and grow up to bear fruit

- Think about this kingdom like food – the Spirit-reality of grace and truth in, glory out

Now, let us understand the kingdom of heaven, as Jesus taught us:

1. John the Baptist, the greatest prophet of the old covenant and forerunner for the King of heaven and earth, i.e. Jesus, came preaching and saying, "Repent, for the kingdom of heaven is at hand!" (Matt. 3:2) – indicating Jesus brought this new heavenly reality with Him to the earth
   - Jesus confirmed the testimony of John, "and from that time Jesus began to preach and to say, "Repent, for the kingdom of heaven is at hand" (Matt. 4:17; Mark 1:14; Luke 4:14)
   - And Jesus told us when this kingdom began: "The law and the prophets *were* until John. *Since that time* the kingdom of God has been preached, and everyone is *pressing into it*" (Luke 16:16); and "from the days of John the Baptist until now the kingdom of heaven suffers violence" and violent men are forcefully advancing against it (Matt. 11:12)
   - Jesus reiterated John's significant importance to the kingdom, "Assuredly, I say to you, among those born of women there has not risen one greater than John the Baptist; but he who is least in the kingdom of heaven is greater than he" (Matt. 11:11; Luke 7:28)

2. Jesus began to teach the multitudes that future residents of the kingdom will be invited to attend based upon the condition of their heart as it relates to the King and their service to Him regardless of title, position, ordination or covenant belief under which you served:
   - "Blessed *are* the poor in spirit, For theirs is the kingdom of heaven" (Matt. 5:3)
   - "Blessed *are* those who are persecuted for righteousness' sake, For theirs is the kingdom of heaven" (Matt. 5:9; Luke 6:20)

- "And I say to you that many will come from east and west, and sit down with Abraham, Isaac, and Jacob in the kingdom of heaven" (Matt. 8:11) – and these three served Jesus as the King of heaven under the Abrahamic covenant before the old or new covenants were established

3. Jesus teaches us some requirements for entering the kingdom of heaven are restrictive:
   - "Not everyone who says to Me, 'Lord, Lord,' shall enter the kingdom of heaven, but he who does the will of My Father in heaven" (Matt. 7:21; Luke 6:46; 13:26)
   - "Whoever therefore breaks one of the least of these commandments, and teaches men so, *shall be called least* in the kingdom of heaven; but whoever does and teaches them, he shall be called great in the kingdom of heaven" (Matt. 5:19;
   - "But woe to you, scribes and Pharisees, hypocrites! For you shut up the kingdom of heaven against men; for you neither go in yourselves, nor do you allow those who are entering to go in" (Mt. 23:13)
   - "Therefore I say to you, the kingdom of God will be taken from you and given to a nation bearing the fruits of it" (Matt. 21:43)
   - "For I say to you, that unless your righteousness exceeds the righteousness of the scribes and Pharisees, you *will by no means enter* the kingdom of heaven" (5:20)
   - "Assuredly, I say to you that it is hard for a rich man to enter the kingdom of heaven" (Mt. 19:23; Mark 10:23-25) – who relies upon and trusts in his own worth, works, righteousness or value system
   - "And again I say to you, it is easier for a camel to go through the eye of a needle than for a rich man to enter the kingdom of God" (Matt. 19:24) – Jesus not only emphatically reiterates His point, but the scriptures have made a distinct link between the kingdom of

heaven and the kingdom of God as operating in oneness on the earth
- "Which of the two did the will of *his* father?" They said to Him, "The first." Jesus said to them, "Assuredly, I say to you that tax collectors and harlots enter the kingdom of God before you" (Matt. 21:31) – and we must all do the will of Him who sent us, just as Jesus did (John 5:30; 6:39;17:4)
- "Do you not know that the unrighteous will not inherit the kingdom of God? Do not be deceived. Neither fornicators, nor idolaters, nor adulterers, nor homosexuals, nor sodomites nor thieves, nor covetous, nor drunkards, nor revilers, nor extortioners will inherit the kingdom of God" (1 Cor. 6:9, 10)
- "Now the works of the flesh are evident, which are: adultery, fornication, uncleanness, lewdness, [20] idolatry, sorcery, hatred, contentions, jealousies, outbursts of wrath, selfish ambitions, dissensions, heresies, [21] envy, murders, drunkenness, revelries, and the like; of which I tell you beforehand, just as I also told *you* in time past, that those who practice such things will not inherit the kingdom of God" (Gal 5:19-21).

4. And Jesus tells His disciples the mysteries of the kingdom are revealed to those who earnestly seek kingdom truth and desire a personal relationship with Jesus:
   - "He answered and said to them, "Because it has been given to you to know the mysteries of the kingdom of heaven, but to them it has not been given" (Matt. 13:11; Mark 4:11; Luke 8:10) – the purpose being not to hide truth *from* us but to hide truth *for* those who search diligently so they may seek and find divine truth (Prov. 25:2), for in these ones the Father delights!

5. As a redeemed child of God, saved by grace and therefore a citizen of heaven, we have an obligation and responsibility to go into all the world preaching the good news:

- "And as you go, preach, saying, 'The kingdom of heaven is at hand'" (Matt. 10:7)
- "Now it came to pass, afterward, that He went through every city and village, preaching and bringing the glad tidings of the kingdom of God. And the twelve *were* with Him" (Luke 8:1)
- "Preaching the kingdom of God and teaching the things which concern the Lord Jesus Christ with all confidence, no one forbidding him" (Acts 28:31)
- "He sent them to preach the kingdom of God and to heal the sick" (Luke 9:2)
- "And heal the sick there, and say to them, 'The kingdom of God has come near to you.'" (Luke 10:11)
- "Now when one of those who sat at the table with Him heard these things, he said to Him, "Blessed *is* he who shall eat bread in the kingdom of God!" (Luke 14:15)
- "For the **kingdom of God** is not eating and drinking, but righteousness and peace and joy in the Holy Spirit" (Rom. 14:17)
- "For the **kingdom of God** *is* not in word but in power" (1 Cor. 4:20)
- "And He said to them, "Assuredly, I say to you that there are some standing here who will not taste death till they see the kingdom of God *present with power*" (Mark 9:1).

6. And ultimately, Jesus explains through parables what the kingdom of heaven will be like "on earth as it is in heaven" when people hear, understand and comprehend this truth:
    - The quintessential timeless message about the kingdom of heaven that is both "upon the earth and in your heart" is found in the "The Parable of the Sower," for it describes the heavenly reality of living life from four different perspectives: the heart as the field of faith, how we accept or reject truth, how we listen, and how we understand kingdom truth... and we must nurture this truth in our garden to mature and produce an

abundant harvest that continues from person to person, from generation to generation and from nation to nation (Mt. 13:1-23)
- "The kingdom of heaven is like a man (*Jesus*) who sowed good seed in his field" but his enemy (*Satan*) came and sowed tares among the wheat and went his way (Mat. 13:24-30)
- "The kingdom of God (*for mankind*) is as if a man should scatter seed on the ground, and should sleep by night and rise by day, and the seed should sprout and grow, he himself does not know how" (Mark 4:26-29)
- "The kingdom of heaven is like a *mustard seed*, which a man took and sowed in his field" – and the smallest of seed grew and matured into a large, life-giving tree that many people sought benefit from (Mt. 13:31; Luke 13:18); Jesus told us "with what parable shall we picture the kingdom of God?" Jesus told us the mustard seed is the "picture" of the visible kingdom (Mark 4:30), in contrast to the invisible aspects of leaven (next).
- "The kingdom of heaven is like *leaven*, which a woman took and hid in three measures of meal till it was all leavened" – whereby the message of Christ's gospel that is invisible and indivisible becomes visibly manifest as it exists in oneness with the bread, whereby it produces a beneficial "leavening" influence and life-altering impact on all people's lives throughout the entire world which will produce beneficial outcomes, sustenance, spiritual increase, abundance and prosperity for their earthly life (Mt. 13:33) as something that can be shared, distributed and partnered with. The kingdom of heaven is like leaven; once it gets into the bread, you cannot get it out, nor can you prevent the inevitable changes that result unless you actively choose to destroy the leavened bread, which is one strategy of the enemy to thwart Christians … who are the visible manifestation of Christ upon the earth.

- "The kingdom of heaven is like *treasure* hidden in a field, which a man found and hid; and for joy over it he goes and sells all that he has and buys that field" – and likewise, we should diligently seek to find the truth of the gospel, and to know the mysteries of the kingdom of heaven (Mt. 13:11), forsaking everything else, so as to take hold of it and establish a fruitful field within our heart as it resides within our earthen vessel, so that we may possess and protect and proclaim kingdom truth (Mt. 13:44).
- "Again, the kingdom of heaven is like a *merchant* seeking beautiful pearls" – found the most precious pearl (the greatest truth) that he had searched diligently for and sold everything to possess it (Mt. 13:45); *this parable and the hidden treasure not only describes our search for Jesus, but it also described Jesus' search for us as we are hidden in a field (earth) with the kingdom of heaven hidden within us (our heart).*

7. Jesus taught us another aspect regarding the kingdom of heaven that acts like an all-encompassing net to gather all things together so that they can be separated as good things apart from worthless, profane things; and things new (spiritually regenerate) from old things (unlawful, unregenerate):
    - "Again, the kingdom of heaven is like a *dragnet* that was cast into the sea and gathered some of every kind" (Mt. 13:47)
    - Then Jesus said to them, "Therefore every scribe instructed concerning the kingdom of heaven is like a *householder* who brings out of his treasure *things* new and old *things*" (Mt. 13:52) – the two things can represent the new and old covenants that Jesus established, or they can represent revelation and the written word
    - "But if I cast out demons by the Spirit of God, surely the kingdom of God has come upon you" (Matt. 12:28)

– in sublime simplicity, Jesus tells us *the kingdom is here*!

8. Principles for effective living and lifeway attitudes in the kingdom:
   - "And I will give you the keys of the kingdom of heaven, and whatever you bind on earth will be bound in heaven, and whatever you loose on earth will be loosed in heaven" (Mt. 16:19) – whereby we have always had the power to forgive sins and any person's offense against us without needing a sacrament or absolution, because whatever we bind on earth also becomes bound within us, and if we do not forgive one another, then our heavenly Father cannot forgive us (Matt. 6:15)
   - "Who then is greatest in the kingdom of heaven?" (Mt. 18:1) – are we not all servants of Jesus and, therefore, are we not also the servant of all
   - "Assuredly, I say to you, *unless you are converted and become as little children*, you will by no means enter the kingdom of heaven" (Mt. 18:3; Mark 10:15) – with childlike faith and lifeway attitudes that are selfless, trusting, playful, happy, kind to all, obedient, sharing, caring, always living in the present – not holding onto yesterdays problems or becoming worried about tomorrows cares… just like a little child!
   - "Therefore *whoever humbles himself as this little child* is the greatest in the kingdom of heaven" (Mt. 18:4) – arrogance and pridefulness are offensive attitudes in God's kingdom, but humility and being poor in spirit are key godly attributes to receive divine favor, mercy and every spiritual blessing
   - "Let the little children come to Me, and do not forbid them; for of such is the kingdom of heaven" (Mt. 19:14; Mark 10:14) – and generations to come. Little children, in this context, are very young and are still in a state of grace (not knowing their left hand from the right) who have not yet known the knowledge of good and evil. In

the kingdom of heaven, we will become like these little children – as living in a state of grace.

9. Jesus goes on to describe Himself and His Father as "a certain" person in varying ways and manners to establish a concrete relationship between the Person and the place as operating inextricably in kingdom oneness:
    - "For the kingdom of heaven is like *a man* traveling to a far country, *who* called his own servants and delivered his goods to them" (Mt. 25:14) – the far country is earth
    - "For the kingdom of heaven is like *a landowner* who went out early in the morning to hire laborers for his vineyard" (Mt. 20:1) – in pre-light darkness, He came as the Light of the world
    - "Therefore the kingdom of heaven is like *a certain king* who wanted to settle accounts with his servants (Mt. 8:23) – and we will all stand before the judgment seat of Christ (Rom. 14:10; 2 Cor. 5:10)
    - "The kingdom of heaven is like *a certain king* who arranged a marriage for his son" (Mt. 22:2) – the church is the bride of Christ, but as we will see, not everyone who was called to the marriage or the wedding feast is living in a state of preparedness with this eternal reality operating within their heart – and thus…
    - "*Then* the kingdom of heaven shall be likened to ten virgins who took their lamps and went out to meet the bridegroom" (Mt. 25:1; five were prepared, but five were not)

10. No one living upon the earth will be able to understand any of this, or comprehend what will happen next, apart from the new birth by the Spirit
    - Jesus answered and said to him, "Most assuredly, I say to you, unless one is born again, he cannot see the kingdom of God" (John 3:3)

- Jesus answered, "Most assuredly, I say to you, unless one is born of water and the Spirit, he cannot enter the kingdom of God" (John 3:5)
- "Now this I say, brethren, that flesh and blood cannot inherit the kingdom of God; nor does corruption inherit incorruption" (1 Cor. 15:50)
- "But if you are led by the Spirit, you are not under the law" (Gal. 5:18)

11. Finally, three keys for effective Christian living according to Christ's kingdom on earth
    - "The kingdom of God is within you" (Luke 17:21) – and since you are a representative of God, you are a citizen of heaven and therefore you are a representative of the kingdom of heaven that Jesus established upon the earth … by grace through faith, but not everyone is living their life with the truth of this reality within their heart – it requires conversion by the Spirit and transformation according to the Spirit to live according to the kingdom of heaven that Christ established
    - "Where two or three are gathered together in My name, I am there in the midst of them" (Matt. 18:20)
    - "But seek first the kingdom of God and His righteousness, and all these things shall be added to you" (Matt. 6:23)

And now, the two greatest commandments shall be added onto the dominion mandate as we establish the kingdom of heaven upon the earth:

> "And (Jesus said) you shall love the LORD your God with all your heart, with all your soul, with all your mind, and with all your strength.' This *is* the first commandment. [31] And the second, like *it, is* this: 'You shall love your neighbor as yourself.' There is no other commandment greater than these." [32] So the scribe said to Him, "Well *said,* Teacher. You have spoken the truth, for there is one God, and

there is no other but He. ³³ And to love Him with all the heart, with all the understanding, with all the soul, and with all the strength, and to love one's neighbor as oneself, is more than all the whole burnt offerings and sacrifices." ³⁴ Now when Jesus saw that he answered wisely, He said to him, "You are not far from the kingdom of God" (Mark 12:30-34).

Listen to His voice, host His presence, have dominion, and love one another.

This is the big picture gospel. If Christ abides within your heart, then you are already abiding in His presence (with Him) within His ever-present reality of heaven itself within you, so now it is up to you to live your life in such a manner, as a workmanship of Christ in you, to let heaven out so that other souls are born anew and saved unto newness of life according to the Spirit of life in Christ Jesus.

Sadly, it seems, for the past 2,000 years, we have been waiting for something… that has already happened.

Jesus came as the King of heaven to usher onto the earth the kingdom of heaven for the earth, and His arrival was neither accidental nor arbitrary. "But when the fullness of the time had come, God sent forth His Son, born of a woman, born under the law" (Gal. 4:4). Jesus came at just the right time and place to declare: "The time is fulfilled, and the kingdom of God is at hand. Repent, and believe in the gospel" (Mark 1:15).

And you are reading this also, at just the right time, to repent and believe in the gospel of Jesus Christ. A moment in time has been prepared for every one of us to hear the gospel and to believe, but if we turn away and refuse His invitation, then we have judged ourselves unworthy to enter into the kingdom of heaven… and have condemned ourselves.

"And Jesus came and spoke to them, saying, "All authority has been given to Me in heaven and on earth" (Matt. 28:18); "He who descended is also the One who ascended far above all the heavens, that He might fill all things" (Eph. 4:10), "That in the dispensation of the fullness of the times He might gather together in one all things in Christ, both which are in heaven and which are on earth—in Him" (Eph. 1:10); and "Then comes the end, when He delivers the kingdom to God the Father, when He puts an end to all rule and all authority and power" (1 Cor. 15:24).

We are in the latter time – even now.

In these last days, "Nation will rise against nation, and kingdom against kingdom. And there will be great earthquakes in various places, and famines and pestilences; and there will be fearful sights and great signs from heaven" (Luke 21:10, 11); "But when you see Jerusalem surrounded by armies, then know that its desolation is near" (v.20); "And there will be signs in the sun, in the moon, and in the stars; and on the earth distress of nations, with perplexity, the sea and the waves roaring; [26] men's hearts failing them from fear and the expectation of those things which are coming on the earth, for the powers of the heavens will be shaken" (v.25, 26).

> "So you also, when you see these things happening, know that the kingdom of God is near" (v.31).

> "Now when these things begin to happen, look up and lift up your heads, because your redemption draws *near* (*nigh, at hand*)" (v.28).

> "We are bound to thank God always for you, brethren, as it is fitting, because your faith grows exceedingly, and the love of every one of you all abounds toward each other, [4] so that we ourselves boast of you among the churches of God for your patience and faith in all your persecutions and tribulations that you endure, [5] which is manifest evidence of the righteous judgment of God, *that you may be counted worthy of the kingdom of God, for which you also suffer*; [6] since it is a righteous thing

with God to repay with tribulation those who trouble you, ⁷ and to give you who are troubled rest with us when the Lord Jesus is revealed from heaven with His mighty angels, ⁸ in flaming fire taking vengeance on those who do not know God, and on those who do not obey the gospel of our Lord Jesus Christ. ⁹ These shall be punished with everlasting destruction from the presence of the Lord and from the glory of His power, ¹⁰ when He comes, in that Day, to be glorified in His saints and to be admired among all those who believe, because our testimony among you was believed" (2 Thess. 1:3-10).

9) Paradigm Shift

> "Wisdom is in the sight of him who has understanding, but the eyes of a fool are on the ends of the earth" (Prov. 17:24).

During the past 40 days, I have been listening to the Lord teach me about a fundamental paradigm shift for the kingdom on earth "as it is in heaven," and how we need to reconsider all "end times" doctrines within the light of "New Earth doctrine" truth,[111] but today, I asked the Holy Spirit "what one thing" is needed to initiate revival to transition the kingdom of this world into the kingdom of heaven.

The earth is at a crossroads and everything that can be shaken is about to be shaken at this time. Waves of change and whirlwinds of transition are becoming tornadoes and tsunamis because two spiritual kingdoms are colliding upon the earth for dominion supremacy – and the souls of men are the point of intersect. In these last days, we will have a choice to make: do you want spiritual revival or tribulation? Both offers are being presented to us at this moment; however... will we choose to live as saints of light, living in truth, or are we going to continue to listen to the children of darkness, disobedience and complacency? Heaven and Hell are two very real choices that we have been experiencing in this lifetime and building in our heart – and times are accelerating quickly the closer we get to the day.

For 2,000 years, we have been preaching and evangelizing feverishly in order to get people into Heaven, but now we need to shift the focus of our attention **to get heaven into people** *as we fix our eyes upon Jesus, the Author and Finisher of our faith.*

---

[111] It is outside the framework of this book to reconsider end times prophecy, but initial reviews seems to put all scriptures into proper perspective once the "heaven-only" determination for man's eternal destination is omitted.

Our attempts to get God into our culture – is contrary– to getting the culture of God into us!

This perspective creates a fundamental shift in how we preach; no longer are we just trying to save many souls alive into Heaven, but we are ushering into the lives of many souls the truth of Heaven to establish the kingdom of heaven onto earth through gateways of grace called men.

Earth is our eternal home – and now it's time to start living like we have something worth inheriting on this planet. Your inheritance – is worth fighting for!

This is our reason for being here in the first place, to get the attributes of heaven into us that Jesus taught us and demonstrated for us, so that, as we focus our eyes upon Jesus, we can establish the kingdom of heaven in the midst of all that we think, say and do.

We were not sent here to get saved and tread water until we ascend into Heaven in the resurrection; we were commissioned to live here as servant soldiers who receive the Lord's salvation through repentance and conversion whereby we are constantly being converted, sanctified and transformed into the awesome image of Christ that you were predestined to be – as a citizen of Heaven living upon the earth with Christ in you and the Holy Spirit's anointing operating through you.

For starters, we need to know, understand and thoroughly comprehend that regenerate man is a citizen of Heaven – but – earth is his eternal home in heavenly places. Selah.

What "one thing" and only one thing is needed to initiate worldwide revival? My mind began to process concepts like "truth, the Holy Spirit, love, grace, faith in Christ alone, *dunamis* and *kratos* power" and these awesome wonderful concepts have been around since the first gospel message was preached and are integral elements of "the one thing," but they are not the one thing to initiate world-wide revival.

A paradigm shift is needed before world-wide revival of titanic proportions can occur – which should begin in the church first, if only the church had ears to hear; but it seems there is "an obstruction" preventing it, as well as a missing "ignition spark" by the Holy Spirit to initiate revival.

What is "the one thing" to initiate global revival? And the Spirit said to me, "Newness."

As God says, "I will make all things new again." "The Lord's mercies are new every morning." "Do not to walk in the oldness of the letter (law) but according to the newness of the Spirit."

A newness paradigm that begets a culture of newness to begin (again) a new way of living, as a born anew Christian with a New Earth doctrine to operate in newness of life according to the Spirit of life in Christ Jesus (Rom. 8:2), has already begun. Newness happens when we embrace "life" in the Spirit! And newness embodies the principle of God's regeneration – in all things.

Stop listening to other people who tell you it cannot happen because it has been tried before – and failed. Indeed, it failed before because they were operating out of a heaven-only paradigm for eternal salvation, but now we know better; and they were operating out of religious traditions, but now the life-giving Spirit of revelation life and truth is converting us to **His** way of thinking.

As John the Baptist said, regarding Jesus, "Behold, the savior of the world." And again, "Behold, the lamb of God who takes away the sin of the world." Not only are unregenerate men worth redeeming unto salvation – but this earth has been redeemed by Jesus and is worth saving as well. The earth is not going to be destroyed – but this worldly system is! The earth is going to be restored in newness… with glory as in the beginning.

Contrary to what many of us have been taught, we do not live in a fallen world (as if the earth did something wrong); we live on a wondrously beautiful earth with dynamic natural processes occurring daily to renew and rejuvenate the earth whose glory has been taken captive to futility by the spirit of darkness upon the earth, i.e., evil. And the sons of God (regenerate men) were sent here as agents of redemption – to rescue lost souls as well as the earth itself from Satan's dominion of corruption and death on account of sin.

Salvation belongs to the Lord – we are not saved for our benefit… but His.

Each time a person has been guided to faith in Christ, they are encouraged to accept Jesus into their heart (or more accurately, to receive Christ by entering the door of Christ that is already in their heart), and to profess Jesus as Lord. Once this bold proclamation has been made, and Christ dwells as Lord in your heart through faith, now the transformational process of turning people from worldly cares (goats) into kingdom-minded sheep is the main function of the church (Eph. 3:9, 10). If the church does not preach this message, then it has become a wolf in sheep's clothing. The church today looks more like the world than ever before because she has adopted the world's system of dominion and hierarchical authority over one another – instead of being joined in partnership alongside of and with one another to build one another up (Eph. 4:1-6)

The Holy Spirit was commissioned by Christ to transform us into His image in order that we should act according to His likeness so as to establish a heaven-like kingdom upon the earth in His name. **It was never about us – it was always about Jesus.** It was never about us getting saved and going home to Heaven – it was always about us entering into the Lord's salvation whereby we become changed, renewed and transformed into instruments of the Lord's peace to overcome the kingdom of darkness through truth, love and obedience. The Earth is our eternal home and it is up to us to transform it into the kingdom of heaven that looks like and becomes a replica of Heaven with every step we take. In doing so, we will be fulfilling the Lord's prophetic declaration that He taught the disciples to pray, "on earth as it is in heaven." But if we keep living like hell on earth and continue to preach an eternal escape into Heaven to avoid the ravages of judgment in the resurrection, then we will also come to learn one thing: our eternal soul with free will remains the same in the resurrection. We cannot bring any worldly garbage or unclean, profane things into the kingdom of heaven, so know this: righteous-fire tribulation happens to ensure the sanctity and holiness of this eternal kingdom.

Only glory remains – everything else will be consumed by fire.

Earth is our eternal home – and now it's time to start living like we have something worth inheriting on this planet (repeated for emphasis).

How can we continue to live according to any other way when the Lord Jesus told us "Thy kingdom come, Thy will be done, on earth as it is in heaven." What is our focus here? Is it not the transformation of Earth into the likeness of Heaven? Unify these three segments into one unified thought: the Lord's kingdom is being established according to God's will on the Earth so that it becomes the likeness of Heaven – as God's will for the sons of men (the host of earth).

Jesus created us in His image to live according to His likeness – and then He came to earth, bringing heaven with Him, to establish a kingdom on earth according its likeness in Heaven.

On Earth as it is in Heaven is not the impossible dream – it is a dominion commandment!

Jesus will move Heaven and Earth to establish His kingdom upon the Earth –not through angelic visitations or wondrous signs and miracles from Heaven, per se, but through the yielded hearts of men who glorify the Lord with their surrendered lives. We are the imperfect things through whom the Lord of glory is bringing perfection (completion) to the Earth.

Saints, we have been looking at our earthly reality backwards for 2,000 years. God told the Israelites that they would inherit the

Promised Land, and thus they entered into Canaan, but followers of Jesus have been given a much greater inheritance according to grace through faith. We have been given the entire Earth as an inheritance for Christ, who is our very great reward!

Am I saying that we will inherit a genesis-type paradise garden as in the beginning? Absolutely! The earth in its current format is merely a type and shadow of the true earth in its former glory as a replica of Heaven – before the war in heaven spilled over onto Earth. "On earth as it is in heaven" was not just a prayer – ***it is a prophetic promise*** when we choose to declare it, live it and usher in a regime change against the spirit of darkness upon the earth – in the name of Jesus Christ.

We were not sent to fix this world – we were sent to kabash and overcome it by bringing a regime change upon it. We are here to change it!

A new way of living was given to us by Jesus – and this living way continues to radicalize the world – and our heart – from the inside out. The Spirit model triumphs over the flesh model every time!

Jesus already won the victory 2,000 years ago – yet now we must understand it, comprehend it and embrace it… as our victory as well that operates within us and through us.

When we try to Christianize the worldly system, we adopt a "less-than" hybridized version of the true gospel of grace. We were never intended to create the change – we were intended to "be the change" according to grace first – and then allow Jesus to create this regime change as a work of the Spirit through us. If we do it, then we take the credit; but when Christ does it "through us," then He gets all the glory. Got it? Great… now live it!

> "…for it is God who works in you both to will and to do for *His* good pleasure" (Phil. 2:13).

You are the salt of the earth and you were sent to season the earth with the living gospel of grace and truth. We are to influence the way in which people think and perceive truth so that the Holy Spirit can begin the transformational process in them like He did in you. The enemy knows that ***the spiritual battlefield is in the mind of man, but the war is won in the heart***. (Read this again and again) Influence minds with the salt of righteous godly living, and hearts will follow. Selah. Meditate on this.

"Do it not" the change – "be" the change He asks you to be. Just be. Live it!

When you live according to righteousness, it either elevates the lifestyle in people around you into life-giving advocates or it turns them into hostile opponents of truth and grace, but if your salt loses its flavor because you have adopted worldly patterns, then what good is tasteless salt?

Transition....

The current pattern of authority and governance in this world is demonic in nature and ungodly in principle. The system of operation in this world promotes an ideological culture of self aggrandizing through selfish motivation, promotion and vainglory. It has the power to control us because we have given it the authority to govern our lives, but when we yield our free will to Jesus Christ to be governed by Him and His sovereignty, then there is nothing this system can do to us except kill us – but that doesn't matter because we are already crucified with Christ (Gal. 2:20) – and we have a guarantee of resurrection into eternal paradise. So you see... no worries!

Living in fear has always been the enemy's primary weapon because it causes doubt and unbelief. Freedom and liberty has always been the reward for those who trust Jesus, so believe the truth and live according to His ways.

Think about every cult practice, evil culture, man-made ideology and religious tradition, like ISIS, for example, and we will always see the primary objective is: world domination. Take a moment to consider this deeply. Is this the Lord's intent? If this was never the Lord's intent, then why has mankind repeatedly adopted this dominion conquest mentality over and over since the beginning of time *if* it were not part of God's spiritual coding for man to begin with? Study the scriptures beginning with Babel to see this truth. Indeed, this was the Lord's intent from day one for man to have dominion! (Gen. 1:26) Indeed, it is God's holy and good intent for man have dominion, but evil (like ISIS) wants domination and they will never stop until they get it – or until they are stopped. Having dominion over the earth is not some wacky, new-world subjugation religion to create a one world government. Jesus is already Lord of heaven and earth – and the governance of the world is already upon His shoulders, but the Lord will not interfere much in the affairs of men regarding how it happens because, why? This planet is our dominion and we can do whatever we want with it, for better or (quite often) for worse. The Lord has given us the intellectual capacity to destroy it with false ideologies and weapons of mass destruction – or we can bow the knee in obedience to Jesus Christ and call on Him to come near whereby we are enabled by Christ to become His hands and feet and thoughts as gateways of grace under the guidance and anointing of the indwelling Holy Spirit.

The Lord never gave man the spiritual mandate to possess world '*domination*,' but rather, to steward world-wide *dominion* and re-creation that overcomes the kingdoms of this world that are hostile to Christ, violently against His kingdom, and in bondage to the dominion of darkness, evil and sin, whereby we transform this world into the kingdom of God according to faith in Christ, as He commanded, "on earth as it is in heaven."

> "He who is not with Me is against Me, and he who does not gather with Me scatters abroad" (Matt. 12:30).

We do not need to go around tweaking all the little fiefdoms in the world, but we must decisively come against all kingdoms and manifest evils of this world that are openly hostile and not aligned with the love and truth gospel of Jesus Christ. Am I talking about a one world religion? Absolutely not! I am talking about a one dominion kingdom under the authority of Jesus Christ. His kingdom according to truth that is lived in reverential relationship with the Divine whereby men continue to live in free-will freedom to do good, and not evil. If you want nothing to do with living for Jesus, then you are part of the old-world problem that will be bypassed during this New Earth paradigm way of living in this current and future kingdom age.

"The kingdom of God is within you" (Luke 17:21).

"God put eternity in your heart" (Eccl. 3:11).

Jesus did not tell us these just so we ponder eternity, but to kick us into high gear to start living according to His kingdom and His dominion.

We are no longer preaching truth to run from earth – but running throughout the earth with His truth – being empowered by the Spirit of Truth.

Too many great ideologies have taught to us to be against something which then becomes a segue to be for something else. The gospel of Jesus Christ is just the opposite.

> "Seek first the kingdom of God, and His righteousness, and all these things shall be added to you" (Matt. 6:33).

When we seek the Lord with all our heart and soul, and this includes seeking His kingdom as well as instituting the righteousness of Christ upon the earth, then we are for Jesus and God is for us, and then all things will be added to us, including the most precious of all divine graces: freedom and liberty.

The Tree of Liberty

Liberty is not a new idea. Freedom and liberty in America was God's idea from the very beginning to show other nations how to live as one nation, under God, that professes Jesus Christ as Lord. The impetus for men seeking the New World in the 1500's was born out of a three-fold yearning: liberty, religious freedom and prosperity (the holding of property). These are not just inalienable rights given to us by our Creator; we were encoded with this internal drive to live life in newness through truth, change and oneness that results in liberty and prosperity whereby we may eternally love and serve God in the manner that glorifies Him throughout all generations. And, in doing so, we shall return to Him a portion of any abundant increase as an acknowledgment that it all belongs to Him – and He means all of it!

America was not just some great Divine experiment to see if newness could happen with Jesus abiding in the hearts of new world men and reigning sovereign in their lives under the guidance of the Holy Spirit (which they sometimes referred to as Almighty Providence) – just so God could see if newness was possible. Balderdash! The new world was the Lord's greatest provision to demonstrate and show forth His glory through yielded and submitted men who desired a godly way of governance according to the Divine model that Jesus instituted among men 1600 years earlier – as being born anew according to the Spirit. This new world was always intended to be the "land of the free" since the creation of the world, and despite all our wrinkles, equality missteps, and civil strife, this country remains standing long after most countries imploded – or were vanquished by another.

The new world of America – is an archetype of the Promised Land – and the New Earth.

The legacy that America has given to the world thus far is innumerable, but if it were not for America's intervention during two world wars, as well as a strong détente approach to preventing other evil empires from rising up and overtaking the world with their doctrines of hatred and self-glorification, we would be living upon a much different planet today. American blood was shed to keep the world safe from tyranny being lorded over other men by evil-minded tyrants, dictators, and ungodly men who do not govern according to the lordship model Christ instituted. All men "are" created equal, as well as upright, very good, beautiful, and precious, being wonderfully made and having been crowned with glory and honor as the object of His affection; men are not things to be governed as subjects, commodities and resources for an altruistic greater good – all men are the delightful glorious image of God who created them as His likeness to have dominion over the spiritual kingdom of darkness upon the earth… "to overcome evil with good."

I am not a patriotic freak… I am a lover of Jesus who understands the role America has played in the global world or nations. Other nations see this clearly, but it seems American leaders distort historical facts to deny this truth exists – and some take it for granted.

Wake up! And listen carefully! America was revealed at just the right time and called according the Lord's manifest destiny to initiate a world-wide revival in the new world newness model upon which it was founded – under the Lordship of Jesus Christ. Living under the freedoms that Jesus affords thereby allows us to govern according to the hearing of His voice in loving obedience. Everything is His! The Earth is His footstool, as well as the abundant increase of our labors – it all belongs to Him (and we are His as well) – and He will put the operation of this Earth under our feet (Psa. 8). We must not continue to elect leaders who live according to a different worldly model and take His things for granted; America was founded upon the new earth model of truth, righteousness, peace and joy in the Holy Spirit, in loving adoration of Jesus Christ, who was sent by the Father to remind us *whose* we are and *why* we are doing *what* we are supposed to be doing upon the earth.

Wake up and pay attention! This is the last chance for revival before the tribulation comes, which, by the way, was a prophetic warning to avert a fiery cleansing of unrighteousness upon the earth, not a global meltdown of judgment forecast to cause paralyzing fear by doom-and-gloom godless naysayers; we are always given a second chance to change according to the truth.

Change can happen – and it begins with Christ in you, by grace through faith, and the hearing of His voice, with the Holy Spirit dwelling in you to guide you into all truth.

There have been several great revivals in the past 200 years and even now numerous birth pangs of global revival have already begun in this country and in many other nations as well, yet now the time of the Lord's manifest presence is being released everywhere across the globe so as to bring to completion God's purpose for this country and all nations: revival, a global revival, that is unstoppable. All the pieces and elements are in place for this to occur, namely, unrestricted access to truth and information via the internet. Newness is about to happen in an unprecedented manner on an unprecedented scale of enormous magnitude. Radical, extravagant worship to love Jesus and host His presence will cause utter amazement in the church – and confusion in the enemy. It will be unstoppable, immeasurable, uncontainable, and the unimaginable that was once considered impossible and illogical will become manifest. Newness happens! The Holy Spirit will move through entire communities to give glory to God, and the spark of revival campfires within families and communities will spread like wildfires across the landscape of America and beyond to announce: Revival Is Here Forever.

Two houses of governance will become one in heart and purpose; two ideologies will bow to the sovereignty of Jesus only; two parties will lay down their agendas to govern according to God's rule of law and reject the counsel of godless courts, judges, justices and special interest groups. We've had our fill of lawmakers and it has corrupted us, so let's return the focus of our attention to the one law that God acknowledges (Rom. 8:2). Until revival is fully birthed, it will get ugly, and evil will rear its ugly head in unprecedented violence to thwart it from happening because it knows the end is near, but when revival has given birth, anarchy will be overthrown and godless governance will be cast out as worthless salt and trampled underfoot. We have tolerated the ways of the godless for too long – and now it's time to let freedom ring once again; freedom from political tyranny, governmental intrusions into religious expression, taxation by special interest representation, taking freedom of speech hostage to "information police," and most of all – allowing the evil things of this present darkness to invade the Spirit's culture of revival. If it is evil, remove it from your midst – and do it decisively.

A New Earth doctrine under the Lordship of Jesus Christ will not be intimidated by worry, fear or doubt; fear has always been the weapon of choice by our adversary to cause worry, doubt and unbelief whereby news medias keep us in bondage to the spirit of fear, but Christ has overcome the darkness of this world and He has bound the strongman as well. If the only thing we have to fear is fear itself, then boldly push past the fear to walk in newness through truth, change and oneness. The old way of living is just that – the old way!

A New Earth paradigm of newness and love according to the truth abiding in Jesus Christ has begun!

There will be a time for patience with understanding while people within the church wake up to this new reality, but I am confident that, even in this, the Lord is able to initiate an accelerated awakening for just such a time as this. Saints, it will only take obedience by the hearing of His voice to watch the walls and strongholds come crashing down. These were only being propped up by false doctrines of humanism anyway; they were just an illusion masquerading as truth.

Do not allow compromise; this is doubt and unbelief.

Do not give in to worry or fear; fear is faith in reverse. Anything not of faith is sin.

Allow the Holy Spirit to renew your mind thoroughly washing it with godly truth.

Do not allow passivity or complacent opinions to teach you unbelief; believe it will happen into completion this time. The time is right – and it has already begun!

Sons of God, our mission has always been to have dominion over the kingdom of darkness upon the earth, but we traded our birthright for an worldly bowl of heaven-less stew, and we were tricked into selling our African brethren into slavery to silence the truth that all men are created equal in the sight of God. We were all created in His image according to His likeness – but the enemy would have us believe some of us are greater, more entitled or more greatly admired by God than another person with a different culture or skin type. Hogwash! We are all the same in sin – and we are all the same in Christ Jesus. God loves the prophet and the prostitute the same!

Sons of God, we were not given dominion for our personal pleasure and vainglory, but for Christ's glory Who was made manifest for our sake to usher in the kingdom of God upon the earth – in His name. It is not about who we are, but about Who is living within us.

> "Then to Him was given dominion and glory and a kingdom, that all peoples, nations, and languages should serve Him. His dominion is an everlasting dominion, which shall not pass away, and His kingdom the one which shall not be destroyed" (Dan. 7:14)

The deliverance of all kingdoms of this world is our responsibility to deliver into Christ's hand. Jesus said, "My kingdom is not of this world" because, at that time, the people of Christ's generation (the Jews) were not willing to fight for and on His behalf. Well then, what kingdom are you building upon the earth within your heart that is not only worth fighting for… but is worthy to be named according to the name above all names, Jesus Christ?

Do not misinterpret this message; we are not called to be vigilantes, but rather, vigilant in the casting down of principalities and powers and strongholds that have raised themselves up against the knowledge of God and Jesus Christ. We are not being called to revolution, but godly revival. We are not being called to violent behavior, but to valiant behavior whereby we are not ashamed to declare Jesus Christ as Lord.

Some evil men openly profess world domination and death to all, but the culture of Christ is not death – but life, love, righteousness, truth, peace and joy in the Holy Spirit. There is no hope in human subjugation under the lordship of any man or beast or antichrist; the only hope this world will ever know is found in Christ alone, who invites everyone into a divine relationship with Him, to enter into His presence, to host His presence, to carry His presence into every facet of our lives so as to release the atmosphere of Heaven residing within us to everyone and everything around us, and to live under the lordship of the only Living and One true God, Jesus Christ, who makes His covenant known through yielded hearts and minds. Hear Him!

In this awesome and wonderful journey upon the earth, the Lord enters into a covenantal partnership with us whereby we are partakers of the divine nature, partners in the gospel of Christ, stewards of His earthly kingdom in righteousness and peace, and caretakers of a planet that is to become our eternal Paradise in the age to come. There is only one Lord, one kingdom and one dominion in this plan, and yet, the Lord will establish His disciples as judges, kings, magistrates and administrators of a New Earth covenant where we will live for all eternity.

I am not proclaiming world-wide revolution… but world-wide revival… to begin in newness within the heart – again!

The great do-over is about to begin. This has always been the perfect plan of God's regeneration upon the earth since before the foundation of the world: *palingenesia* – genesis again! Either you are with Christ or against Christ. The choice is yours. Obedience in Christ is not some mandatory criteria for living on this earth, just yet, since there was never a call to violence by Christ to kill anyone other than the worldly man that is already death within you. Jesus invited us to life abundantly because *He is* the life – but we were never invited to live in abundant living. Never! Generous provision has always been a vehicle for generous benevolence. If your church is hoarding riches for its vainglory, then ask Jesus which kingdom He wants you to pour your abundance into. Be transformed – and then be transformers.

You will always have free will, even into the millennium and forever in eternity, but the evil that is in our midst must be forcefully eliminated because it is an abomination to God's love and is an affront to the truth of Jesus Christ. We will always have free will, in this life and the hereafter; however, being passively ambivalent to ostensibly hostile, hateful, violent, vitriolic, malevolent slaughterhouse evil was never what God intended. If you want peace, then live in peace, but if you profess fanatical evil and declare death to all, then you shall have according to your religion; beginning with your ideology… let hate consume itself! But the righteous shall stand, living by faith, and will be raised into resurrection life to live in newness and peace – again.

Why Earth, Lord?

>"O earth, earth, earth, Hear the word of the Lord!"
>(Jer. 22:29)

What is so important about the earth? It is just one celestial body in the universe of perhaps millions that are capable of supporting life and thousands that are identical in nature with the potential to inhabit life as we know it, so I ask again… why earth? What is the Lord doing here as a show-forth of His strength and sovereignty whereby He demonstrates throughout the heavens that Jesus is Lord over the earth – and in the earth? What is the message that He is communicating to principalities and powers seated in heavenly places? Once we understand this aspect of Christ's Lordship, then we will be able to comprehend much about this new earth life.

And here is one key to help us understand: Jesus is the Branch. In this context, Jesus is the connective life-giving Spirit that enables everything upon the earth to live. When Jesus said, "I am the Life" and "I am the resurrection and the life," He is saying very simply: I am Life. Apart from me there is nothing that is alive nor can it live because… "I am the Life." Jesus does not have life that He dispenses as a commodity, much like human power or truth or wisdom (which are also His); Jesus is life, Jesus is power, truth, and wisdom. These are not just elements that make up who He is, nor are these just character attributes of His divinity that God must have in order to be God; Jesus is life. Jesus is the Branch through Whom we get life. Our life comes from The Life! We have life because Jesus gave us life – His Life.

> "I am the true vine, and My Father is the vinedresser. ² Every branch in Me that does not bear fruit He takes away; and every branch that bears fruit He prunes, that it may bear more fruit. ³ You are already clean because of the word which I have spoken to you. ⁴ Abide in Me, and I in you. As the branch cannot bear fruit of itself, unless it abides in the vine, neither can you, unless you abide in Me. ⁵ I am the vine, you are the branches. He who abides in Me, and I in him, bears much fruit; *for without Me you can do nothing*. ⁶ If anyone does not abide in Me, he is cast out as a branch and is withered; and they gather them and throw them into the fire, and they are burned" (John 15:1-6).

By now, I hope that you are able to see that Jesus is all in all, in Him the universe was created and in Him all things consist. If you have ears to hear – everything that you see is an expression of Who He is… as He manifests Himself in all creation… as Creator. This is a Divine Mystery: that even while *everything* is His and it all belongs to Him and *everything* that grows and bears fruit is an increase that is attributed to Jesus Himself having produced the increase[112] as the Branch, He has entered into a Divine partnership with man to live by grace with free will so that we manifest His kingdom and His dominion in the earth. This is why He created us as His image bearers… to live on the earth as His "imaged" representatives so that – in all we think, say and do, we give Him all the glory as an outward expression of our inward posture as servants under Christ's lordship – as one more expression of His manifold glory made manifest in us.

It's all about Jesus – and God gets the glory

How can you buy or sell the land[113] if it all belongs to Jesus? Truly, we can build houses and cities on the land, but when we breathe our last breath, then what we have built is given to another to inhabit according to their free will choices. What happens after that? Well, it becomes someone else's – and so on. This is wisdom: we are simply caretakers and stewards and sojourners who manage the Lord's benevolent resources upon the earth; however, while it is a divine privilege to transition this accumulated wealth and prosperity and blessing to future generations, we have also seen just how quickly empires with seemingly unlimited wealth and provision can vanish overnight if someone thinks they can live upon earth apart from His provision and His life. Lord, help us understand.

Everything belongs to Jesus. It is all His – and He can do whatever He wants with His things.

> Jesus said: "Is it not lawful for me to do what I wish with my own things? Or is your eye evil because I am good?" (Matt. 20:15).

---

[112] And that also includes your wealth, since everything means everything… including your money in the bank, the bank, the land the bank is on, the physical materials to print money, and the air the bank uses to breathe.

[113] An Indian quote attributed to Chief Seattle during "an undocumented" speech in 1855.

There is a divine plan for the earth that far exceeds man's human capability to comprehend. It concerns spiritual matters in the heavenly realm that wise spiritual men have been struggling to understand since time began.

Why the earth? Of all the planets in the universe, why did Jesus choose earth to demonstrate His manifest glory? So, I asked the Lord this question and this is the understanding that came to me:

> *Jesus didn't choose it… Satan did. His free will actions resulted in his expulsion from heaven, and this is the truth behind all free will created beings: our actions determine our final determination.*

Lucifer (Satan) was cast out of heaven and he fell to earth because he exercised his free will, as a created being, in an attempt to exalt himself above God and take God's glory unto himself. And likewise, if any person lives according to their free will but *not* according to God's grace, and chooses *not* to exalt God or give Him the glory that belongs to Him, then they are just as condemned as Satan to an eternal life in the bottomless pit of hell in the coming judgment.

A judgment has come against Lucifer, and a similar judgment is coming to this world – and Jesus is the Judge, who will judge everything on the earth according to His sovereignty.

So, what does this have to do with the earth? Well, the earth in its' current form is only temporary. The earth is full of the glory of the Lord, but the glory of this earth has been taken captive by Satan and, one day, Jesus will return this earth to its' full and former glory after evil is vanquished and all evil things are burned away. In the meantime, Jesus sent sons of men to populate, steward and redeem the Earth, but Satan has deceived a great many people with lies and proud, haughty thoughts who think this Earth belongs to them simply because they are living on it, but this is wisdom:

> "The earth *is* the Lord's, and all its fullness, the world and those who dwell therein" (Psa. 24:1).

The earth, the world and the people therein – are the Lord's. He made all things, both material and invisible, and He is responsible for all things which have been happening upon the earth for centuries – which, by the way… constitutes merely a few seconds in the eternal timeline. We are living just one season in eternity upon the earth, and yet, what we do on the earth during the brief time that we are allotted will determine where we spend the remainder of eternity – and in what capacity, as an eternal reward for our faithfulness to Christ. When we live our life according to grace through faith, and we give God all the glory through Jesus Christ our Lord, then we shall continue to live upon a future, glory-filled, paradisiacal earth where only goodness dwells – after the resurrection and the regeneration of all things.

God is going to make all things new again. God is going to restore the heavens and the earth to their former glory – and we who live according to true faith in righteousness *will* inherit the earth. Yes, we will inherit the earth from Jesus, who will live with us eternally upon the earth; but those who choose to live in rebellion will inherit eternal torment. (I know, some people are still struggling with the concept of Jesus on the throne in heaven and living on earth at the same time, but this next revelation may put the pieces in to context)

Of all the places in the universe, why does the spiritual battle between good and evil have to be here… on earth? If earth is man's eternal home from beginning to end, then why, Lord, why did the battle have to happen here on earth? Satan could have landed upon Mars or Jupiter, but he landed here. Again, why? Well, he landed here for two reasons:

1. To continue his war of rebellion against God – by waging war against the sons of men
2. He was in the neighborhood

We have learned thus far that men do not go to (ascend into) Heaven, that Eden and Paradise represent Earth in its spiritual/heavenly dimension, that angels ascend and descend from heaven to earth just by 'anabaino' going a little farther, that the kingdom of God is within man (by grace through faith) and the kingdom of heaven was established on earth by Jesus so that it may abide in the hearts of those who love Jesus with all their heart, mind, soul and strength in order that they may also release and establish the kingdom of heaven upon the earth in servant obedience.

And here is the key to unlocking many spiritual mysteries: earth is paradise. Earth is Eden, the Garden of God, and this same Earth is the glory-filled Paradise that Satan took captive when he fell to Earth. As a general rule, I never study or read about Satan or demonic things because I choose to focus my eyes upon Jesus (and I strongly suggest this to everyone), but then the Lord followed up the "why earth" question by showing me how Satan came to earth.

Satan began his journey as an anointed cherub angel and star of heaven on God's holy mountain *in Heaven.* Then, one day, he decided to take God's glory captive in heaven and began a war of rebellion whereby he swept away one third of heaven's angels and all of them landed on earth. As you read these scripture references, I want you to keep track of four things: a) heaven is referred to by two other names, as God's holy mountain *and* Eden, the garden of God; b) Satan's expulsion from heaven was a two-part process of being cast out and then cast down; c) Satan has several names, like Lucifer, the devil, the anointed cherub who covers, son of the morning, "the man," star, angel of the bottomless pit, accuser of the brethren, dragon, great dragon and the fiery red dragon, and d) angels are referred to as stars *and* fiery stones. Now, regarding Lucifer/Satan:

> "You *were* the seal of perfection, full of wisdom and perfect in beauty. [13] **You were in Eden, the garden of God**; every precious stone *was* your covering: the sardius, topaz, and diamond, Beryl, onyx, and jasper, Sapphire, turquoise, and emerald

with gold. The workmanship of your timbrels and pipes was prepared for you on the day you were created. ¹⁴ "You *were* the anointed cherub who covers; I (God) established you; **you were on the holy mountain of God**; you walked back and forth *in the midst of fiery stones.* ¹⁵ You *were* perfect in your ways from the day you were created, till iniquity was found in you. ¹⁶ "By the abundance of your trading you became filled with violence within, and **you sinned; therefore I cast you as a profane thing out of the mountain of God; and I destroyed you**, O covering cherub, *from the midst of the fiery stones.* ¹⁷ "Your heart was lifted up because of your beauty; you corrupted your wisdom for the sake of your splendor; **I cast you to the ground**, I laid you before kings, that they might gaze at you. ¹⁸ "You defiled your sanctuaries by the multitude of your iniquities, by the iniquity of your trading; therefore I brought fire from your midst; it devoured you, **and I turned you to ashes upon the earth** in the sight of all who saw you. ¹⁹ All who knew you among the peoples are astonished at you; you have become a horror, and shall be no more forever""" (Ezek. 28:12-19).

"How you are **fallen from heaven**, O Lucifer, son of the morning! How you are **cut down to the ground, you who weakened the nations**! ¹³ For you have said in your heart: '*I will ascend into heaven, I will exalt my throne above the stars* of God; I will also **sit on the mount of the congregation** on the farthest sides of the north; ¹⁴ I will ascend above the heights of the clouds, I will be like the Most High.' ¹⁵ Yet you shall be brought down to Sheol, to the lowest depths of the Pit. ¹⁶ "Those who see you will gaze at you, and consider you, saying: '**Is this the man** who made the earth tremble, who shook kingdoms, ¹⁷ who made the world as a wilderness and destroyed its cities, who did not open the house of his prisoners?" (Isa. 14:12-17).

"Then the fifth angel sounded: And I saw *a star fallen from heaven to the earth*. To him (the fifth angel) was given the key to the bottomless pit. ^{2} And he opened the bottomless pit, and smoke arose out of the pit like the smoke of a great furnace. So the sun and the air were darkened because of the smoke of the pit.".… "And they had as king over them *the angel of the bottomless pit*, whose name in Hebrew *is* Abaddon, but in Greek he has the name Apollyon. ^{12} One woe is past. Behold, still two more woes are coming after these things" (Rev. 9:1-2, 11-12; Satan's name, Abaddon, means *destruction or destroyer*).

"And He (Jesus) said to them, "I saw Satan fall like lightning from heaven" (Luke 10:18).

"And war broke out in heaven: Michael and his angels fought with the dragon; and the dragon and his angels fought, ^{8} but they did not prevail, ***nor was a place found for them** in heaven any longer.* ^{9} *So the great dragon was cast out, that serpent of old, called **the Devil and Satan**, who deceives the whole world; he was cast to the earth, and his angels were cast out with him.* ^{10} Then I heard a loud voice saying in heaven, "Now salvation, and strength, and the kingdom of our God, and the power of His Christ have come, for *the accuser of our brethren*, who accused them before our God day and night, *has been cast down*. ^{11} And they overcame him by the blood of the Lamb and by the word of their testimony, and they did not love their lives to the death. ^{12} Therefore rejoice, O heavens, and you who dwell in them! *Woe to the inhabitants of the earth and the sea! For the devil has come down to you,* *having great wrath*, because he knows that he has a short time" (Rev. 12:7-12).

"And another sign appeared in heaven: behold, a great, fiery red dragon having seven heads and ten horns, and seven diadems on his heads. ⁴ *His tail drew a third of the stars of heaven and threw them to the earth*" (Rev. 12:3, 4)

Ok, so let's put this in some sort of chronological order:

A. Satan wages war against God in heaven (called the holy mountain of God, and also Eden, the garden of God, which is known as "earth" in her pre-captive Paradise glory)
B. Satan's attempt to take God's glory captive and ascend above heaven (higher than God) results in him being cast out of heaven and then cast to earth, and the appearance of this angelic star's departure from heaven looked much like lightening, according to Jesus
C. God casts Satan out of heaven (Eden) and then he casts out rebellious angels
D. God casts Satan down to earth along with one third of heaven's angels (also called stars or fiery stones)
E. Satan was destroyed by God and turned to ashes, and being full of great wrath, he searches to and fro over the earth to torment men, but he cannot take human life (see the book of Job)

So, let me ask you just three additional questions:

1. If Satan is cast out of Heaven by God, and Heaven is referred to as Eden, then how did Satan get back into Eden to tempt Adam and Eve? (Gen. 3:1-5)
2. If Satan is cast out of heaven onto the earth, then how can Satan enter Heaven again with "the sons of God" when they must present themselves before the Lord? (Job 1:6; 2:1)

3. If Satan has been utterly destroyed and turned to ashes, then how is Satan allowed to have "seed" that will wage war against Eve and her "seed"? (Gen. 3:15)

Like I said, there are going to be many unanswered questions, but before we go one step further toward a giant spiritual paradigm shift, let me ask you this: where do you think hell is? It seems many of our traditions and religious perceptions regarding the location of hell are seemingly universal across all cultures, historical time parameters, faiths and beliefs. So, I ask you again… where do you think hell is? This is not a trick question, so just say it out loud (or under your breath). OK, I am very happy to tell you that you are correct.[114] Your understanding is the same as everyone else's – and if we know that this spiritual place of eternal torment has a physical counterpart (type and shadow) as a pit in the earth… then what might we also say about heaven's counterpart in the earth?

Heaven, as a spiritual place, also has a physical counterpart (type and shadow) in the earth – and it is often referred to as God's holy mountain. Heaven has many physical attributes that describe it as a most holy place, above the clouds, higher than the highest heavens, higher than the stars (the realm of stars or celestial bodies), glorious in splendor, etc. If hell's physical counterpart is in the bowels of the earth, then heaven's physical counterpart is spiritually on a mountaintop called Mount Zion.

Heaven is the place where angels ascend and descend in order to assist men when an intervening hand is needed, or to wage war against the demonic forces that are upon the earth, including Satan himself. Angelic responses to human utterances for divine assistance often take less than a second for them to manifest themselves, so, why is that? How is that possible if Heaven is way out beyond the sphere of earth in another galaxy near Alpha Centauri?

---

[114] The physical location of hell is traditionally considered in (the center of) the earth.

I want you to think spiritually for a moment and consider the distance between the physical reality and the spiritual reality as not being restricted by space, place, time or other physical matters; governed, yes, but restricted, no. As I mentioned earlier in our study regarding 'ascend' – *'anabaino'* simply means "to ascend, to go a little father," but now... I do not want you to think of the distance between Heaven and Earth as being less than 24" – I want you to think of this distance as being as thin as a piece of paper. I want you to close your eyes for just a second and to imagine a very thin veil between your body (the physical reality) and the spiritual reality that surrounds you. The spiritual reality surrounding you is all around you and even in you, but you cannot see it because there is "a veil of separation" between the eyes of the natural man and the eyes of the spiritual man that is unable to *'oida'* perceive and completely comprehend what he sees because "apart from the Spirit" we know nothing (John 3:3; 16:13; 1 Cor. 2:11-14; 1 John 5:6). Can you sense the closeness of Heaven all around you? Can you perceive that the kingdom of heaven is in your midst? If you answered yes, and if you have spiritual ears to hear, then the eyes you need to spiritually see are separated by a thin little veil called: perception. Yet many living apart from the Spirit... "They will look and will not perceive" (Matt. 13:14).

The kingdom of heaven is not complicated, but faith merchants operating under the spirit of religion have made the spiritual reality that surrounds us far too complicated to comprehend (and I may be guilty of many words as well, but new spiritual concepts require truth that must be defensible). So, in an effort to make it very, very simple:

The kingdom of heaven is at hand – here now is! The kingdom of heaven can be experienced by you – here and now – if you have been born anew according to the Holy Spirit. The kingdom of heaven is all around you, but it cannot be seen or experienced through the eyes of sinful man. It can be perceived... but it cannot be experienced apart from repentance and conversion through faith in Jesus Christ.

Now, let's go back and assemble the following thoughts in our mind together:

1. Heaven is a spiritual place, as is Hell, and the spiritual "barrier" preventing anyone from ascending into Heaven from Earth – is the hovering "Holy Spirit" (Gen. 1:2)
2. Heaven is referred to as Eden, the Garden of God *and* also the holy mountain of God (Ezek. 28:13, 14)
3. Earth is a heavenly place under Heaven that is *also* referred to as Eden… and Paradise
4. This same earth where the Garden of Eden is situated is where the Tree of Life is located. Now, follow the linear thought of these next bullet points:
   - "The Lord God planted a garden eastward in Eden and there He put the man whom He had formed" (Gen. 2:8); and "Now a river went *out of* Eden to water the garden" (V.10). A river went out of Eden to water the garden in Eden makes no sense… unless you can see this story is about two gardens that were created by God in "the land of Eden" whereby every garden that God establishes on earth for man to tend that gives praise and glory to God is another "domain" of Eden within God's dominion
   - "Then the LORD God took the man and put him in the Garden of Eden to tend and keep it" (Gen. 2:15). You need to see this: God took Adam from "his" garden and put him in "His Own" garden in Eden. It is essential to see these two gardens residing alongside one another wherein man works his garden for "x" days and then returns to God's garden to maintain intimacy and fellowship with God – on God's day[115]
5. The Earth is Eden, the Paradise of God, and this garden that God created "on earth" for Adam to tend is an extension of Eden – and every garden place that we establish on Earth that gives praise and glory to God is an extension of God's

---

[115] This is a Paradise paradox, so read "Gateways" section titled "Paradox - Glory Alongside."

dominion upon the earth by a process called: redemption! It retakes captive territory in the name of God and renames it: Eden – the Paradise of God

6. The future place that men enter in the resurrection of the faithful is called Paradise – where the Tree of Life is located – on Earth. Paradise was, is and forever will be upon the Earth and she will be restored to her original heavenly beauty and glory in the regeneration of all things after she has been liberated and set free from Satan's captivity. Paradise is the heavenly place that still spiritually resides in the earth, but this is not Heaven, which is the throne of God, which is the highest Heaven above all heavenly places which man cannot ascend to

"God created a garden for Adam eastward (of) Eden to tend and "then" the Lord brought him into His presence to tend His Garden called Eden (aka Paradise). This is highly significant: God created a garden for Adam within the domain of Eden, but when Adam fell from grace (as did we), he was driven out of Paradise and put back into his own garden (the wilderness) in a place now called "this world" – by the Spirit (Luke 4:1). And this is where we find ourselves today… living in this temporary "eastward" place alongside Eden during one season of eternity to be tested and proofed within a worldly wilderness before we return home again – to Paradise.

"It is important to see the larger implications of life on earth – as a paradox. For example, the nation Israel wandered in the wilderness for forty years… yet the Promised Land was alongside them the entire time. The Israelites had to wander forty years for that corrupt generation to pass away before they could consecrate and rededicate their life is service to God. Sampson did not re-consecrate himself, so he perished, and Israel didn't do this, so that generation perished. Everything we are going through in this life is "to get something out of us" in order to "get something into us." If you have not consecrated and rededicated your life to God, then you should not expect the Promised Land when it was withheld from multitudes of others who were/are just like you.

"Consider the prophets who dwelled in wilderness places to get closer to God... to be tested and proofed and changed by Him, yet afterward as coming out of the wilderness when called by Him... they had messages to deliver. Let this become an application metaphor for your life.

"Heaven is alongside us and God wants us to establish the kingdom of heaven through us, but first... we need to consecrate ourselves, get the stinking thinking and sinful ways of the old man out of us, and then be filled with the Holy Spirit so that God can release heaven through us."[116]

We are living in a Paradise Paradox. We are living alongside glory with a pearl of glory within us for this purpose: to redeem the land, advance the kingdom of heaven and produce more glory on the earth – in the name of Jesus!

Yet many of our doctrines have been inverted to promote another narrative. Adam's garden was planted "in this world" as a type of beach-head to come against the kingdom of darkness. Adam was sent to live in a fallen world – and so were you and me. This fallen world was not caused by Adam's fall from grace, as many of our doctrines teach; he allowed the desire for the things of this fallen world to tempt him, whereby Adam and Eve acted in rebellion and fell from grace.

The sin of this world was already here. Darkness was upon the earth (Gen. 1:2). Through one man, sin entered this world – and his name is Lucifer, and Satan (Isa. 14:12-17). Yet through another Man, Jesus came – to take away "the sin of the world" (John 1:29).

By this single solitary act, Adam delivered his authority, his glory and his garden to Satan, but have no fear because... Jesus got it back and returned this authority to His disciples.

---

[116] IBID.

You were not born "in sin" as a permanent spiritual condition akin to all humanity that was passed down to you through your parents; you were born a child of grace; yet you were born "into" a sinful world whereby all have been tempted and succumbed the allure of this fallen world under the dominion of Satan… to act independently of God and take God's glory captive. We have all forfeited grace through willful disobedience, yet through repentance and faith in Jesus, grace is restored unto us.

The sad part of the Eden story is: the scriptures never indicate they repented and re-consecrated themselves. Some may say… perhaps they didn't know that's what they were supposed to do – to which I counter: if any of us don't know what to do, then ask the Lord – and seek His counsel. If they had repented… we might not be going through the mess we're in now.

Not knowing what to do is a lame excuse. You were sent here to have dominion over darkness. If you don't know or can't remember what you are supposed to be doing, then ask Jesus – and then wait for His response. Our quest for answers can always be found within the ask-seek-knock inquiry with Jesus.

> "So they will say, 'This land that was desolate has become like the garden of Eden; and the wasted, desolate, and ruined cities *are now* fortified *and* inhabited" (Ezek. 36:35).

The regeneration will happen; you can count on it! The New Earth will be wonderful, indeed!

It's all about Jesus – and God gets the glory!

The Oneness Condition

Good and evil cannot be manifest in the same location; however, there is one condition whereby all three (God/man/Satan) are co-manifest in Heaven/Earth/Hell – and that is within context to man. The spiritual reality is invisible and will not make sense to any unregenerate persons without faith; apart from the Spirit's indwelling and transformational work within them to renew their mind... unregenerate reasoning will always result in futility when unsaved persons try to envision Heaven or Hell as physical places... because the kingdom of heaven resides upon earth within the heart of regenerate man!

Heaven and eternity abide within the heart of godly men or women – who abides in Christ!

Repent... because we have an adversary who continues to wage a spiritual war against us in very close combat for earthly dominion. Religion tells us that all we need to enter into heaven is faith, but 'faith' is insufficient because even demons believe and tremble; we need 'conviction faith' to produce 'saving faith.' We must host Christ in our heart with "saving faith" so He may abide in us and dwell with us, as we live for Jesus with saving faith in our heart. Jesus is not a patch we wear on our shirtsleeve to prove we made a verbal profession of faith as an utterance from our mouth. If you have not yielded your heart to Him, and He does not abide in your heart even now, then patches, sacraments and ordinations don't count.

Co-manifest Upon The Earth

If you do not believe in the devil, then that is your opinion, albeit, a very narrow-minded one, but if you do not believe that God/man/Satan are co-manifest in your presence, then continue reading and allow spiritual truth to wash your mind.

The Apostle Paul wrestled with the mystery of iniquity. He was perplexed when he did things he did not want to do and, conversely, he did not do the things he purposed to do.

> "For the good that I will to do, I do not do; but the evil I will not to do, that I practice. [20] Now if I do what I will [purpose] not to do, it is no longer I who do it, but sin that dwells in [the flesh of] me. [21] I find then a law, ***that evil is present with me***, the one

> who wills to do good. ²² For I delight in the law of God according to the inward man. ²³ But I see another law in my members [body], warring against the law of my mind, and bringing me into captivity to the law of sin which is in my members. ²⁴ O wretched man that I am! Who will deliver me from this body of death?" (Rom. 7:19-24).

Paul discerned a force greater than himself – caused him to do things against his will, which he referred to as "a law." There is the "law of the Spirit in Christ Jesus" and there is the "law that evil is present with our members." Man is able to co-manifest good and evil nearly on top of one another… but Paul also discerned "another law in my members [body], warring against the law of my mind." How this occurs – and why it happens – perplexed Paul tremendously, so let's recap the lessons learned in "Commission" regarding our human construction.

You don't have a soul, per se… you are a soul.

"The soul was *made* (Gen. 1:26 – the expression), then we were *created* upright by Jesus in rightness and goodness, as men of goodwill, according to "His Own" likeness (v.27 – the manifestation), and then we were *formed* of the earth (v.2:7) to multiply goodness and glory upon the earth – in us… and then the spirit was formed in us (Zech. 12:1) in order to help man glorify God and return to Him all the glory we (our soul) produced on the earth – through us. In us *and* through us – this is our manifold reason for being on earth whereby all other reasons are either secondary or superficial to our primary purpose as we have dominion in His name… and give Him all glory."[117]

The body connects you to earthly things, while the spirit connects you to spiritual things. Our soul is the intersect between these two realities: one earthly and the other heavenly (spiritual).

---

[117] Excerpt from "Commission" section titled "Soul With Spirit."

Our body and our spirit are two "instruments" placed in dynamic tension alongside our soul that God purposed (intended) to pull us in two directions in order to sanctify our soul.

"The dynamic tension between the living organism placed upon "the soul with spirit" creates a mysterious union of Mr. Hyde upon Dr. Jekyll for one season of eternity on earth for this reason: our soul's sanctification. Why did the Lord intentionally create us to function in this manner? This is the mystery of iniquity and the mystery of sanctification (combined) that is at work upon us and within us to proof our allegiance to Jesus. Why did the Lord ordain this? This is an excellent question that you must ask Him yourself. It is my 'opinion' that this was done as the most loving and kind way of reconciling the kingdom after the war in heaven broke out (Rev. 12:7). Rather than judging us in that moment, the Lord purposed that *we would judge ourselves* based upon the litmus test of life on earth to determine our allegiance to Jesus *and* our willful obedience to love Him *and* serve Him despite having the presence of evil all around us. We are being tested… and it is we who judge our selves worthy or unworthy of redemption!

"We are on probation[118] (having been sent from heaven) to attend class whereby you determine your future place in the kingdom of God (of which there are at least 14)[119] based upon your deeds of righteousness and your faithful obedience to Jesus – or the lack thereof. We are in class to learn at least three things: 1) to love the Lord and one another, 2) to remember our three-fold purpose on earth[120], and 3) to remove all seeds of doubt."[121]

---

[118] Term was used by Matthew Henry: "We must aim at the glory of God in all. We must glorify Him on the earth, which He has given unto the children of men, demanding only this quit-rent; on the earth, we are in a state of probation and preparation for eternity." Matthew Henry's Commentary on the Bible, St. John, Ch. 17:1-5; II.(2).[1].3.2; p. 1153.

[119] Read "Here" chapter 6 to learn about "I go to prepare a place for you" as one of fourteen places in the kingdom.

[120] Our three-fold purpose: dominion, sanctification, glorification.

[121] Excerpt from "Commission" section titled: "Mystery of Iniquity."

The flesh upon us and the spirit within us creates a dynamic tension within every one of us that strives to be holy and good before the Lord according to the spirit within us, BUT the flesh wages war against the spirit man the Apostle struggled to comprehend: the mystery of iniquity.

The mystery of man on the earth is: sanctification. The mystery of iniquity is: we were created with weakness to be susceptible to lawlessness.

Your soul (by thoughts of the mind) must make this determination (as an act of your will) to choose between glorifying God through your spirit or glorifying self in your body!

> "For you were bought at a price; therefore glorify God in your body and in your spirit, which are God's" (1 Cor. 6:20).

> *God loves us and wants us to choose wisely in the mind of our soul –*
> *to operate according to the spirit within us rather than the flesh upon us.*

Paul stated eloquently this dynamic tension of sanctification whereby we must rely upon the empowering of the Spirit through our spirit to strengthen our spirit within us against the weaker member placed upon us that is susceptible to sin.

Yet he also deduced something else: "another law in my members [body], warring against the law of my mind, and bringing me into captivity to the law of sin which is in my members" (Rom. 7:23). Our soul must decide how it wants to think, will and act – either through the spirit within us or the flesh upon us. Modern translation bibles are unable to communicate what Paul said a couple verses later, so allow me to show you what is stated in the Greek:

> "For the mind [*phronema*-5427] of the body is
> death, but the mind [5427] of the Spirit is life and
> peace" (Rom. 8:6; Greek).[122]

Have you ever heard the expression: "Your body has a mind of its own" or "follow your gut?" Well, the above scripture is proof that the body has a mind of its own (as does our spirit).

"Mind (in the scripture above) employs a word (*phronema*-5427) that is different than previous occurrences in Romans (mind-*nous*-3563) which is: "the mind, the intellect, the seat of reflective consciousness comprising the faculties of perception and understanding."[123] '*Nous*' – the intellect – is where "*oida*-1492' i.e. perfect knowing, perception, understanding and comprehension occurs – in the mind of the soul.

"'*Phronema*-5427' "denotes what one has in the mind; (the content of the process expressed in '*phroneo*-5426' which means: "to exercise the mind; to be mentally disposed in a certain direction; to think; to be minded in a certain way."[124] The body and spirit were given to us by God and are "minded in a certain way" to operate according to a certain (predetermined) manner.

"Here, now, is the perplexing part of our construction: the mind of the body and the mind of the spirit were predetermined to operate in unity through faith – or in opposition toward one another in sin. Through faith in Christ, God reconciles these two instruments to become one man – a new man! We literally become… a new creature (creation) – as a new heart and spirit within a quickened body (Rom. 8:9-11) – through the born anew baptism by the Spirit!"[125]

---

[122] Sarx-4561 is most often translated "flesh," but when placed in context with soul and spirit, "body" seems to be the proper term.
[123] Strong's Concordance.
[124] Strong's Concordance.
[125] Excerpt from "Gateways" section titled "Many Minds."

> "Therefore, if anyone is in Christ, he is a new creation; old things have passed away; behold, all things have become new" (2 Cor. 5:17).

When we operate according to sin, our members are divided, but when we operate by faith according to the Spirit, and are born anew… our members are unified "one in Spirit" to create one "new man" out of two. By faith, we become a new creation that didn't exist beforehand, which is why God "remembers our sin no more" because it was attributed to the "old man" and not the 'new man" that is being transformed by the renewing of his mind to be conformed to the image of Christ.

How are we able, at this point going forward, to continue living in sin once we've comprehended the grace at work within us? If we truly comprehended grace, we would desire holiness. It seems, however, that even Paul struggled against a weakness within him that we all continue to struggle with as well. The law of our members (according to sin) is warring against the law of our mind (nous - the mind of our soul) for supremacy. The Apostle Paul struggled with it, the author struggles with it, as do all pastors, priests, prophets, evangelists and a great cloud of witnesses who have gone before us, but the issue is: the mind of the soul must have mastery over the mind of the body in order to operate according to the mind of your spirit.

Beloved, until your soul is able to exercise mastery over the mind of your body (flesh), then you will spend more time at war within yourself rather than doing the will of the Lord, which is to operate with a sound mind – in oneness of your spirit with the Spirit – to make war against principalities and powers seated in heavenly places that are in rebellious opposition to Christ!

The Apostle Peter also struggled with it. Examine these scriptures carefully regarding the close proximity of God and Satan in regard to how we co-manifest good and evil within our 'self':

- Peter had just proclaimed Jesus as "the Christ, the Son of the living God" (Matt. 16:16) as revelation having come by the Spirit of the Father… and then a few moments later, this same apostolic giant strongly *rebukes* the Lord Jesus, who is God (Peter rebukes God), for talking about His death, whereby Jesus says, "Get behind Me Satan" (v.23). We have been taught Jesus rebuked Peter for his words, but look carefully to read what Jesus says and then it becomes clear… Jesus "turned to Peter" and then "spoke against Satan" who had just influenced Peter's opinion about Christ's death and resurrection. Let me say this again… He turned to Peter and spoke to Satan, as if Satan and Peter were co-manifest and co-existing in the 'same place'

The Co-manifest Kingdom

In order to comprehend what is happening within you, it is important to also comprehend what is happening around you. The kingdom of God is comprised of two kingdoms: the kingdom of heaven and the kingdom of darkness. When Jesus told us: "The kingdom of God is within you" (Luke 17:21), He is stating clearly: there are two kingdoms at work within you that are governed by two princes: the Prince of Peace and the prince of darkness (the prince of the air). We are being tested and proofed through sanctification to determine our eternal allegiance to serve one or the other, "For no man can serve two masters."

There are numerous indications in the scriptures of a co-manifest kingdom reality that surrounds us even now.

Jesus was led by the Spirit to be tempted by Satan in the wilderness (as an on-earth place) *and* the devil "took Him up *into* the holy city, set Him on the pinnacle of the temple" (Matt. 4:5) *and then* the devil "took Him up on *an exceedingly high mountain* and showed Him all the kingdoms of the world and their glory" (v.8)… *and afterward*, when Jesus could not be tempted, "the devil left Him and angels came and ministered to Him" (v.11).

- What is the "exceedingly high mountain" on earth that Jesus was taken up to? Could this be "God's holy

mountain" that we just talked about, that is also referred to Eden, the garden of God... which is a spiritual place that has always been upon the earth?
- What is "the holy city" that Jesus was taken up to? Could this be the "new Jerusalem" that is prophetically written about as "coming down *from out of* heaven," that is... from God's holy mountain?
- Indeed, the spiritual reality of heaven, aka God's holy mountain/the garden of Eden, is a spiritual place that resides upon and co-exists within the physical reality of earth, and is co-manifest with this earthly planet that man cannot ascend to. The reason we don't need to ascend into Heaven is because Heaven surrounds us even now – always has and, one day, the earthly glory of this planet will be revealed once again... in regenerate-newness, as the New Earth along with the New Jerusalem

Just six days after Jesus rebuked Peter (co-manifest with Satan), Jesus led Peter, James and John up on *a high mountain* "and He was transfigured before their eyes" (Matt.17:1, 2). These three apostles saw Jesus transfigured with Elijah and Moses "on a high mountain"... and "as they came down *from out of* the mountain,[126] Jesus commanded them, saying, "Tell the vision to no one" (v.9).

- This Heaven/Earth co-manifest event happened within the context of a spiritual vision
- This "high mountain" was none other than the spiritual heaven that resides upon earth
- Now, here is the kicker... were Elijah and Moses (who are in Heaven) sent back to earth to appear on an earthly mountain – *or* – does it make more sense that Peter, James and John experienced going up "a high mountain" into a

---

[126] The Greek words: down from "*ek* - out of" the mountain, are the same words to describe our eternal habitation, resurrection clothing as coming – from God "*ek* – from out of" heaven (2 Cor. 5:2), and these are the same words to describe the New Jerusalem as coming – *from* (*apo*-as something near God) out of (*ek*) heaven (Rev. 21:2)!!!

co-manifest heaven/earth vision[127] on earth whereby they "pierced the veil" that separates Heaven from Earth as an earthly event experience while they were in the presence of Jesus – upon the Earth?

We have focused so much attention on the transfiguration of Jesus that we failed to see the 'who, what and where' transcendence of the other five men that all appear during this magnificent spiritual moment: three earthly men meet two heavenly men as they have one singular event in a heaven-like place *with* Jesus. So, I want you to consider the nature of these two types of men (heavenly and earthly) – and where this event took place:

- Did Moses and Elijah come back to earth from heaven?
- Did Jesus take three earthly apostles up a high mountain into heaven?
- Did Jesus take three apostles *into* a heavenly vision on earth?
- Or – did all six people transcend a physical reality on earth to meet in a heavenly realm?

This is a paradigm paradox! There is only one condition whereby all four theories are valid – and this is when all six men appear in the spiritual reality of Paradise (the kingdom of heaven) on earth as they became co-manifest "*in* the presence of Jesus" paradigm!

The spiritual reality of heaven is neither up nor down – but in – and all around us.

And this is why we must be born anew according to the Spirit – so we can perceive the kingdom of heaven (and conversely, the kingdom of evil) that surrounds us.

---

[127] Visions are spiritual glimpses (and encounters) into the spiritual reality that is all around us, which our spirit can experience as a working of the Holy Spirit in us to establish the kingdom of heaven upon the earth.

There is another interesting biblical event we need to look at in order to conclude this co-manifest theory. Scoffers doubted Jesus was the Messiah and they told His disciples that Elijah would come first to prepare the way of the Messiah (Mark 9:11, 12), but no one as yet had seen Elijah, or at least they had not... from their point of view. In response to these scoffs, Jesus said, "Elijah has *also* come, and they did to him whatever they wished" (v.13; referring to John the Baptist). Now, with the ideas of co-manifesting and co-existing in your mind, consider this comment by Jesus about John: "For all the prophets and the law prophesied *until* John. And if you are willing to receive it, *he is Elijah* who is to come. He who has ears to hear, let him hear" (Matt. 11:13, 14). How can John the Baptist be Elijah... unless they are co-manifest by the same spirit within one spiritual reality? Consider how Elisha asked for, but could not receive, the double portion of Elijah's spirit <u>unless</u> he is "present to witness" his transcendence when the Lord takes him into Heaven? Or how the Spirit that was on Moses was also put upon the elders (Num. 11:17, 25)? Or how the apostle Paul tells us we have diversities of gifts, but it is the one and same Spirit that works all these things... as He wills (1 Cor. 12:4-11)?

If this seems hard to believe, then how can you also co-exist with Jesus who is co-manifest within you – and – is seated at the right hand of the Father in Heaven?

Certainly, I tell you, most people do not perceive the oneness of Jesus *within* them in this manner because... they still think they are doing it, which is why most people say that they don't need God or that "religion stuff" because they really believe they are doing it – until some tribulation event overturns their applecart – and then they run to God to fix a problem that God did not give them in order to save them from something they created that they typically blame Him for later.

Some people may have a hard time trying to fathom this mystery about the dual spiritual reality of good-evil/heaven-hell that surrounds us and is at war within us (in our mind), so let me explain it a couple different ways:

- Jesus cast out 6,000 demons named Legion that co-existed *within* a man living amongst the tombs in Gadarenes (Luke 8:26-33)
- Jesus cast out an unclean, convulsing spirit *from* a young boy (Luke 9:37)
- Jesus is the Door in your heart which leads to the Father (John 10:7), the Holy Spirit is the Doorkeeper of the Door (v.3), sin lies at this door and its desire is to have you (Gen. 4:7) and Satan also waits at this door to devour you – all this – within your heart

The universe was designed to operate in oneness, both material and spiritual… both visible and invisible… to operate in oneness under the Lordship of Jesus Christ; however, we have an adversary who creates division because he wants you to serve him, but he is quite content for you to live with a divided heart and double-minded thoughts if it keeps you from one thing: living in oneness of the Spirit with Jesus.

Hear Him. Know Him. Love Him. Trust Him. Understand Him. Serve Him. Live for Him.

We keep trying to figure out the "where" part of eternity and the spiritual reality of heaven, but our eternal resting place is not "where" – but rather – it is "*in*" Whom we worship.

Worship Jesus. In Christ, we live in oneness – in the Oneness of Christ – as we co-exist *with* Him in our heart and abide *in* Him to live eternal in heavenly places in oneness *with* God our Father *through* Jesus Christ our Lord.

"I and My Father are one" (John 10:30).

Think about this statement *very carefully*. Jesus is God. God is in Heaven. Jesus is on earth. Jesus and God are one – in Heaven and on Earth. Since Jesus is God upon the earth, then this can only mean one thing: that heaven and earth co-exist in oneness *in the presence of Jesus*:

> "No one has ascended to heaven but He who came down from heaven, that is, the Son of Man *who is in heaven*" (John 3:13).

We seem to have greatly misunderstood the epiphany that resides within this one scripture!

Since Jesus abides in oneness with you, through faith, and you are manifesting His presence as a gateway to release God's grace upon the earth, *then you are co-manifesting Jesus as He co-exists in "heaven-and-earth" whereby you, as a co-laborer for Christ, are establishing the kingdom of heaven "on earth as it is in heaven" in the similitude of Christ*!

How awesome is that!

"No one has ascended into heaven except He (Jesus) who has descended"… is a heavenly truth that should send shockwaves of revelation through the church – that is – unless you already understand who Jesus is, and who you are, as someone who existed in God's presence before the foundation of the world. Yet it is the Lord's fourth point within this single sentence of exquisite importance: Jesus is standing on earth when He says, "Who is in heaven." How can Jesus be on earth and in heaven at the same time? This is not difficult if you fully understand Who Jesus is – and what Heaven is – so I invite readers to read "Image" and "Here" to learn more.

The kingdom of heaven… is wherever Jesus is!

Since we cannot ascend into Heaven – heaven descended into us, through faith!

Jesus is the King of Heaven, and wherever King Jesus goes – He establishes His kingdom. Jesus is the Divine Doorway through whom the kingdom of heaven is being established – and since

King Jesus abides in you, through faith, then the kingdom of heaven is being released through you – through the Spirit of Christ. Now go ye therefore and release heaven into this world!!!

Jesus never promised us Heaven, the apostles never preached it and our creeds don't teach it. Spend a year or a lifetime searching this truth and it will liberate you from the bondage of numerous manmade doctrines and ordinances which contradict what Jesus purposed to accomplish through you – since the beginning! You were activated by grace through faith to operate as Christians (Christ in you) and as disciples of Christ to usher in a regime change on earth – from the kingdom of darkness to the kingdom of heaven! You are dual citizens of Heaven and Earth, but your rightful place and proper '*oiketerion*' domain is – Earth!!!

> Jesus said, "Believe Me that *I am* in the Father and the Father in Me, or else believe Me for the sake of the works themselves" (John 14:7-11).

As a co-manifest child of God and disciple of Jesus Christ, you are to live life as a saint of the Most High God, with Christ in you, with the Father in you… with you abiding in Them… to complete the works which our heavenly Father began, which He is completing through you as "Christ's workmanship" to restore the kingdom of God in you – and through you – in order to establish the kingdom of heaven upon this earth!

Jesus said, "I and My Father are one." Jesus made a claim of Divine relationship with the Father – and so can we! Jesus is Divine – and you have a divine nature (2 Pet. 1:4). Jesus is the Archetype of a better Way, the Branch of life, the Firstfruit of many brethren – and He showed us, by example, the only way anyone can enter into divine relationship with the Father – is through faith in the Son. Since Jesus is in you, co-existing and co-manifest with the Father, now therefore, you are *also* able to say these words: "I and my Father are one."

You co-exist with the Father… and now He wants to co-manifest His works through you.

Through faith in Christ, because Jesus abides in us, we are able to claim a special right of divine relationship with our heavenly Father, just like Jesus; "you and your Father are one." You are manifesting the Father as you live in oneness with Him – and because you are in the Father and the Father co-exists *with* you, *in* you, and *through* you, others may also come to the same knowledge of Christ "for the sake of the works themselves" that the Spirit accomplishes through you. Therefore, you are now a heavenly herald and messenger of the gospel in the similitude of Jesus… to co-manifest His works and *glorify* the Father *on* the Earth (John 17:4). By our works, our 'spiritual father' is made known to others (John 8:41, 44).

With Jesus abiding in oneness with us, we can do the same miracles and works Jesus did – and now – Jesus promised we will do even greater works – and these are about to begin.

And because the Father, Son and Spirit abide with you (in your heart-house), now you have become like Jesus in this regard: "In whom the fullness of the Godhead dwelt bodily" (Col. 2:9; 1:19).

We are here to proclaim newness – through truth, change and oneness – and God gets the glory!

God is everywhere and God exists in everything – and that includes both redeemed and unregenerate persons (they just don't know it yet). When God reveals Himself to you, as the One who co-exists *with* you, and you come to understand Him as Divine Father, Christ and Holy Spirit… as the God who "is at hand" and abides *with* you, Who delights to reveal Himself and make His mysteries known to His children, as Creator and Savior of the world Who takes away all sin that separates creation from intimacy *with* Him – and how He delights to co-manifest Himself *through* you to demonstrate His power and glory to the lost world that surrounds you – then truly – a supernatural event has occurred! You are the divine miracle the Father predestined *for* you *in* Christ *before* the foundation of the world! Embrace your salvation – and live it!

When Father, Son and Spirit dwell in you – the fullness of the Godhead dwells bodily in you!

Now that you understand *why* the fullness of the Godhead abides within you *and co-exists with* you... the Spirit desires to take your faith to the next level: *to co-manifest Himself through you with greater works.* The hands that you place upon another person for healing are releasing a flow of His power through co-manifest hands of grace (your body, His hands); the prayers you offer are co-manifest petitions to release His grace whereby His kingdom may be established upon the earth; and the works you do as a gateway of grace are being done as co-manifest expressions of the Father's continuous work upon the earth through the Spirit in the similitude of Jesus Christ – whereby God gets all the glory!

Amazing grace! "To the praise of the glory of His grace" (Eph. 1:3-6)

God is doing "all things through Christ who strengthens us." It is not "I" doing it... as in "I can do all things"... it is God doing it – through Christ – and Christ is doing it through you according to the Spirit who is at work within you; therefore, when God does these works through us – and even the greater works, we must never take credit for it, because by doing so, we are robbing God of His glory... and we must always remember...

...we were created for His glory!

God is doing it, by His grace... through faith. Contrary to what the spirit of religion teaches, there are no special prayers, magical incantations, higher offices or ordinations, anointed ministries, or Holy Spirit sanctioned conferences to help us manifest God's power; God is looking to manifest *Himself* through meek, humble, contrite, poor in spirit, everyday people just like you to release His glory through you. The God of all grace and glory delights

Himself in such, which is why "the meek shall inherit the earth" (Matt. 5:5; Psa. 37:11).

The kingdom of God is in you – and Jesus wants you to let the attributes of heaven out.

> "And I will give you the keys of the kingdom of heaven, and whatever you bind on earth will be bound in heaven, and whatever you loose on earth will be loosed in heaven" (Matt. 16:19).

Perhaps, now, this scripture makes more sense… knowing that Earth is the kingdom of heaven. As a "child of God" and a member of "the host of earth," the Lord has given us His divine authority, as we partner with Him, to engage in stewardship activities upon Earth whereby Heaven is being released through us to establish His kingdom and dominion on Earth.

Think about this for just a second… why else would Jesus tell us something so fantastic, such that the earthly activities we conduct on earth are thereby bound in heaven… unless Heaven and Earth are residing within the same place. The spiritual reality of Heaven and the physical reality of Earth are two realities that both reside in oneness upon the Earth, and the "on earth as it is in heaven" prayer by Jesus reinforces this "same place" perspective. We are surrounded by Heaven, but we cannot understand or comprehend this spiritual reality apart from the new birth by the Spirit of God (John 3:3), nor can we comprehend that heaven and eternity reside within regenerate man.

When Elijah prayed for the eyes of his servant to be opened so that he may see the heavenly army that surrounded them, the army was already there – and this same army is still surrounding us today. Elijah did not pray for the army of the Lord to be sent from Heaven, the army was already there – he simply prayed for his servant's "spiritual eyes" to be opened.

Our ability to "see" this reality is through a thin veil called: '*oida*' perception.

It is we who are residing in the midst of Heaven, not the other way around. Too many prayers have been piously offered for Heaven to come to Earth, and for Heaven to be made manifest in our presence, and for Heaven to open its doors and pour forth a blessing upon us, but Heaven has been '*dianoigo*' thoroughly open in our midst the entire time; it is we who need to be made aware of this reality because we are supposed to manifest Heaven on Earth as "the kingdom of heaven" is manifested in us and through us.

Earth, as a vessel for the spiritual reality of Heaven and the physical reality of this world, was created by God to operate in oneness with Heaven; likewise, man is also a vessel for the spiritual and physical reality that constitutes the soul of his being as he sojourns through this planet to establish the kingdom of heaven upon the Earth by overcoming evil with good, lies with truth, darkness with light, and pride with meekness, God's grace and the Lord's manifest presence.

If you do not loose Heaven and release it into the Earth, then who will?

> "No one has ascended to heaven but He who came down from heaven, that is, the Son of Man *who is in heaven*" (John 3:13).

Consider this scripture on the basis that Jesus, who came as God in human flesh, who lived in the same manner of all men, who performed all his miraculous works as an ordinary man filled with the Holy Spirit, is standing upon the earth "in heaven." And now the fifth lesson to be learned from this scripture is this: so are we! If we have been born anew, and have received the baptism of the Holy Spirit, we are walking in the fullness of the Spirit and we are hosting the Lord's presence, then we are also "in heaven." Heaven is wherever the King of Heaven is!

Jesus came as "the Way," to show us how to walk in liberated freedom under the anointing of the Spirit, to live according to the truth, so that we may also proclaim the truth, just as Jesus did...

Repent! The kingdom of heaven is at hand!!!

The reality of heaven on earth is already here. Jesus didn't bring the kingdom of heaven to earth – it has always been here – but it was taken captive by rebellious sinners in the likeness of Satan. When you manifest the fullness of the Spirit, as Jesus did, then you are already walking in kingdom truth, kingdom power and kingdom promises. When you move in the fullness of the Spirit, you are engaged in the Holy Spirit's work and you are living within the spiritual paradigm of Heaven on Earth. Heaven is not coming to Earth; we need to be walking in the midst of the spiritual reality of Heaven that is behind the veil. The glory of "heaven on earth" was stolen by the enemy and we were put here to take that glory back. I don't know why a critical mass of 6 billion or 60 billion people is needed on this planet to accomplish the work that God prepared in Christ Jesus since before the beginning, but that is the way it is. Heaven is here! We are here to establish the spiritual reality of heaven in the midst of the demonic kingdom that Satan built – in the face of all God's enemies. Through the Spirit, who is our intercessor, Who comes alongside us, Who has partners with us and enables us to walk in the fullness of the Spirit to establish the kingdom of heaven on Earth – in the similitude of Jesus Christ.

Two Kingdoms in Conflict

Jesus said: "My kingdom is not of this world" (John 18:36) and "The kingdom of God is within you" (Luke 17:21) and Jesus came preaching, "The kingdom of heaven is at hand" (Matt. 10:7). There is only one condition whereby all three of these proclamations by Jesus are consistent: *the kingdom of God goes with you, wherever you go, when Jesus abides in you.*

Now do you see why the soul of man is the spiritual intersect between these two spiritual kingdoms – and why the mind of man is the battlefield between Gods' good and Satan's evil to build one kingdom or the other in your heart – and why God gave us dominion over this earthly kingdom so that we can build God's kingdom in our heart and establish it upon the earth in the face of His enemy? So, I ask again… what kingdom are you building in your heart?

Jesus said, "My kingdom is not of this world"… because the kingdom Jesus came to establish upon this "earth" resides within every heart that yields its' sovereignty and authority and dominion kingship into the Lordship of Jesus Christ – who is King of kings and Lord of lords. Until you yield your sovereign will into His Divine authority, your heart will never be at peace – or be able to rest in His peace. ***The doorway to the Divine – is in your heart***! Seek it diligently… find it in your heart as one seeking a pearl of great price… then knock… and the kingdom of God will be opened unto you by Jesus Himself.

It's all about the heart! Home is where your heart is!

> …but some will not understand because of the hardness of their hearts (Mark 8:17).

Christian life is not about awesome preaching or great theology, or miraculous signs and wonders. If you completely comprehend in your heart how much Jesus truly loves you, and how God wants to live in co-manifest oneness with you, and you have dedicated your life in obedience to Him, then a supernatural miracle of infinite spiritual magnitude has already happened *in* you. When Jesus is Lord of your life and He is living within your heart, then the issue of Heaven or Hell really doesn't matter – now, does it? Heaven is *in* you!

And now we know why Solomon, the wisest man who ever lived, wrote these words:

> "He has made everything beautiful in its time. Also ***He has put eternity in their hearts***, except that no one can find out the work that God does from beginning to end" (Eccl. 3:11).

No man can find out, that is, *apart from the Spirit*! The spiritual reality and the manifest reality of Heaven and Hell are both in the Earth – and they co-exist within the heart of man – but man cannot find out this marvelous work apart from the new birth by the Spirit. Either you will love the one or hate the other, or serve the one and rebel against the other – but you cannot do both!

You cannot stand in between two ways with a one-kingdom kind of heart.

Please understand this: all people must stand before the judgment seat of Christ and give an account for their actions, but only one kingdom shall remain after the judgment: HIS! Everything else will be disregarded and thrown into the firepit.

Very few people can perceive this dual reality, but God's holy prophets can, which is why "the Lord God does nothing, unless He reveals His secret to His servants the prophets" (Amos 3:7), "which in other ages was not made known to the sons of men, as it has now been revealed by the Spirit to His holy apostles and prophets" (Eph. 3:5). If your church traditions do not allow God's prophets to speak, then how will you ever know what God is going to do next?

Our mind is the interface with the Divine, and your heart is the spiritual processor to determine the origin and authenticity of the message!

Listen up! A moment is going to happen very soon in which the veil of separation between earthly things and spiritual things will be changed, and angelic activity will be experienced by many faithful saints in obedience to Jesus Christ – as He promised (John 1:53). Our angelic brethren are here to assist us in the midst of this sojourn to remember what we are supposed to do as we oppose the Lord's adversary… and ours as well.

Listen up! We have already won! Christ has been victorious over His enemy for over 2,000 years and He invited us to have a share in this victory, so now it's time for us to rally behind Him in obedience to Him and take this Earth back from the enemy – and give God all the glory!

Listen up! The veil of separation is called doubt, worry, fear and unbelief. Believe in Jesus as Lord God Almighty, keep your eyes focused on Jesus and let the Holy Spirit guide you into all truth to help you know Him, understand Him and spiritually perceive the heavenly reality that surrounds you so that you may thoroughly comprehend the wonder, beauty and majesty of God's heavenly kingdom that is not only around you – but is also *within* you according to faith.

God knows that we are dust, formed in weakness with imperfection so that Perfection may reign within us and God's Sovereign Strength may flow through us; therefore, we must remain steadfast and faithful to Jesus, regardless of what Satan may do to us, and we will be rewarded in the hereafter.

And now it seems clear, doesn't it… that man got caught in the middle of a heavenly war between good and evil, and all he has to do in order to escape the fire of eternal torment is to believe *in his heart* that Jesus Christ is Lord, trust the Lord for salvation – and obey His voice.

That seems simple enough, doesn't it? Well, there is much more going on than we may be able to comprehend. ***Everything that man is going through on earth is in preparation for eternity*** – and this includes our sanctification. The mystery of man is this: our soul needs to be sanctified. In order for God's things to avoid the Spirit's fire that will burn away all unrighteousness, ungodliness, sin, every unholy profane wicked and evil work, and every demonic principality and power, God's things must be saved unto salvation by faith through sanctification, righteousness and holiness – apart from these, no one can see God.

> "For we are His workmanship, created in Christ Jesus for good works, which God prepared beforehand that we should walk in them" (Eph. 2:10).

If you are a tool of the Lord and you are not being used, then you are a liability; but if you are a tool that is being used, then you are an asset to the kingdom of God – and you will be rewarded exponentially for your faithful obedience to Jesus. Eternal life – with benefits! Hooray!

Learning from Job

One way we may begin to understand this cosmic predicament where man stands as an intersect point between two kingdoms (God's good and Satan's evil) is to read the book Job. This is considered by some to be the oldest book in the Bible, and in my opinion, more answers can be learned about man's predicament by reading Job than any other book. God knows Job as His servant, but Satan is asking God for permission to sift his life. Why he selected Job after going to and fro *through the earth* is not the message of this story; Job's quest to understand why bad things are happening to him is not the message either; maintaining one's righteousness in the face of extreme difficulty is not the message either. The message of Job is this: <u>*life is not about you*</u> – or trying to figure out why bad things are happening to you… but rather… knowing WHO will help you through it? Indeed, only the Anointed One can help any of us get through our many ordeals upon the earth – and His name is Jesus Christ. Jesus has been with us the entire time to help us in our time of need, not so much to get us out of the messes we create or the problems foisted upon us by others, but to help us "get through it." This earth is covered in darkness and sin on account of Satan's kingdom, but a way of escape has been prepared for every one of us… and its' called "the Way of Grace" through faith in Christ… and Christ alone!

When trials, tribulations and afflictions abound, pray for more grace… and hope for deliverance.

Many things must happen before Jesus comes to gather together all things that belong to Him. It is nearly impossible to know what all these "things" are, but we can trust the One who does know and understands our situation completely because He came to earth like one of us: as a Man. Jesus completed His mission and then left earth to "prepare a place for us," yet before He left, He promised to send the Holy Spirit (the Spirit of Jesus Christ) to be our Paraclete, to come alongside us to teach us and to guide us into all truth and understanding. Jesus never left us – and Jesus is coming back again for us..... yet several things need to happen, like global revival and the final harvest, the great tribulation, the millennial reign with Christ, the rapture (though not necessarily in that order) and then the end comes before the regeneration occurs.

So I ask you: if the rapture occurs "before" the great tribulation, then how is such a great multitude of people going to profess faith in Jesus and be saved (Rev. 7:8, 14, 15)… if all the teachers, preachers, pastors, evangelists and ministers of the gospel are in heaven? If you suggest the Holy Spirit will do it, then you are (once again) being derelict in your duty as a soldier in the host of earth to save other souls alive.

The Earth became chaotic and disorderly when Satan fell to the Earth – and the end of times will culminate in a spiritual battle between Jesus and Lucifer to restore the manifest glory of Jesus in the Heavens and the Earth, but until then, the Lord is testing the sons of men to see if they are willing to bend the knee in sovereign allegiance to Christ's Lordship to become sons of God – again – and do His will to overcome evil with good.

Why didn't the Lord just turn the Earth (and Satan) to toast *before* man appeared on Earth as in Genesis? Because the plan of God delegated the operational management of this planet to men – and despite a perilous beginning in Eden, this is still our mandated responsibility. There are many spiritual things going on that we may be unable to understand, so trust in the Lord and He will help you get through it. Consider now, these words from the Lord:

> "I would have said, "I would dash them in pieces, I will make the memory of them to cease from among men," had I not feared the wrath of the enemy, lest their adversaries should misunderstand, lest they should say, "Our hand is high, and it is not the Lord who was done all this" (Deut. 32:26, 27).

The faithfulness of God is on display. We often look at faithfulness from man's perspective as we consider our successes and failures, but we rarely consider faithfulness from God's perspective. His integrity is at stake and His enemies are looking to see if He will keep His word to protect us from calamity. And furthermore, God is more interested in maintaining His integrity according to His faithfulness than upholding the integrity of any person or any nation.

The End of Earth?

There are some scriptures that support the future judgment of the Earth that ends in global fireball whereby mountains melt like wax, so let me ask you this: do you really think Jesus would completely annihilate something that He created along with His glory in the earth, or is there perhaps another explanation? Peter mentions how the earth *and the works* that are in it will be utterly burned up (2 Pet. 3:10), John talks about the darkness of this world and the lust of it will pass away (1 John 2:8, 17) and Revelation describes how 'the woman on the beast: Babylon' will also be judged and utterly burned by the Lord God (Rev. 18:8), but is the Earth going to be literally destroyed, or just the worldly antichrist system of Satan? Certainly, all evil, sin, including all works of lawlessness and rebellion will be burned in the ensuing judgment, but why do trees, mountains and oceans need to be melted with them? Beloved, the Lord's regeneration is about a culture of newness, not annihilation. The things of "this world" will destroyed, yet "the Earth abides forever" (Eccl. 1:4).

Removing the Elements

By now, we have seen that the kingdom of heaven is neither up nor down – but in you.

And now we shall see that the kingdom of heaven is all around us, not as a *place* we enter in, nor as something that is to be released in our midst, but as the material substance that already exists around us and within us which many cannot enter in to on account of sin.

> "Behold! The Lamb of God who takes away the sin the world!" (John 1:29).

From this scripture, we are able to grasp another one of the primary missions of Jesus: to take the sin of the world away. When Jesus came as the truth, the light of His testimony was a frontal assault against the kingdom of darkness and the dominion of sin that so easily ensnares all humans on the earth with lies and doubt. Sin, in this instance, is not the bad things we do; sin is an evil spiritual entity that desires to have us (Gen. 4:7), devour us, and separate us from the love of God. Sin has taken us captive by leading us away because of our sinful desires, and has placed us in spiritual bondage and slavish servitude to the prince of darkness.

Sin does not enter into us, but rather it is we who enter into sin… which we enter willingly.

When humans choose to walk away from the divine relationship, our action constitutes a banner of sin we placed over us that represents our willingness to live within the midst of rebellious attitudes that we've hidden within our heart. It is like a spiritual neon sign flashing over our head that says who our spiritual father is. We are thus sinners who enjoy the sin, justify the sin, make excuses for the sin and then make casual jokes about the life of sin we delight in doing. Thus, we are living in sin – surrounded by a sea of sin – within the kingdom of darkness.

But this is not our nature according to the manner in which we were created; we were never created for sin – we were created for righteousness! When we were created, we were crowned with glory and honor (Psa. 8) and we are the apple of our Father's eye, but we turned away from Him like the Prodigal Son to live a life of decadence and depravity – but the Father never stopped looking toward the horizon for our repentant return back to Him.

There is only one way of escape from this hellish existence upon earth; there is only one door that leads to safety – and His name is Jesus, and He stands as the door of your heart to restore the heavenly gateway that was temporarily taken away on account of sin. In truth, Jesus never left you – it was we who turned and walked away from Him. And the person who is guiding and revealing to each of us the way back to Jesus is the Holy Spirit. Only the Holy Spirit can guide you to Jesus because He is the discerner of the thoughts and intents of our heart (Rom. 8:27); He is the Doorkeeper (John 10:3) who guides us back to Jesus… and Jesus is the only One who knows the way back to the Father. Anyone who teaches otherwise is a thief, a liar and a destroyer of souls, both human and demonic.

> Jesus said, "For this cause I was born, and for this cause I have come into the world, that I should bear witness to the truth. Everyone who is of the truth hears My voice" (John 18:37).

Why Not Here, Why Not Now

If all the elements of darkness and sin were removed from Earth and your divine relationship with the Father was restored to you, would you consider this new place Heaven – or not? And if not, then why not? Would you call it Paradise? And if not, then why not?

For nearly 2,000 years, we have been taught that man must be taken from this world of sin to enjoy the rewards of Heaven, but the opposite, in fact, is true. We are supposed to be in the world… but not of it (John 17:15-17). The Lord wants us to be sanctified and the sin removed from us, but it seems we have many doctrines that remove man from the earth which is the exact opposite of God's plan for redemption. We are gateways for God's redemption on planet earth.

Sin must be taken captive and removed from this world, and then the earth and all therein may enjoy the rewards of Heaven upon the Earth. It is not we that are taken from this earth to enter into Heaven, but rather, sin is removed from the Earth and the Father is thus restored unto us – on earth as it is in heaven. Man is not leaving – sin and principalities are removed.

Our "heaven only" theology has been falsely teaching us to run away from the very truth we should be running toward. The world to come and eternal life hereafter, as our Creeds teach, represent the eternal reality of Heaven that already surrounds us, on Earth, which we cannot see because a veil prevents us from perceiving this spiritual reality. We should not be attempting to escape Earth – we should be turning away from sin that ensnares us to escape the ravages of spiritual death and eternal damnation which are the penalties for unforgiven sin.

If Christ is in you, then you have already passed from death to life according to Galatians 2:20; and physical death no longer has any fearful meaning anymore. If Christ is in you, and Jesus is the Resurrection, then the power of the resurrection is already within you – "it" just hasn't happened yet. You are living eternally – even now!

So, let me ask this again… if all the evil, corruption, wickedness, deceitfulness, depravity, mean-spirited, hateful, vengeful, violent, degrading and horrific *elements* of this world were removed, would you want to live here on Earth? If everyone loved one another and cared equally for one another, without partiality and without any regard for position, rank or prestige, without sickness, without pain, without tormenting thoughts, without persecution, without cruelty of any kind – would you still want to leave Earth?

Take away all this negative worldly junk – and we can call this – living in Paradise!

The negative and destructive things I described above are "the elements" of this world which are going to be burned away in the future judgment. These elements are just as real as mountains, hills, grass and all other things which revelation scripture says will be burned away, but (keep in mind) only the spiritual elements of darkness and the works of the enemy will be burned away, including the mountain empire of sin upon which Satan sits which will melt like wax. It seems we have forgotten who rebelled against the King of Heaven and where he fell to establish his kingdom. We were sent to *kabash*... to subdue, overtake, and disregard all the works of the enemy and take authority over all principalities and powers in the name of Jesus, but the enemy has turned our theology upside down and inside out so that we fight against one another and against other denominations, instead of coming against the enemies of the Lord! They want us to run away and sing our pious songs about Heaven because they want us to leave; this world is their home, but now it's time to take the fight to the enemy that is subjecting us and the kingdom of heaven to violence. Saints, it's time to turn and fight! Vanquish evil from your midst. Silence lies with truth. This battle is the Lord's!

This battle is more than just the Lord's... the earth is our eternal home, and we should be fighting for our birthplace, our homeland and our inheritance!

Everything that has been redeemed will be restored in the regeneration of all things – whereby both man and the earth will embrace heaven at hand!

No longer separated by sin, we shall be united to our heavenly Father in oneness for all eternity.

Much has been said about "the elements" melting like wax when the Lord returns, with special emphasis to imply "physical elements;" however, the Greek word *stoicheion* (4747) has a variety of meanings, such as the substance of the material world (2

Pet. 3:10, 12) as well as delusive speculations, vain deceit and the rudimentary teachings of the world (Col. 2:8, 20; Gal. 3:4, 9).[128] Therefore, material elements can also refer to immaterial realities... and also vain philosophies and ideologies.

We must also remember the material world came from the immaterial, spiritual reality.

> "By faith we understand that the worlds were framed by the word of God, so that the things which are seen were not made of things which are visible" (Heb. 11:3).

However, there are things on this planet that do not belong here that we must *kabash*, and other things on this planet that we must protect. When we consider God's original plan of creation for man and the Earth, there are many things here that are "out of place" and do not qualify as being "very good" (Gen. 1:31); these things need to be shaken because they do not belong here. This is what the writer of Hebrew's is trying to convey when he quotes Haggai 2:6:

> "Yet once more I shake not only the earth, but also heaven." [27] Now this, "Yet once more," indicates the removal of those things that are being shaken, as of things that are made, that the things which cannot be shaken may remain" (Heb. 12:26, 27).

God is removing (present tense) those things that do not belong in His creation. He is shaking everything that can be shaken for one reason: so that only the glory of the Lord remains. If it does not give all glory to Him and acknowledge Jesus as Lord of all, then it will be consumed.

> "Therefore, since we are receiving a kingdom which cannot be shaken, let us have grace, by which we

---

[128] Strong's Concordance, study of *stoicheion* (4747).

may serve God acceptably with reverence and godly fear. ²⁹ For our God is a consuming fire" (Heb. 12:28, 29).

"Beware lest anyone cheat you through philosophy and empty deceit, according to the tradition of men, according to the *basic principles* (*stoicheion*) of the world, and not according to Christ. ⁹ For in Him dwells all the fullness of the Godhead bodily; ¹⁰ and you are complete in Him, who is the head of all principality and power" (Col. 2:8-10).

Temple Type and Shadow

We are currently living in the shadow, and not the substance, "which are a shadow of things to come, but the substance is of Christ" (Col. 2:17).

This physical, worldly reality is just a shadow reality that is very much like the Matrix movie… except in reverse. The spiritual reality of heaven that gloriously awaits the restoration and regeneration of all things is the "red pill" of repentance that we must take to realize that this world we are currently living in is the fake – the counterfeit reality! We have all swallowed the "blue pill," and we are currently living on earth in this sinful world within the kingdom of darkness, which is deceitfully wicked, but take the "red pill" of faith to embrace Christ Jesus as Lord, and thus, heaven enters into us. We are saved… and this is the element of grace which the Lord has done for us! Christ Jesus saved us! And this, He did, before the foundation of the world, no less (Eph. 1:4).

We do not enter into salvation – our Salvation enters into us! And His name is Jesus.

The redeemed of the Lord are never taken out of this earth! Sin is taken away – and those who remain upon the earth will abide with God "on earth as it is in heaven" for all eternity.

"The righteous will never be removed, but the
wicked will not inhabit the earth" (Psa. 10:30).

"For evildoers shall be cut off; But those who wait
on the Lord, They shall inherit the earth" (Psa. 37:9;
see also v.34).

"Ask of Me, and I will give You the nations for
Your inheritance, and the ends of the earth for Your
possession" (Psa. 2:8; the Father is speaking to
Jesus).

Faithful followers of Jesus will inherit the earth, and Jesus will inherit the nations, as well as the ends of the earth. We are inheriting one another for all eternity – on earth!

When the Lord takes away the sin that so easily ensnares us (Heb. 12:1), as well as the veil that separates us, our ability to perceive the heavenly reality that surrounds us is precisely what Elijah, the prophets, and the apostles experienced. We do not need to become perfect for this to occur; however, we are made perfect when we embrace our Perfection, Jesus, for even Elijah "was a man with a nature like ours" and was similarly affected by like passions (James 5:17).

It has never been about you – or anyone. We cannot make it right – we can only be made right by grace through faith via sanctification. It has always been about "Christ in you" and the sanctification of the inner man unto salvation and greater works. Especially greater works!

The temple was designed by God – not to keep people out, but to teach us about the spiritual reality all around us. God does not dwell in temples! God does not reside in the Arc! The veil in the temple that separates the inner court from the most holy place is just a tangible, physical reminder administered by God to teach us that only a thin veil separates us from God Most High. The High Priest was allowed to enter only once a year, but that old covenant veil was torn from top to bottom and rendered obsolete according to the New Covenant in Christ Jesus. Therefore, the only veil that separates you from the Father, and the spiritual reality of Heaven that surrounds you, is the veil (or wall of unbelief) that you think in your mind and construct in your heart.

> "But their minds were blinded. For until this day the same veil remains unlifted in the reading of the Old Testament, because the veil is taken away in Christ" (2 Cor. 3:14).

> "And every priest stands ministering daily and offering repeatedly the same sacrifices, which can never take away sins" (Heb. 10:11).

Elijah prayed that the eyes of his servant be opened so he could see the heavenly reality surrounding him; the scales fell from his eyes and he was able to perceive the angelic army all around him. The Apostle Paul saw a brilliant light on the road to Damascus that blinded him, but it wasn't until Ananias prayed that "the scales" fell from his eyes and he could see again (Acts 9:17, 18). And the same is true with you and me today. We should be able to see, but the scales need to be removed. This alone is a work of grace by the Spirit. We cannot do it or believe it or will it by faith or prayer; the new sight to perceive the heavenly reality is done to us as a work of grace by the Spirit (John 3:3) whereby we are able to comprehend spiritual truth and all things with spiritual understanding.

The scriptures have many references for "things" that should be removed and taken away from our midst so that we may be righteous before the Lord. Anything that gets in between us and Jesus is a vain work resulting in disobedience and sin. God is more interested in circumcised hearts than circumcised foreskins, and He is more interested in baptized hearts than baptism rituals. God is after the heart of man so that He may establish an everlasting covenant *with* him.

> "Circumcise yourselves to the Lord, and take away the foreskins of your hearts, you men of Judah and inhabitants of Jerusalem, lest My fury come forth like fire, and burn so that no one can quench it, because of the evil of your doings"(Jer. 4:4).
>
> "For this is My covenant with them, when I take away their sins" (Rom. 11:27).
>
> "As the heavens for height and the earth for depth, so the heart of kings is unsearchable. ^{4} Take away the dross from silver, and it will go to the silversmith for jewelry. ^{5} Take away the wicked from before the king, and his throne will be established in righteousness" (Prov. 25:3-5).

We are not the ones who are leaving this Earth; the wicked will be removed by angels (gathered like tares) and thrown into eternal torment in Hell's fire. Then the righteous will inherit the Earth, but unrighteous ones will be judged and condemned to Outer Darkness. We were all taken captive to darkness by sin; yet the redeemed will arise with righteousness in their wings, but all unredeemed and unclean things will be lead captive to remain captives forevermore (Psa. 68:18). God sent us here to have dominion over darkness, "to rule over sin" (Gen. 4:7) and establish His kingdom of heaven upon the earth; we are the "called out ones" with a mission to *kabash* the enemy and take authority over every principality and power that will not submit to the sovereignty of Jesus. We who were once taken captive and made obedient to sin have been liberated and been set free from bondage to lawlessness and sin in order to take unrighteousness captive to the obedience of Christ.

We are here to establish a regime change in the name of Jesus Christ.

> "He who overcomes shall inherit all things, and I will be his God and he shall be My son" (Rev. 21:7).

We should not be running away from the enemy – but rather, we should be running toward the enemy with truth and redemption on our lips, proclaiming once and for all...

> Repent! The kingdom of heaven is at hand!

Restoring the Kingdom

> "Lord, will You at this time restore the kingdom to Israel?" (Acts 1:6)

Moments before Christ's ascension, the disciples asked Jesus that question, but they were asking about the divided kingdom of David... not the divided kingdom of Heaven and Earth. It seems clear, now, that Jesus disregarded the question due to of their lack of comprehension to address the larger kingdom issue: the restoration of Heaven and Earth.

The kingdom of God was bifurcated into Heaven and Earth, and God sent the sons of men to Earth to have dominion and take back from the enemy that which was stolen from God in the great rebellion led by Satan. This is our mission on Earth; if you need a purpose in life, then now you know – so stop wandering aimlessly looking for "my purpose in life."

Yet the enemy continues to wage war today. So what is your purpose in life: to come against the kingdom of darkness. Initiate your purpose with prayer.

Jesus told His disciples... "It is not for you to know times or seasons which the Father has put in His own authority" (v.7), and this He said in regard to the restoration and the regeneration of all things. Jesus did not tell us the day or the hour that the Father would culminate the end of times to unify the kingdom; He simply said... "You shall be My witnesses."

There are two types of servant messengers in the kingdom of God: heavenly angels and earthly men. We are spiritual brethren (Rev. 19:10) who do the Lord's will to speak and declare and decree the wisdom of God in spirit and in truth. Our life is not our own. We are kingdom servants who belong to the King of heaven and earth, Jesus Christ, and we are His servant messengers to declare and proclaim freedom to captives (from darkness and the spirit of rebellion) and liberty to slaves (of sin). Before the resurrection, all men were slaves, but now, we are slaves by choice. We were set free from the bondage of slavery in sin by Christ's victory over sin and death, as well as the works of the enemy in this worldly system that operates in rebellion against Christ... which is antichrist.

This dual reality in which we are living is much like the snow-globe; when you shake it, the snow swirls around as it passes through an invisible substance. And such is life on earth. We are spiritual beings with physical form who are swirling through an invisible spiritual reality; we cannot see it, but we know it's there because of the "evidence not seen." Many saints have seen angels and approximately one-third of us have experienced some form of angelic encounter or life-saving divine intervention. This may never be enough proof for some because of the hardness of their heart; they don't know because they do not want to know. For them, truth is relative... and inconvenient.

Christians are seekers of truth. If you claim to be a follower of Christ, but you are not living with the conscious awareness and certainty of Christ abiding in you, or you are not able to hear His voice, then how do you know if the manifest presence of "Christ in you" has occurred? Our salvation is predicated upon it!

Don't just settle for "I think so." Search diligently to establish a divine personal relationship with your Salvation, Jesus Christ. Listen for the sound of His voice. Your life is dependent upon it – both in this world and the world to come.

A New Culture For Living

> "Behold, I create new heavens and a new earth" (Isa. 65:17).

Newness is one aspect of creation that man comprehends. Every day is a new day with a unique sunrise, and new events happen every day, but newness that happens over and over can become quite redundant and uneventful, often resulting in spiritual mundanity and complacency.

However, spiritual newness and awakening is not like physical and natural newness; spiritual newness is exciting, invigorating, joyful, patient, hopeful and expectant. Man's salvation is wrapped in newness, and when a person decides to dedicate their life to the Lord, to reverence Him as Lord, Master and Savior, then, by grace through faith, they are considered a new creation (or creature). The old man has passed away and now a new person is standing in their place (2 Cor. 5:17). When the old man (self) voluntarily surrenders their will in order to establish Christ on the throne in their heart, as the inward expression of heartfelt conviction and a new awakening according to the spiritual renewal process that is happening within them, then they have become a new creation.

So, what happened to the old body? Did the old body pass away and now before you stands a brand new person? Absolutely not! The outward vessel of the body remains relatively the same (except for an obvious change in countenance and joy)… the inner drive and motivational purpose has been reconfigured to operate in a different manner, according to Christ who now dwells as Lord within your vessel. Old man – with new purpose. The old man wasn't melted in a fireball before you could become a new creation; you are a new person, by grace – and now you are being transformed into newness from the inside out.

You are not new in terms of time – but new in regard to character and culture.

And this is how the kingdom of God works. These old things, having been created at a certain time to perform a specific purpose and function, having become either worn out or obsolete, become like a temporary shadow to be disregarded in accordance with the will of God so that a transition into newness can happen. The old man is being transformed by the renewing of his mind into the new man to live according to righteousness and peace and truth, and similarly, the world in which we live is also being transformed by the same Spirit according to the eternal purpose and will of God – to be renewed according to Christ. The old man is reckoned dead so that we may discover what our eternal purpose with new life is – through Jesus Christ our Lord.

Even earthly seasons are natural cycles of God's transformational power and renewal on Earth.

You have an eternal purpose. The Earth has an eternal purpose. Heaven has an eternal purpose… and so does Hell. Much of what I write about is in regard to God's people discovering their eternal purpose in life, because – once you know what you are supposed to do, as having been re-purposed by the transformational work of the Holy Spirit to do it, then your life becomes very intentional, spiritually meaningful – and dynamically worth living for.

Forgetting the old and disregarding it – let us advance on into newness.

There are two words in the Greek for "new":

- *neos* (3501) – new as in time
- *kainos* (2537) – denotes that which is new or as yet unaccustomed; not new as in time, but new as to form or quality; in the spiritual sense, it can be described as different in nature, character or culture from that which is contrasted as old. Nearly all of the spiritual newness found within the new covenant teachings and gospel of Christ Jesus, are '*kainos*' His new commandment (John 13:34) and the new wine of the kingdom (Matt. 26:29 etc.), and

'kainotes' – newness (Rom. 6:4; 7:6; 2 Cor. 5:17). The new man born anew through faith (Eph. 2:1-10, 15) is *'kainos'* who begins a *'neos'* new-in-time experience as a newness *'kainotes'* person in Christ who is being molded according to the new pattern of Christ (Eph. 4:24).

God is in the business of making all things new again – <u>*not making all new things*</u>. God didn't destroy you because of your sinfulness before you were made a new creation – He redeemed you because He loves you. God finished creation on the sixth day, rested on the seventh from all His work… and then He began His greatest work upon the earth on the eighth day: the regeneration of all things. God's regeneration principle goes to the heart and soul of Who God is – and it is the core and substance of Who He is as He manifests Himself within His creation in the face of His enemy. Jesus is God's representative for the earth as "the God Who manifests Himself" and for this reason He delights to manifest Himself to complete the works of the Father because God is love – and love conquers all!

Passed Away

When we use the term "passed away" in regard to the decease of a person's life, the term is loaded with much meaning *and* just as much ambivalence. We understand that this person has passed from life into death, but how come we know so little about death and what happens afterward? Well, if we see ourselves as humans rather than spiritual beings having a human experience – and we envision "the great escape" from earth through "heaven only" lenses, then our ability to comprehend eternity and our purpose in life will just not make any sense, but – if you can see yourself from God's perspective and that you are a spiritual being first and foremost, then there is no longer a need to escape – because you will abide wherever Jesus will be.

There are two words that are used to describe the earth as "passing away," but we must remember foremost that it is inconsistent with God's character to destroy His creation if He plans to keep it, restore it and make it new again. If the glory and the blessing are still in it, then He will regenerate it. Consider now the scriptures Rev. 20:11, 21:1 and 12:4 ...

1) The earth and "the heaven" (singular) will *"flee away"* (*pheugo*-5343) from the judgment throne of Christ and *"no place was found for them"* (Rev. 20:11), whereby scripture commentators say they were "burned up" even though the scriptures do not say this, but similar terminology is used regarding the casting of Satan and his angels out of Heaven:
   - "And war broke out in heaven: Michael and his angels fought with the dragon; and the dragon and his angels fought, [8] but they did not prevail, *nor was a place found for them* in heaven any longer. [9] So the great dragon was cast out, that serpent of old, called the Devil and Satan, who deceives the whole world; he was cast to the earth, and his angels were cast out with him" (Rev. 12:7-9)
   - To "flee away" (v. 20:11) – because evil cannot remain in Christ's dominion (See 1 Tim. 6:11)
   - But I ask you – isn't "fleeing away" unnecessary if they have been turned to ash?
   - But again I ask– is melting consistent with the nature of Christ's salvation?

2) A new heaven and a new earth are mentioned in Rev. 21:1 because the old ones *"passed away"* (*parechomai*-3928). This word is a combination of two words (*para*-near,from,by + *erchomai*-2064-to come or go) which is translated with much diversity of meanings. A similar word (*dierechomai*-1330) with a different prefix (*dia*-through) means: "to come or go through" as in "to pass through" a town or village which conveys the idea of passing through without stopping. A similar sense should be applied when translating *parechomai* as in "to come or go by" or "pass near"
   - The word itself (pass) is heavily burdened by various meanings within the English language. When this word

is mentioned of a person (pass, passing, passed away), it conveys the death of the body (to perish) and their non-existence among the living. When this word is associated with Heaven and Earth in the scriptures, we apply this terminology (pass away) with the same measure of non-existence and, in some cases, utter destruction. Heaven and Earth are two permanent places within the kingdom of God, so this meaning cannot be implied – and some other term must be applied
- The word (pass) occurs 126 times in the New Testament, yet is only translated from a specific word as follows: *parechomai* (19x), *dierechomai* (6x), misc. (5x) = 30, which means there are 96 instances when the term (pass) appears in order to convey some meaning without a specific word associated with it (i.e. "it came to pass")
- This makes even less sense even when we see *parechomai* attributed 18x to Jesus (pass, pass away, come, go) including "Heaven and Earth will pass away"
  - Matt. 5:18 (2x) – "For assuredly, I say to you, till heaven and earth *pass away*, one jot or one tittle will by no means *pass* from the law till all is fulfilled"
  - Matt. 24:34, 35; Mark 13:30, 31 (3) – "Assuredly, I say to you, this generation will by no means *pass away* till all these things take place. [31] Heaven and earth will *pass away*, but My words will by no means *pass away*"
  - Mark 14:35 – "He went a little farther, and fell on the ground, and prayed that if it were possible, the hour might *pass* from Him"
- There are instances when the appropriate meaning is applied to *parechomai*
  - Mark 4:29 – "But when the grain ripens, immediately he puts in the sickle, because the harvest has *come*"

- Luke 12:37 – "Blessed are those servants whom the master, when he comes [2064-*erchomai*], will find watching. Assuredly, I say to you that he will gird himself and have them sit down to eat, and will *come* [*parechomai*] and serve them"
- Luke 17:7 – "And which of you, having a servant plowing or tending sheep, will say to him when he has come [entered] in from the field, '*Come* at once and sit down to eat'" is literally translated: "Come immediately recline" (rhetorically) as something a master would never say to a slave
- Thus, the meaning suggested by Greek translators (passed away) needs to be reconsidered with proper terms applied to convey what Jesus meant: perhaps "to come near" or "to come aside/come beside" or "to pass by" rather than pass away.

3) Another similar term (*aperechomai*-565) with a different prefix (*apo*-from, of, out of) means to "come or go from" (as away from something near)[129] or perhaps "away from something near at hand." Let's see these terms used in context with one another:

> "Now I saw a new heaven and a new earth, for the first heaven and the first earth had *passed away* [3928]. Also there was no more sea. ² Then I, John, saw the holy city, New Jerusalem, coming down out of heaven from God, prepared as a bride adorned for her husband. ³ And I heard a loud voice from heaven saying, "Behold, the tabernacle of God *is* with men, and He will dwell with them, and they shall be His people. God Himself will be with them *and be* their God. ⁴ And God will wipe away every tear from their eyes; there shall be no more death, nor sorrow, nor crying. There shall be no more pain, for the former things have *passed away* [565].

---

[129] Strong's Concordance.

⁵ Then He who sat on the throne said, "***Behold, I make all things new***." And He said to me, "Write, for these words are true and faithful" (Rev. 21:1-5).
- To pass away (Rev.21:4) – the former things departed from the presence of the Lord because (tears, death, sorrow, crying, pain) must cease once Christ dwells with us
- The former things "go away" because they have been rendered obsolete and are of no value in the regeneration of Heaven and Earth in Christ's dominion

4) None of these scriptures ever mention Heaven or Earth are burned up, only that evil unredeemed things must "flee away" from the throne of Christ where "no place" is found for them in the midst of (among, beside, near) heavenly things

God is not going to make all new things – He is going to make all things new again. This is the regeneration principle that God instituted and implemented on Day 8. Just because Satan fell here and rendered the earth chaotic… enveloped by evil darkness, God could have turned Earth and Satan to toast at that moment and then started new again… but He didn't. Why? For two reasons: 1) Because that is man's job, and 2) Because Jesus is doing something on Earth that will demonstrate to all created beings with free will, once and for all eternity, as they live within His universe – if you choose to live in joy and peace, then you will honor the Lord, exalt His name above all names and give Him all the glory – or be ready to spend eternity in eternal torment with those angels who rebelled against Him (2 Pet. 2:4). The choice is yours… always has been.

> "Yours, O Lord, is the greatness, the power and the glory, the victory and the majesty; *for all that is in heaven and in earth is Yours*; Yours is the kingdom, O Lord, and You are exalted as head over all" (1 Chron. 29:11)

The spiritual things happening upon the earth are a cosmic demonstration to show forth, once and for all, that Jesus is Lord of all. It seems Satan tried to exalt Himself higher than God, but he soon learned that he underestimated just exactly Who Jesus is: Lord God Almighty! Before you come to the altar thinking Jesus is your brother or companion or friend (which you are, by grace through faith, when you do all that He commands), then you had better exalt Him and give Him all the glory He is due. Don't make the same mistake Lucifer did.

> "Now therefore, do not be mockers, lest your bonds be made strong; for I have heard from the Lord God of hosts, a destruction determined even upon the whole earth" (Isa. 28:22)

The prophet Isaiah is telling us exactly what the Lord Jesus told him: destruction is destined _upon_ the earth (not for the earth). The extent of this destruction by a "spiritual fire" is thorough and complete except for two things: seeds and roots. One generation after another for the past 100 years, in the Scofield (1909) tradition, was heavily influenced by the global atrocities of World War1 and has been teaching an end to the world by physical fire in the end-times judgment, but what do the scriptures teach us?

> "One generation passes away, and another generation comes; but the earth abides forever" (Eccl. 1:4)

> "For as the new heavens and the new earth which I will make shall remain before Me," says the Lord, "So shall your descendants and your name remain" (Isa. 66:22)

The earth abides forever! Stop living with a foxhole mentality and start advancing the kingdom! Is Jesus a God of chaos, confusion and destruction, or is Jesus a God of order, sound reason and life-giving sustenance? Jesus did not come to bring destruction to earth or condemnation to men, but to bring judgment *to the ruler of this world and to destroy his mountain and all his works.*

Now, let's look at the miraculous works that Christ accomplished to see if we are able to comprehend His kingdom building mission and commission for man upon the earth, such as:

- In the old covenant, if a leper touched you, you became unclean, but when Jesus touches a leper, the leper becomes clean
- In the old covenant, if you touched a dead person, you became unclean, but when Jesus touches a the dead person, they become alive again
- In the old covenant, a woman in her monthly cycle was considered unclean, but when the woman with a bleeding issue for 12 years touches Jesus, she becomes healed, and then Jesus commends her for her faith
- To the woman caught in adultery, her sin was an issue because of the law, but when Christ confronts her accusers, grace becomes an issue of redemption for everyone
- They were just 12 ordinary men, but when Jesus called them to walk with Him and host His presence, they became apostolic world-changers

Do you see a recurring pattern here? It didn't seem to matter to Jesus what the old covenant laws or traditions were; He was demonstrating to them, and to all future generations as many as are called, how to live according to the Spirit within a new spiritual paradigm reality to understand the kingdom of God by challenging many false assumptions. When Jesus manifested Himself and His glory, He lived according to His new covenant whereby the lame walk, the blind see, the dead are raised to life – and the poor have the gospel preached to them (Matt. 11:4-6). Jesus came to promote life, not destroy it; Jesus came to liberate us from bondage in a corrupt worldly system that refuses to give glory and honor to God... Jesus came to set us free from bondage to sin and the consequence of sin (death) so that we may live life in abundant reverence to Him.

You may be stuck in a self-made prison or perhaps you are surrounded by raging storms in your life that the enemy has orchestrated to destroy you, but if you are in the boat with Jesus, even the wind and waves must obey Him (Mark 4:39-41). Jesus said, "My peace I leave with you" (John 14:27) and this is the "world peace" that this world cannot attain apart from faith in Christ.

Jesus wasn't teaching us new rules – He was teaching how to think like He does… and to live anew within His new covenant reality according to the manner in which we were first created – as when we walked with Him in the Garden and hosted His presence.

Miracle Man

The first miracle by Jesus was to turn a foot-washing urn full of dirty, despoiled water into fine wine (John 2:1-11), so if you still think Jesus came to planet Earth to turn this forsaken dirty sphere of darkness into a nuclear fireball, then you do not understand why Jesus came to earth. He did not come to destroy – but to save; He came to destroy darkness – but "For this purpose the Son of God was manifested, that He might <u>*destroy the works*</u> of the devil" (1 John 3:8) with the light of truth; nor did He come to condemn us – but to justify us and lead us in truth to the Father. Jesus came as our salvation to redeem and "offer us the way of salvation" through faith in Him, as ones being rescued from darkness into the light of truth. Jesus also came to "take away the sin of the world" (John 1:29) so that "through Him the world might be saved" (v.3:17).

Jesus is the Savior of the world (John 4:42) and because He lives, *the earth has already been saved…* and now we are His workmanship to finish the work on earth that He began.

Why would Jesus save the world – if He plans to destroy it? That reasoning is utter nonsense!

The second miracle by Jesus was to heal the son of a royal officer of a local governing authority, which was probably under the rule of Herod Antipas. If you think Jesus came to heal only those with the right theology, religious affiliation or political influence, then guess again. Jesus came *to heal as many as came to Him*, and many came – and all were healed. Jesus didn't heal some and then refuse to heal others; He healed all on account of faith because that is Who Jesus is – our Healer, our Redeemer, our Deliverer, our Salvation, and our Resurrection.

The third miracle by Jesus was to drive out an evil (unclean) spirit from a man. When Jesus came into the synagogue to teach, the evil spirit cried out with a loud voice, "Let us alone! Did you come to destroy us? I know who You are – the Holy One of God!" (Luke 4:34) Consider, now, the words of this demonic spirit: it speaks on behalf of many evil spirits, it knows who Jesus is – and then it wants to know if Jesus came to destroy them. Demons know and operate within the spiritual realm; they know Jesus is "the Son of the Most High God" (Mark 5:7) and they also know He is coming to destroy them – just not now.

If you still think Jesus came to accuse, condemn and destroy men and the Earth, then you obviously have Jesus confused with someone else.

Jesus is the Truth and the Life; our condemnation and destruction is something we do to ourselves by choosing to live 'apart' from Him.

> "Concerning the works of men, by the word of Your lips, I have kept away from the paths of the destroyer" (Psa. 17:4).

He didn't come to fix the world; He came to change the way we think about life – with newness.

The reason we call it a "paradigm shift" is because it requires us to change the way we think!

In the reality that Jesus lives in, there is no sickness, there is no illness, there is no leprosy, there is no more death or remorse, there are no more stormy seas or depression, there is no more sadness or pain, there is no sin and, therefore, there is no more condemnation; there is nothing unfruitful… all things are wonderful and glorious in the Paradise of Heaven on Earth that Jesus resides in. This is the way He approached life according to the way He thought about life – His life, that is, the life that He manifests in everyone and everything. The life that Jesus manifests in every one of us is verily heaven on earth. When we live with Jesus dwelling within us, then verily – the kingdom of heaven is at hand… and Paradise "here now is" is upon the Earth!

When Jesus was asleep in the boat that was being tossed around by the wind and the violent waves, the reason He wasn't affected by the natural elements which He made – was because – there are no storms of life in the reality that Jesus is living in. His disciples came to Jesus and said, "Teacher, do You not care that we are perishing?" (Mark 4:38) Of course, Jesus cares if *any* of us are perishing, but the reason Jesus castigated His disciples for their lack of faith was because they were consistently unable to assemble the truth of the spiritual reality of Christ "in their midst" *within their mind*; they did not *'suniemi'* comprehend His truth, and therefore, they did not comprehend the reality of His kingdom that Jesus had given to them which includes His authority and power to live according to the dominion mandate He gave us.

The kingdom of heaven is *on the Earth* "within" the heart of every believer when Christ Jesus abides within us – so now it's time, saints of God, to let heaven out! My earnest prayer is that your eyes may be opened to perceive the heavenly Paradise of Earth that is all around you, so please… stop looking at your circumstances and situations, stop looking backward at your troubles and failures, stop comparing yourself to others or considering how other people think of you, stop asking blind religious leaders what the Holy Spirit is saying (ask Him yourself), *stop living in the past, stop living in fear and stop believing false reports* – Jesus is alive in you – so start living anew in the newness paradigm of faith which Jesus taught us to live according to.

In this reality, even when Jesus was required to pay a tax from the worldly reality, a fish was summoned to provide a coin so that the temple tax could be paid – and if you think paying a worldly tax is an injustice, just consider this: Jesus is the manifest Temple of God, incarnate. Jesus was being asked to pay a tax – 'on Himself' – so get off your soapbox and stop your pity party. Change the way you think about the new reality of Christ in you – and be the paradigm shift Christ has called you to be. Be the light of the world that Jesus said you are and start changing this world for the better… and let heaven out!

Live according to the kingdom of heaven within you… and then let heaven flow like a river of goodness out of you! Overcome evil – with good!

Apart from the Holy Spirit at work within you – you can do nothing of yourself. Focus on Jesus as you are guided by the Spirit to walk in newness.

The old worldly way of thinking considered the wilderness a sinful, dark and dangerous place where demons resided, but Jesus goes into the wilderness so He can be closer to His Father – and so it is today. It doesn't matter where we go or what we do… when the kingdom of heaven is in you, and you host His presence, then the old realities of this world must bow in the presence of Christ. Start living in the light of this truth!

The old worldly way to encourage an unfruitful tree was to dig a trench around it and fill it with fertilizer (manure/animal waste) and give it another year (Luke 13:6-9). But when Jesus sees a fig tree that is not yielding fruit, Jesus cursed it whereby it withered and died (Matt. 12:33-37). While this may seem like a harsh thing for Jesus to do to a tree or any living thing, especially since this tree was not in the proper season for bearing fruit, we must remember this: you can tell a tree by its' fruit – *and* by its flower. Even though this tree was out of season for fruit, there would have been fruit-bearing flowers to give evidence of future fruitfulness. If anything hinders the Gospel of grace and truth, and does not produce the fruit of the kingdom, or at least produce flowers leading to fruition, then we are to disregard it and move on – *why try to fix something that doesn't want to be fixed. We are agents of change* in this world on behalf of the kingdom of Christ! Jesus said many things that we might take offense with today, like telling another of His disciples… "Let the dead bury their own dead" when he asked to be released to "let me go first and bury my father" (Matt. 8:21, 22). Dead people go around mourning the dead, but people alive in Christ rejoice in the resurrection because this is our hope of life eternal. Keep it simple. Focus on Christ. Declare the good news. Preach the gospel of salvation… but, if any person does not want to listen, then treat them like dead wood and just keep moving. You are not here to convince and fix – you were sent as an agent of change to declare the truth and shift the atmosphere. Stop trying to resurrect dead people – that's Christ's job! And it is the Holy Spirit's job to bring conviction to the heart so He can transform people and transition them to walk in the newness of Christ. We are not soul-winners, the Holy Spirit is. We are not soul harvesters, the Spirit of God is. As Christ said, "Let the dead bury the dead," and just keep moving forward with the Gospel. Some people, like unfruitful trees, are just taking up space… so *speak the truth in love* and, then, move on! Jesus came to offer salvation to everyone, but know this: some people do not want to be saved. In this case, the Spirit says: NEXT!!! Some churches do not want to be changed. NEXT!!! Keep moving forward with the Good News of the Gospel to people who have ears to hear with softened hearts. And if anything becomes an impediment to proclaiming the good news or His calling for your life, like the "mountain" that Jesus mentioned, then we are (by faith) to cast it into the sea (Matt. 21:20-22). It is not about our faith – it is about walking in His truth to advance God's kingdom upon the earth with the confident assurance and certainty of Spirit-anointed faith that knows, understands, and comprehends the truth – and therefore – lives according to the Spirit *in* the truth of Christ!

"He who is not with Me is *against* Me, and he who does not gather with Me scatters abroad" (Matt. 12:30).

"Therefore I say to you, every sin and blasphemy will be forgiven men, but the blasphemy *against* the Spirit will not be forgiven men" (Matt. 12:31).

"Either make the tree good and its fruit good, or else make the tree bad and its fruit bad; for a tree is known by *its fruit*. [34] Brood of vipers! How can you, being evil, speak good things? For out of the abundance of the heart the mouth speaks. [35] A good man out of the good treasure of his heart brings forth good things, and an evil man out of the evil treasure brings forth evil things" (Matt. 12:33-35).

These three scriptures, back-to-back, reveals much about Christ's New Earth doctrine.

Be Like Angels

In this new paradigm whereby we continue to live upon Earth as a heavenly place in the hereafter, supernatural events will happen all the time, which is why Jesus told us, "In the resurrection, we will be like angels (that are) in heaven." We will still be on the same Earth with the same gravity and the same weather patterns, but the power within us will be greater than the power of gravity or the forces of nature, thereby allowing us to walk on water like Peter did – and to be physically translated from place to place like Philip and Elijah. Only a thin veil of doubt and unbelief currently separates us from the heavenly reality that already surrounds us where the miraculous and supernatural – become spirit-normal events!

But, you say, I do not see Paradise on Earth where I live; all I see is pain, despair, death and destruction. Yes, there are some places where the angel of darkness and demonic strongholds have overtaken an area or a region with death and destruction, but now you know it doesn't have to be that way. Change it! For even while martyrs were being tortured, they were, albeit painfully, still giving praise to God. This is not mind over matter or the power of positive thinking; these are newness ways of thinking that allows the Spirit-guided river of life to flow through your heart like a torrent with life-changing-attitudes of faith and joy. I know what I speak about: even as I write this, at this very moment, a significant life changing event happened to me just 10 hours ago… and I was not shaken or moved by it; the bank repossessed my house for non-payment of mortgage due to three years of unemployment. In my reality, there are no problems… there are only opportunities waiting for the Lord to tell me about His solution. When anyone lives by grace and walks in the Spirit – newness will happen – because the Lord God likes to reveal His majesty and power in our weakness and seemingly hopeless situations.

Keep moving forward – advance – and don't look back!

But, you say, how can Paradise be upon Earth when I see natural disasters happening with loss of human life? Well, during the time that Jesus was upon the earth, a tower in Siloam fell and killed eighteen people, so what did Jesus have to say? Was it the result of sin? Was this a judgment from God? No! Jesus simply said, "Unless you repent you will all likewise perish" (Luke 13:5). Bad things are going to happen to every one of us eventually; none of us are getting out of "here" alive; however, when we repent from the old way of thinking to put our faith in Jesus and trust Him to take care of us as we live according to His way, then it really doesn't matter… because He is the Resurrection and the Life.

But, you say, can you give me an example of paradisiacal heaven on Earth? Yes I can, now go… and take a vacation. Think about it (that is, if you can envision it, or if you cannot, then read poetry with Spirit-guided imagination), whenever a person plans a vacation, they are planning to step away from one reality to enter into another reality in a work-free, stress-free, worry-free existence where they can experience joy, peace, happiness and bliss. That, my friend – sounds like Paradise to me. When we visit a National

Park, a Botanical Garden, or ocean seashore, we can sense God's presence more often in these places than in gothic cathedrals.

But, can Earth be Paradise? Yes! Earth is Paradise – behind the veil! Only those with spiritual eyes to perceive the heavenly reality that already exists all around them will understand what I am talking about; and naysayers are selling this planet short, having been duped by many lies from the deceiver because his desire is to destroy us – and Paradise with us. Every now and then we get a glimpse of our heavenly Paradise on Earth when we see a vacation commercial to visit a tropical island with white-sand beaches, hike an alpine trail surrounded by hillsides of blooming flowers, snorkeling with exotic fish swimming around you, gazing at the grand canyon at the exact moment to marvel a rainbow, watching a hummingbird drink nectar from a cactus flower that blooms for only a couple hours a year, or standing beneath a giant 300' Sequoia tree to consider eternity was happening for this tree when Christ was still walking upon the earth.

Paradise is all around us – the kingdom of heaven "now is" – but many prefer to live in bondage to the old way, which Jesus referred to as "Ye of puny confidence." We must be transformed by the renewing of our mind if we are ever going to have dominion as Jesus commanded us according to the power and authority He commissioned us with.

If, by hearing of His voice, He has told you to do anything, then He has also given you the power, the authority and the provision to live according to it! Trust and obey!

Jesus is the Branch, the Vine, the Life, the Redeemer, the Anointed One, the Chosen One, the Resurrection, the Way, the Truth, the Door that leads into eternal life, the Manifested One, the Messiah and Christ who came to save us and the world, because the Earth is full of His glory – and that includes not just you and me but everything *in* the whole entire Earth. Jesus is our Creator; He created the dust, then formed dust around our soul to create our human body, and then back to dust and ashes our body will return. Everything belongs to Him – and that is why…

It's all about Jesus – and God gets the glory!

Jesus is the Resurrection. For too many years we have been taught that we will enter into a resurrection "event" whereby we will ascend with glorified bodies into Heaven. Let me say this again: Jesus is the Resurrection. If Jesus is abiding in you, then the resurrection and the power of the Christ's resurrection are already within you, through faith. When the moment comes for us to be raised for resurrection, we will be raised up in Jesus Christ Himself before we ever leave the ground because the resurrection and its' power goes with our soul unto salvation. The idea that you will be raised up is because the Resurrection is already within you – and the supernatural power that will raise you from the dead has already happened to you… the moment you gave your life to Jesus. Regardless of when, where, or how you die, the resurrection has already happened to your eternal soul. Easter is not just a day in which we celebrate "resurrection day" and then go about our life the remaining 364 days to do our own thing; faith in Christ is a supernatural miracle that transformed you into a new person whereby the resurrection of Christ is operating within you 24/7/365. If you die but Jesus is not already abiding in your heart, through faith, then eternal life will be impossible for you at that point, because if Jesus is not abiding in you, then the resurrection into newness of life is not in you either. So, repent – and believe in the Good News of Jesus Christ!

It's all about Jesus – and God gets the glory!

And Jesus is God!

The earth is not just His inheritance – it represents one manifold expression of His manifest presence in the universe. He created your body as a vehicle to host His presence in much the same way He created the Earth to host His presence… so don't you think it's time to give Him all the glory He deserves, which includes releasing the glory that was taken captive in all captives by lies and deception – as well as the glory that was also taken captive in the Earth?

We are being changed from one glory that already resides within us as adopted spiritual sons and daughters of God into a future resurrection and regeneration glory of all things according the Spirit of life in Christ Jesus. We do not know what we will be – but we will all be changed – and we will be raised in glory to enter into the glory of our Lord Jesus Christ.

> "But we all, with unveiled face, beholding as in a mirror the glory of the Lord, are being transformed into the same image from glory to glory, just as by the Spirit of the Lord" (2 Cor. 3:18).

Likewise, sons of God will release the glory in the earth so that, once again, Earth's Paradise is revealed. Isn't this why creation groans… waiting for the sons of God to be revealed so that creation can release the glory that is already in the Earth? (Rom. 8:18-25) *We are already living in Paradise and the kingdom of heaven surrounds us*, but sons of God seem to be looking through "heaven-only" lenses – waiting for a heaven-bound train that has no station stops on Earth for ordinary men.

Destroy the earth? Do you now see that this is inconsistent with the mission of Jesus and our mission as sons of God? What do the scriptures say will happen to those who destroy the earth? They themselves will be destroyed!

> "The nations were angry, and Your wrath has come, and the time of the dead, that they should be judged, and that You should reward Your servants the prophets *and the saints*, and those who fear Your name, small and great, *and should destroy those who destroy the earth*" (Rev. 11:18).

Destroy the Earth in order to create a new one??? Can we now see that this is inconsistent with the character of who Jesus is? He is going to make all things… new… again. This is the message of the resurrection and this is the principle of regeneration: to make new again. Any religious tradition that teaches Christ as destroyer goes way beyond even what demons believe.

The kingdom of heaven is like a man who sowed seed:

- A seed will sprout up
- A shoot will spring up
- A branch will arise
- A mustard seed will ascend up
- The spiritual leaven of Christ will cause the earth to rise up – again
- And yet, we like to focus our attention upon the mountain being cast into the sea…
- Oh ye of puny '*pistis*' (little faith)

Jesus is growing, building, establishing, arising, ascending, increasing, multiplying and blessing everything in the Earth for one reason: to magnify and glorify the Lord of glory *in* the Earth.

Jesus wants us to be busy about His business and our Father's business to finish the work at hand: HAVE DOMINION!!! To condemn and destroy are *inconsistent* with His Divine character and mission for the Earth. He came as the Light of the world to dispel the darkness – and He called us sons of light to move through this Earth with equal disregard for the darkness. Now, go, and overcome evil with good – bear fruit of righteousness, in newness and oneness, with love toward one another.

> "I am the vine, you *are* the branches. He who abides in Me, and I in him, bears much fruit; ***for without Me you can do nothing***. [6] If anyone does not abide in Me, he is cast out as a branch and is withered; and they gather them and throw them into the fire, and they are burned. [7] If you abide in Me, and My words abide in you, you will ask what you desire, and it shall be done for you. [8] By this My Father is glorified, that you bear much fruit; so you will be My disciples (John 15:5-8).

Jesus is the Branch of eternal life. Now, read Jeremiah 23 to see Jesus as Branch, Righteousness, and the Lord of glory.

Worldly Kingdoms on Earth

The words 'earth' and 'world' represent two very different concepts, and the word 'mountain' is often used to represent these two very different types of operating systems upon the earth.

- Earth – '*ge*' (1093), the planet; God's celestial vessel for creation, as a habitation for all life and mankind, as well as a vessel for His glory
- World – '*kosmos*' (2889), the universe; creation that is ordered and arranged according to one operating system or another, Godly or ungodly

The Lord's operating system created the Earth and mankind *with His glory in it*, but the second operating system of Satan purposed to rob and defraud God of His glory and honor in the earth, as well as mankind. These two spiritual operating systems have been at war with one another since the war in Heaven spilled over onto Earth.

Many authors of books about Heaven fail to make a distinction between world and earth; using them interchangeably thus creating much confusion… and theological error. Earth refers to the planet as well as the soil, but "world" refers to the current operating system that is opposed to Christ and uses 'sin' to separate us from the reality of God's kingdom upon the Earth. At times they are used coincidentally, but clarifying light should be used in reference to end-times theology. Jesus said, "My kingdom is not of this world…" thus referring to the kingdom of darkness and the dominion of Satan that has enslaved both Earth and all inhabitants of Earth, which awaits the regeneration of all things. And yet – the glory of the Lord fills the Earth!

If these two operating systems are functioning concurrently, then how can anyone discern one from the other? Excellent question! First: only the Holy Spirit reveals and brings understanding and only born anew Christians are able to discern and comprehend spiritual truth. Second: it all has to do with giving glory to God. But what does this have to do with the Earth – and man – and end times? It has everything to do with redemption, resurrection, restoration, and the regeneration of all things – the culmination of this age and the age to come – but it seems end-time prophets and doom-and-gloom teachers are more interested in life hereafter in Heaven rather than living life according the assurance of hope right now in preparation for the New Earth age to come.

Think about this for a moment: why has God's plan for redemption taken so long? Why has this age lasted this long? If we look at the plan of salvation with finality, then it seems to be taking forever for the culmination to occur, but when we see that God's plan includes man's eternal command to have dominion over the Earth as a "continuation" of God's plan for the Earth, then this may explain why it has taken so long… and may even take longer. Remember, there is also a millennium period to go through, and then Satan will be released for a short period, which brings up even more questions about God's plan for us to have dominion over the Earth.

There are only two conditions whereby the Earth and man will cease to exist in the coming age:

- If the Lord's judgments and ordinances cannot be found in the earth, and there remains no more glory in the earth on account of sin and godlessness, then, indeed, the Lord will destroy the earth as He did with the flood in the day of Noah (yet leaving a remnant)
- If the Lord's glory cannot be found in man's reflection as His image bearer, then God will utterly destroy all the inhabitants of the earth as well

If these two conditions can be met, then the annihilation will happen, but if there remains even a remnant of a few who have not defiled the glory of God within them, as in the case with

Abraham's request of Sodom and Gomorrah, then the Lord will relent for the sake of the remnant. Even Elijah felt the land was destitute of God's glory at one time, but the Lord told him there were "7,000 who had not bowed their knee to Baal" (1 Kings 19:18). It sometimes seems that there are few – if any – with a remnant of God's glory in them, but I can assure you that the "hidden" abide in great multitudes waiting for "the day."

For even if the Lord does utterly destroy the Earth, the life *in* creation will still remain within the seed and the root as a manifestation of God's eternal glory in Christ Jesus as Creator, whose fingerprint upon and within all creation fills the Heavens and the Earth with His glory. The Lord's glory remains forever! The Lord's Spirit will always remain with His things to give Him all glory – even to the end of the age – because He blessed it and His blessing remains "in it."

There is a Godly mountain where the Lord resides, on Mount Zion, where the glory of the Lord is exalted above all created things:

> "They shall not hurt nor destroy in all My holy mountain, for the earth shall be full of the knowledge of the Lord as the waters cover the sea" (Isa. 11:9).

And there is a mountain of wickedness that represents the worldly system controlled by Satan:

> "Behold, I am against you, O destroying mountain, who destroys all the earth," says the Lord. "And I will stretch out My hand against you, roll you down from the rocks, and make you a burnt mountain" (Jer. 51:25)

These spiritual mountains represent two operating systems upon the Earth: Godly and demonic. The mountain in the Earth that the Lord will burn (melt) and be utterly destroyed is the worldly dominion and demonic system that operates according to Satan that exalts itself above God's glory in an attempt to take from Him what belongs to Him – or destroy it in the process.

> "Behold, the eyes of the Lord God are on the sinful kingdom, and I will destroy it from the face of the earth; yet I will not utterly destroy the house of Jacob," Says the Lord" (Amos 9:8).

> "Behold, the LORD makes the earth empty and makes it *waste*, distorts its surface and scatters abroad its inhabitants" (Isa. 24:1; then read Nah. 9:2 for the only other occurrence of '*balak*'(1110); also read Micah 6 to see that God's judgment is against the godlessness in the earth in the manner of Kings Balak, Omri and Ahab; v. 5, 16 and then read to see "what the Lord requires of thee" v.8).

These two scriptures refer to the Lord's annihilation of a *spiritual* worldly kingdom upon His physical Earth; however, these scriptures must be read within the context of their entire chapter regarding nations that worship 'other' gods and even combine Godly worship with ungodliness (sensuality and worldly passions) because they do not give glory to God; this *must not* be construed as the destruction of the *entire* Earth in the coming judgment unless the "lack of glory" conditions have been met – or a blessing no longer remains "in it."

> "Thus says the Lord: "As the new wine is found in the cluster, and one says, 'Do not destroy it, *for a blessing is in it*,' so will I do for My servants' sake, that I may not destroy them all" (Isa. 65:8).

The Lord is rich in mercy and compassion; His faithfulness is everlasting; He will throw out the water of dirty, despoiled foot-washings if a potential blessing to yield the finest wine still remains within the vessel. It is inconsistent with His nature to annihilate anything if a remnant of His glory remains "in it."

The Lord of glory has given us the ability to bless and to curse, to build up or to destroy, to ascend or to descend, to give life or to take it, to live according to the glory within us – or to glorify ourselves above the King of kings and exalt ourselves above God Most High like Satan.

> "Behold, I set before you today a blessing and a curse" (Deut. 11:26).

> "Now it shall be, when the Lord your God has brought you into the land which you go to possess, that you shall put the blessing on Mount Gerizim and the curse on Mount Ebal" (Deut, 11:29).

What the Lord requires is very simple: honor the Lord and give Him all the glory; acknowledge Him as Lord through your sovereign allegiance to Him, and then… do all that He commands! Live as a manifestation of His blessing upon the earth according to the manner in which you were created – as a blessing, with a blessing in it, to be a blessing… as His image bearer!

> "And every creature which is in heaven and on the earth and under the earth and such as are in the sea, and all that are in them, I heard saying: "Blessing and honor and glory and power *Be* to Him who sits on the throne, And to the Lamb, forever and ever!" (Rev. 5:13)

We have all been given a very simple choice to make: give God all the glory and live as a divine continuation of His blessing in the earth by the hearing of His voice – or don't… but…

> "If you will not hear, and if you will not take it to heart, to give glory to My name," Says the Lord of hosts, "I will send a curse upon you, and I will curse your blessings. Yes, I have cursed them already, because you do not take it to heart" (Mal. 2:2).

It's your choice: either build up or tear down; either rejoice in gladness and joy – or pursue worldly happiness in futility; either live according to one kingdom's operating system or the other – *because it is impossible to live in supernatural abundance if you live double-minded in a one-heart reality.*

The Promise

The Lord is coming back and He will reward all according to their deeds. To those saints who dwell in righteousness, they will be "a light of the world, like a city set upon a hill that cannot be hidden" (Matt. 5:14).

When we live according to His precious promises, we will live forever with Him in Paradise, in a city always filled with His glorious light, as the New Jerusalem that comes "from out of" Heaven upon His holy hill – Mount Zion. Welcome, once again, to the New Heaven and the New Earth – which is literally, Paradise on Earth – "As it was in the beginning, is now, and shall be forever: *world without end.* Amen." [130]

The Lord's promises are not too fantastic to believe… unless you prefer the uphill climb on your self-righteous knees upon the mountain of worldly religion. By grace you are saved, through faith… and grace alone! Jesus only! There is no other way, but to trust and obey.

---

[130] Doxology, *Gloria Patri*, often said after the end of many Orthodox and Catholic prayers.

The Essence of a New Day

This is the beginning of a new day. You have been given this day to use as you will. You can waste it or use it for good. What you do today is important because you are exchanging a day of your life for it. When tomorrow comes, this day will be gone forever; in its place is something that you left behind... let it be something good.[131]

---

[131] The Essence of a New Day; quote attributed to: Sucessories, Inc. 800.535.2773

10) New Earth Residents

> "He has delivered us from the power of darkness and conveyed us into the kingdom of the Son of His love" (Col. 1:13).

The Church has been preaching a theology of eternal life in Heaven for 1600 years, but now it is clear that those saved unto salvation will be resurrected into a New Earth with a New Jerusalem which comes down "from out of" Heaven. The obsolete theology of Heaven as our eternal destination was never able to tell us what we will be doing while we are in Heaven, and for some, it really didn't matter as long as it we did not end up on Earth or in Hell. "Heaven only" was the goal – and this goal, regrettably, became a calling higher than seeking Christ Himself.

Once this New Earth doctrine is embraced as truth, a new way of reading the scriptures will be revealed to all of us and we will see just how marvelous His plan is for those who love Him – and how marvelous this Earth is going to be for those who put their hope and trust in Christ. Familiar terms like birthright, inheritance, homeland, redemption, hope fulfilled, promised land, great reward and many others will come into focus once sojourners embrace Earth as our eternal home… as something worth living for – and as something worth fighting for to reclaim and redeem.

Many months after this book was written, and as yet unpublished, the Lord revealed a monumental truth to me that needed to be inserted into the fabric of this book.

> "The meek shall inherit the earth" (Matt. 5:5)

Many of our denominational doctrines have taught us how to get saved and who shall enter into Heaven, but these things only have I found thus far that describe "ordinary believers" who enter into the Lord's salvation in the New Earth:

- John 17:3
- They follow Jesus by hearing of His voice (John 10)
- The Spirit of Christ is within them (Romans 9)
- As they forgive others, their heavenly Father forgives them (Matthew 6)
- They have a personal relationship with Jesus and He knows them (Matt. 7:21-23)
- They live by grace according to Spirit – in meekness

Meekness is not a word that is readily defined.[132] Many of our Bible dictionaries, commentaries, expositories and concordances use the term "humility" or "gentleness" to describe meekness; however, humility is an attitude – but meekness is an attribute. Let me explain.

- Attitudes are elements of our character which define us according to how we behave
- Attributes are grace gifts from God which define us according to His character in us

Meekness is not the attitude of humility, which is one way to esteem yourself; rather, meekness is a Godly attribute of grace whereby you esteem God higher than "self" and others "ahead of self."

Meekness is a Godly attribute which Jesus used to describe Himself: "I am meek and lowly" (Matt. 11:29). Meekness is the greater grace which the apostles preached that comes to us as a grace gift by the Spirit, whose transformational work within us is to transform us into the very likeness of Christ.

Meekness, by definition, is selflessness, a Divine attribute that puts God and others ahead of self; selfishnessless. And Jesus, our Example and High Priest, lived according to meekness – as should we.

---

[132] Excerpts about meekness were taken from an as-yet unfinished book by the author about grace and greater grace.

Christ performed multitudes of miracles, but He always gave all the glory to God. He didn't profess to be a prophet or somebody of any report; He simply directed all attention to God. And yet, being fully God, He lived His life in such a manner that He "did not consider it robbery to be equal with God, but made Himself of no reputation" (the essence of lowliness; Phil. 2:6, 7) because His mission was to teach us how to live as ordinary men who live "out of God's presence," as in the beginning in Garden of Eden. Being God, yet living subordinate to the Father, Jesus taught us how to live according to the Spirit in the fullness of the Spirit that gave all glory to God – and God alone! Every time someone tried to pay Him a compliment, like Nicodemus (John 3:2) or the lawyer who called Him "good teacher" (Matt. 19:17), Jesus always deflected the comment in such a way to give all the glory to His Father. And we must imitate Christ's example.

There were many times when Jesus drew away from people into wilderness areas to abide in oneness with His Father, but when He returned, His ministry involved teaching the truth and ministering to the needs of others – at the same time – because one is inseparable from the other. In this regard, some teachers, evangelists, prophets and pastors stumble. We are all ministers of Christ's gospel and our lives need to be conformed to the pattern exemplified by Jesus Himself – with love for one another, as we walk in meekness and lowliness. When we live out of love, and out of our spirit, then we *will* live according to meekness because that is the way of love!

We need to esteem others *ahead* of "self" in this Earth – and this is how we will live in the new earth kingdom to come. We are not to esteem other people better than ourselves, for we are all the same in Christ; we are to esteem others *ahead* of self. Jesus put the needs of others ahead of self, and likewise, we must imitate Christ's example.

John the Baptist, the forerunner of the Messiah, said it perfectly, "He who comes after me is preferred ahead of me because He was before me." John put Jesus ahead of "self" and, likewise, so must we.

We were created in meekness by Jesus, our Creator, and born with meekness, but it didn't take long for the pattern of this world to negatively impact that inner child to alter our heavenly perspectives on life – and our sense of "self." As adults, we cannot begin to undo all the negative things that have happened to us, which is why the Holy Spirit is here to help us "change into" the person we were created to be. We would spend far too much time and ill-focused effort by going backwards to "fix" all the broken elements of our life, which is why we must allow the Spirit to transform us. We must look forward – to walk in newness, never focusing upon the past, or we risk ending up like Lots' wife.

Trying to "fix" instead of entering into "change" assumes two things: 1) that which was broken can or must be fixed, and 2) God's grace for today is insufficient for who I am right now.

Walk away from brokenness and despair – and walk into grace!

God's grace is *all* sufficient for what happened to you, who you are now, and who He predestined you to be. Grace is the divine attribute of God that makes all things new again. The pattern of this world seeks to entrap us in the past and keep us crippled in worry and unbelief, but the grace of God always moves us forward in hope – and into His destiny for those who believe.

Part of our problem is: we think grace is an element or "thing of God" when grace is everything that God is. Grace is not something we can appropriate or an attitude we can adopt, because grace constitutes the elemental nature and fullness of who God is! Grace is an attribute. Grace is God's nature and His divine attributes being revealed in us – which is a work of the Spirit in us. The gifts of the Spirit and the fruit of the Spirit are all grace gifts and Divine attributes of who God is (Gal. 5:22) and they are given to us as "spirituals" by the Spirit to transform us into the likeness of Christ. So, let's keep it simple – and live according to the Spirit of Grace in the spirit of meekness.

Changed By Truth

Truth is wonderful, as is wisdom and understanding, but *if* the acceptance of Christ's truth does not result in a transformational change whereby a believer adopts the attributes of Christ in their life, especially meekness, then truth was minimized, marginalized or not believed because it did not result in some noticeable change by the believer into the likeness of Christ upon the earth.

A major element of newness through truth, *change* and oneness – is meekness. Change apart from truth is meaningless, and change without meekness is arrogant futility, because without meekness, we cannot enter into the Oneness of God. This is something that I needed to learn as I found myself recently in the crosshairs of the Spirit on this matter. Even though I was focusing on God, I was still focusing too much on "self" – and I needed to "change." There was too much "me' and not enough "Thee" in my thoughts and deliberations – and manner of living.

So the Spirit directed my study on meekness and this is what I learned:

1. "The meek shall inherit the earth." Jesus said it and His words of truth can be believed. We are Christ's inheritance and the earth is our inheritance for those saved by grace *in* faith. Now consider this: why would God want anyone in His kingdom that refuses to live out of His presence and refuses to put the needs of others ahead of "self"?
2. Meekness is an attribute of God's nature and His grace whereby you esteem God higher than "self" and others *ahead* of "self."
3. Meekness is a change in perspective from "self" to selflessness. It is living so totally "other-centered" that we become like Christ as a life-giving spirit. Living according to this pattern comes against the kingdom of darkness and selfishness on many levels.

4. Meekness will always put God first. As our highest priority, God must always be first in our life, and then others, lest we seek to serve men ahead of God.
5. Meekness is a paradigm shift that commands attention. We must change!

> Jesus said, "Take My yoke upon you and learn from Me…" (Matt. 11:29)

The yoke of Jesus is the coupling together of a true believer that operates in oneness *with* Christ, not just according to those things given by Him, but also those things that are shared *with* Him, including meekness. When we become joined, bound, knitted, yoked, glued and united in Christ whereby we walk in the manner in which Christ identified Himself, as "meek and lowly," then we will exhibit the greater grace called meekness – and, in resurrection blessedness, we shall inherit the New Earth at the regeneration of all things.

Meekness is a divine attribute that enables us to live according to love, because without love, no one will see God, for God is love. Meekness enables us to satisfy these two commandments, 1) love God, and 2) love one another; and meekness enables us to live according to the new covenant commandment Jesus gave us, "Love one another as I have loved you" (John 13:34).

> "Jesus said to him, "'You shall love the LORD your God with all your heart, with all your soul, and with all your mind.' [38] This is the first and great commandment. [39] And the second is like it: 'You shall love your neighbor as yourself.' [40] On these two commandments hang *all* the Law and the Prophets" (Matt. 22:37-40).

Meekness and love are yoked together… and this is a mystery revealed in Christ.

The true meaning of life is to live the true meaning of love.
Living life according to love in the spirit of meekness is the way of Christ – and we have all been called to live in this manner.

> "Beloved, let us love one another, for love is of God; and everyone who loves is born of God and knows God. ⁸ He who does not love does not know God, for God is love" (1 John 4:7, 8).

Meekness is one of the four keys the Lord has revealed to me about the kingdom of heaven and the age to come in the new earth. Selah… meditate on this.

And may we live accordingly.

> It's all about Jesus – and God gets the glory! Amen!

11) America, The New World

> "One generation passes away, and another
> generation comes; but the earth abides forever"
> (Eccl. 1:4).

Have you ever lived in a place where it felt as if life's vitality and the flow of creative energy were being sucked out of you – and you just had to get out of there? Is this the place where the unacceptable has become acceptable and then normalized to become an integral part of the culture, so much so, that "that's the way we've always done it" was the only reason why people did it, whereby you were admonished "you need to know your place?" This is not a place of wisdom and understanding; it becomes a deathtrap of the human soul – and you need to escape.

Such was Europe in the 1500's at the height of the Renaissance following the discovery of America in 1492. The human spirit had become crushed, disillusioned, hopelessly downtrodden and heavily burdened following the aftermath of mysterious plagues, wars lasting over 100 years, political conquests over trivial boundary disputes, the nationalistic crave to become the single dominant supremacy world power – and one intolerant religion that would crush science and the pursuit of knowledge if it felt threatened in any manner. Worldly dominion was everywhere... and it was oppressive. People grew up upon lands that were entirely owned by others and unavailable unless handed down to you through family lineage, the wilderness had been tamed such that the wolf was extinct and old growth forests were nonexistent; your marriage was planned for you and every aspect of your life was, well, so constrained, controlled and manipulated that life's vitality could only be experienced by reading poetic writings, that is, if you were taught to read and then given permission to read.

And then one day, as you are walking down the street, someone tells you about a new world that has been discovered on the other side of the ocean. It is described as a veritable paradise with unlimited potential, land for the asking and the freedom to satisfy all your unfulfilled dreams and expectations. This was a land of promise and opportunity, a land of freedom and liberty to become who you were destined to be; it was a new world full of adventure that offered one thing that Europe could not: hope for the human condition.

If one word could summarize the promises offered by this new world, it would be "freedom."

The idea of freedom was sown within the human soul, and it was only a matter of time before people began to devise plans to start life anew – somewhere – and now there was a new world opportunity on the other side of the earth. The idea of beginning anew had been birthed in our consciousness and now it was available, if only you could financially pay for passage to America – or offer seven years of your life as an indentured servant to pay off the debt. It was the adventure of a lifetime; an entirely new world waiting to be explored. The human spirit saw the first faint glimmer of hope in nearly 1,000 years – and it was mesmerizing.

Students of American history understand the paradox of the European flight mentality and the veritable deathtrap that this new world paradise eventually became for the vast majority of settlers. Jamestown Island, c.1607, became the final resting place for six out of seven would-be colonists – and they were buried on the island by the thousands. But as we know, "hope deferred makes the heart sick," and people continued to pursue what would later be known as "the American dream." Their soul and spirit craved something more… something much, much more.

They wanted freedom from – and – to be free for.

These are two sides to the freedom coin. You can flee some worldly trappings that rob or restrict your freedoms, only to become ensnared again in another worldly trap – or you can seek to be free from all worldly systems in order to be 'who' you were destined by Almighty Providence to be. Freedom from and free for… this is the dynamic tug of war within the human soul and spirit; this is a spiritual search that occurs within every one of us and continues as a push-and-pull within us until we eventually find the peace we desperately seek.

How does this relate to America? For starters, we need to see America as a piece of land that God's sovereignty controls. This land has always been here, but it wasn't until just 500 years ago that European's knew it existed (I don't say discovered, in this sense, because Native Americans could not discover what they had always known as their home). America was an unknown country that was withheld from European awareness until the fullness of time, that is, the fullness of God's timing for the kingdoms of this world. God does not reveal all that He has done or will do until the time is right – and we are living in such a day in which all things are going to be revealed so that the nation's themselves stand in awe of God's purpose and plan.

We may not know what the fullness of God's plan is, but the truth is being made known by searching the scriptures to reveal His heart's desire through the Spirit's anointing within the renewed mind of man that is being sanctified and transformed into the likeness of Jesus Christ.

God's global plan for regeneration is at the core and substance of His loving, Divine and eternal plan for man and the earth. [As I write … this seems like such a foreign concept because I have been taught that "man and the earth" are spiritually separate and distinct entities that will be eternally separated by death, but now that I know that earth as the kingdom of heaven is where mankind will reside for all eternity, it seems I am having, right now at this moment, a paradigm shift of some spiritual magnitude that I had not anticipated. Yes, I know that we are the host of earth, a.k.a. sons of men in the flesh and sons of God according to faith, but my focus has always been about God's regeneration of man "to make all things new again," yet not fully realizing how God's plan of redemption and regeneration for the earth is equally fantastic. According to the same power that raised Jesus from the dead, which by the way, is the same resurrection power at work within regenerate man, is also the same power that will regenerate the earth again... in newness. The same Divine power from God – is for the regeneration of "man and the earth." Just as man will be raised up incorruptible in the resurrection, likewise the earth will also be renewed incorruptible. Both man and the earth will be regenerated for God's glory – according to His glory that already resides within us and also within the earth. ---- I know this sounds like new age teaching, but the counterfeit culture can only exist if there is a genuine and authentic culture from which to base it upon... so consider it from that perspective.]

How does the New Earth relate to America? Or, better yet, how can it *not* relate to America? Look at world history and you will see something very unique that happened to America. This country became a "place" for a fresh start and a new beginning for millions of foreign nationals seeking a better future and a better hope. They left an old worn out and obsolete world behind to "begin anew" with little more than the clothes they wore. They came to build a future that could not be physically or politically taken from them without just cause. They came expectantly to freely worship God apart from nationalistic mandates, requirements and religious obligations.

They came by the millions seeking to be free... and to begin again... in newness.

This is the America that God intended. Freedom loving people living life – free from tyranny, free from religious control, free from bondage and servitude, free from slavery, free from corruption, oppression, extortion, bigotry, idolatry, prostitution, injustice, senseless violence, worldly evils, and every human evil that exploits human weakness for sinful gain. This is the America that God intended whereby His people could be set free to worship Him "in spirit and in truth." No longer slaves to the world, but spiritual servants to live in freedom upon the Earth as He intended – as in the Garden of Eden. America is a type and shadow of "the Promised Land" that we shall experience as Paradise – in the New Earth.

America was not some grand social experiment in human democracy; America is the land of the free and it became "the land of we."

The Land of We

America stands upon the Constitution and the Bill of Rights, which begins with a very profound statement: "We the People." It does not say: we the government, we the traditions of our fathers, we the religious caretakers of humanity, we the judges and lawyers of the law, we the entitlement class, we the 'whatever fill in the blank.' It simply says, "We the People." This nation is a self-governed nation of God-fearing individuals "by the people, for the people" … well, at least it used to be until "we the people" complacently allowed the government of-by-and-for the people became dominated by political institutions, lawyers and special interest groups. This book is not about America's governmental and social failures; it is about America – God's providential hope for ALL humanity – as a city of light set upon a hill.

"We" find these truths to be self evident…

God has always allowed mankind to do what it wants upon the earth as long as it does not violate one aspect of His sovereignty: the earth's dominion. The spiritual plan for American never included world domination, but rather, *spiritual dominion* over principalities and powers that are evil and demonic in nature. When America ceases to defend the rights of men to live in freedom from evil-minded men yet defends the democratic choice to freely murder unborn children, then know this: a spiritual line has been crossed. A reckoning is due, and unless we repent and convert (change our way), a judgment is coming. If America ceases to be what God intended America to be, then why on earth should God tolerate our evil any more than He tolerates ISIS? Either we are establishing His dominion of righteousness and peace upon the earth that initiates global revival that gives all the glory to Him, or we are living in fantasyland. America was predestined, but she can also be forsaken. If God can disregard His chosen nation, Israel, because they refused to listen to His voice and obey His truth concerning Jesus, the Messiah, then what hope is there for an entire nation that allows freedom of speech that cannot use the "F" word for fear of an "R" rating but routinely takes the Lord's name OMG in vain?

If any nation other than America can arise to become the next wave of revival, then judgment shall come to her. There have been repeated warnings, but false reports of security were written by bureaucrats sitting behind the safety of their government pensions. Enough! Change is coming – and it is a spiritual tsunami!

Nations rise and nations fall, yet this is the Lord who has done this, not the will of man. Human history has witnessed many great nations rise and other nations take their place; most were overthrown by more powerful nations while others were vanquished from within. We now live within a moment of human history when any nation can arise to fulfill the Lord's mandate to "have dominion" and usher in the final great revival, but one nation above all nations was established, consecrated and set aside for this purpose: to begin anew again. This is America: the New World. It is as if her boundaries had been determined beforehand with great expanses placed on all sides to protect her from the conquest of other nations in preparation for this incredible moment: to initiate global revival.

The Lord is a nation builder

He made promises to Abraham to be a father of many nations; He led the Israelites out of Egyptian bondage as a mighty nation to dwell in a new and better land according to His promise; He brought them to His holy mountain and gathered them around to hear His voice and enter into a personal relationship with Him, but sadly, they refused. They preferred to have Moses intercede on their behalf as their leader – and God responded by giving them written laws and ordinances that no one could faithfully follow.

God has always been interested in forming nations to establish His kingdom upon the earth – by the hearing of His voice! He gave man His ***dominion mandate***: occupy the land, listen to My voice, host My presence, believe all that I tell you – and do what I tell you, as you remember who you are and live out of relationship *in* Me. This is the manner of life that God instructed Adam and Eve to live out of – until they disobeyed the Lord when the serpent deceived them through lies by twisting the truth. When they considered the lies, they: doubted God's authority, they questioned His instructions, they forgot who they were and then they acted out of character in disobedience. In this moment, the first couple struggled with insecurity, inferiority and insignificance, and it seemed the plan of the enemy was working successfully, but God planned a new beginning whereby He would reset the spiritual clock upon the Earth *beginning with* the transformation of the inner man to regenerate the old man first – and then – regenerate the Earth.

Regeneration – is God's secret weapon!

When it comes to nation building, God does not want us to reinvent the wheel, He just wants us to listen to Him, do what He says, and follow His leading as the Holy Spirit guides us into all truth as *He* establishes *His* dominion for man upon the earth. *He owns it – we manage it.*

> "Thus says the Lord: "Behold, a people comes from the north country, and a great nation will be raised from the farthest parts of the earth" (Jer. 6:22).
>
> "Thus says the Lord of hosts: "Behold, disaster shall go forth from nation to nation, and a great whirlwind shall be raised up from the farthest parts of the earth" (Jer. 25:32).

America was envisioned as a new covenant country in which the Lord desired to demonstrate His glory. America came from "a people from the north country" (England) to become a great nation "raised up from the farthest parts of the earth." America was divinely intended to be a nation built upon a covenant agreement with faith in Jesus whereby all men may live in freedom to worship the Lord Almighty in holiness and truth, and it began with the Charter of 1606 to create a Virginia colony in America. Our history books teach us this was done for economic reasons alone; however, reasons for this venture were multifaceted, being economic, personal, political and religious: The Charter of 1606 says in part:

- "to make Habitation, Plantation, and to deduce a colony of sundry of our People into that part of America commonly called VIRGINIA"
- "to divide themselves into two several Colonies and Companies" (Virginia and Plymouth)
- "We, greatly commending, and graciously accepting of, their Desires for the Furtherance of so noble a Work, which may, by the Providence of Almighty God, **hereafter tend to the Glory of his Divine Majesty, in propagating of Christian Religion** to such People, as yet live in Darkness and miserable Ignorance of the true Knowledge and Worship of God, and may in time bring the Infidels and Savages, living in those parts, to human Civility, and to a settled and quiet Government: DO, by these our Letters Patents, graciously accept of, and agree to, their humble and well-intended Desires."[133]

If we want to see where America got off track, then look no further than this First Charter of 1606. Are we tending to the Divine Majesty of His glory? Have we propagated the Christian religion? Sadly, we are now being labeled as intolerant – instead of advancing it.

All readers need to begin their own spiritual inquiry to see the Divine origins of America and what God planned since day one. Many of our history books have taken a dramatic left turn toward liberalism with a progressive agenda to remake America into a non-sectarian , non-Christian, religion-less society that has already become enslaved to radical revisionist ideologies with very strong anti-Christ agendas. Search the internet for the topic:

---

[133] The First Charter of Virginia, 1606.

America/Godly Heritage/ Christian Heritage/ Christian History – and search the testimony of our Founding Fathers, and you will see that they all knew God, the vast majority had a personal relationship with Christ – and also knew that God always had a plan for America. For example:

- "It is hoped that by God's assistance, some of the continents in the Ocean will be discovered....for the Glory of God." *Christopher Columbus*
- The Liberty Bell was not given its name because it rang on July 8, 1776 after the signing of the Declaration of Independence, but is the name given to the bell in regard to the inscription that was cast into it: "Proclaim liberty throughout the land, to all the inhabitants thereof" (Leviticus 25:10)
- "It cannot be emphasized too strongly or too often that this great nation was founded not by religionists but by Christians, not on religion but on the Gospel of Jesus Christ. We shall not fight alone. God presides over the destinies of nations. The battle is not to the strong alone. Is life so dear, or peace so sweet, as to be purchased at the price of chains and slavery? Forbid it, ALMIGHTY GOD! Give me liberty or give me death!" *Patrick Henry of the Constitutional Convention*
- After America's revolutionary success over Britain, the English Bible was now allowed to be printed in America and approved by Congress on Sept. 12, 1782 with their endorsement: "Whereupon, resolved, that the United States in Congress assembled... recommend this edition of the Bible to the inhabitants of the United States."
- The term "separation of church and state" was never intended to protect the state from the excess of religion, but to protect the freedoms of religion from excess control by the state or mandating the establishment of a state-sanctioned religion
- "Laos Deo" is written on the east side on top of the Washington Monument – meaning "Praise Be To God"

- "God who gave us life gave us liberty...... indeed, I tremble for my country when I reflect that God is just; that His justice cannot sleep forever." *Thomas Jefferson*

For over 400 years, this country has experienced much testing and many threats against her unique role and identity in the world of nations, to be a show-forth and demonstration against tyranny on behalf of God's liberty and freedom. The true legacy of America is not about her ability to influence nations with seeds of democracy, but rather, her spiritual role in converting nations with the love and truth gospel of Jesus Christ. Her methods have not always been admirable, even against her own indigenous peoples, but in such a time as this, we need to see her role as a representational beacon of hope and as a tool against every form of evil and injustice against every person upon the planet who desires one thing more than anything: spiritual freedom. America is not just a place for religious freedom... America is a beacon of hope with spiritual liberty that other nations may seek to imitate and replicate.

However, in recent times, our own governmental leaders have listened to the wrong advisors… and the occasional misstep with words has now become a culture of lies, distorted truth and overt deceptions to mislead a nation that was founded upon the truth. Anathema! We were founded upon the truth of Jesus Christ as Lord of all, but… we prefer to be a nation of laws that we can break, violate and manipulate (and even invent) whenever we want… and then hire the best lawyers to beat the conviction. The double-standard must stop!

The time has now come for all leaders in America to tell the truth. We have tolerated a CYA culture long enough and now we need a CYH culture of truth: clean your house! Our government was established upon biblical principles, the Ten Commandments, and an unwavering faith in Jesus Christ, whereby the institution itself cannot continue to stand without these three pillars. Any solution to national or worldly problems without understanding Jesus is the Solution, is rooted in failure.

> "We have staked the whole of all our political institutions upon the capacity of mankind for self-government, upon the capacity of each and all of us to govern ourselves, to control ourselves, to sustain ourselves according to the Ten Commandments of God. *The future and success of America is not in this Constitution, but in the laws of God upon which this Constitution is founded.*"
> (James Madison, Father of the Constitution)

Listen up! If your leaders cannot control themselves, then *why* do you allow them to control you... and your children? If your leaders do not love God, then get rid of them!

"It is impossible to rightly govern the world without God and the Bible." (George Washington)

Sadly, we routinely elect leaders that do not govern themselves or control themselves, choosing to place their ideology above the law itself – and above God – and embrace their culture of lies to justify their agenda. A day has now come whereby every word will be brought into the light of truth and all lies will be exposed by... "The Spirit is truth." This new day is now at hand.

> "These six things the LORD hates, yes, seven are an abomination to Him:
> [17] A proud look, a lying tongue, hands that shed innocent blood,
> [18] A heart that devises wicked plans, feet that are swift in running to evil,
> [19] A false witness who speaks lies, and one who sows discord among brethren" (Prov. 6:16-19).

Twice it says, "a lying tongue... and a false witness who speaks lies" are an abomination because they are from the kingdom of hell where darkness, lies, deception, manipulation and death are produced by sin. Can you see the actions of your political leaders manifested by any of these seven abominations? If yes, then these leaders must go. If you do not take a stand for God, then you will fall for anything.

> "For the wrath of God is revealed *from heaven* against all ungodliness and unrighteousness of men, *who suppress the truth* in unrighteousness" (Rom. 1:18).

It has been said, "Noble thoughts based on a lie lose their nobility." It is time to tell the truth, clean house – and let freedom ring, once again, throughout this land.

Leader of the Free World

Freedom has always been God's promise to the world and His gift to America. If America is no longer willing to walk within her destiny, then the Lord will raise up another nation to take her place as the next manifestation of the Lord's revival in the world. If this happens, America will cease to be according to her manifest destiny – and no longer need to be – and there are many liberals that have been clamoring for this to happen by plotting in secrecy. There have been many superpowers upon the Earth, even recently, yet only one remains now, but this… is only for another season, unless America returns to her original destiny to be the strong arm of the Lord's grace and truth against the face of evil and tyranny upon the Earth.

A New Day Begins

In early morning pre-dawn darkness, you do not need a clock to know when the sun is rising; every day begins with the faint chirping song of the sunrise sentinel to announce: new again… new again. Wake up… wake up, it's time to begin again.

And likewise, so it is with living life in the awareness of the spiritual reality that surrounds us. It is as if a giant reset button is pushed every morning and a fresh new day is given to us that is full of expectant promises to receive, dreams to fulfill, and hopes to be realized; a brand new day is waiting to be experienced. This same new day will be experienced by two very different types of people: born anew Christians with truth, hope, goodness and spiritual understanding, or human beings that do not comprehend that they are living deadened lives surrounded by a sea of darkness. The life you live does not come with a label to tell others which of these you are – your actions and resultant fruit will reveal the outward evidence of your inward reality.

Fruit provides evidence of several things: what kind of plant you are, how healthy you are and the type of growing conditions affecting you. External factors affecting the plant will become manifest in the fruit – for better or worse. The same is true with people, families, denominations, communities and nations. We may not be able to judge a book by its cover, and for this reason we must not judge by outward appearances, but much in every regard can be known by examining the fruit that is produced – even the blossoms beforehand.

What do sunrise and fruit have to do with "the new world?" These are two spiritual principles that all creation operates according to… to begin *anew* each day, and bear fruit. All creation exists: A) to create and sustain life, and B) and give glory to God (bear fruit). What you do and why you do it are fundamental to the kingdom you live in. If you do not agree with this simple assessment of earthly living, then the spiritual awakening has not happened to you – or not yet.

Jesus said, "Render to Caesar what is Caesar's, and render to God the things that are God's" (Matt. 22:21). When we walk in the truth of Christ, we will teach the way of God and we will have regard for the person of every man (what has been entrusted to him). It is entirely within the will of God for men to build cities, nations, tall towers and whatever industry you apply yourself to, but we must do "all these things" while giving glory to God, or we are violating His will for man; just ask Cain; just ask Jonah; consider Sodom and Babylon. Render to this world those worldly things, but if you are a spiritual being that is having a human experience, then render everything and do everything "as unto the

Lord" and give Him the glory in all that you think, say and do. Honor Him, reverence Him, listen to His voice – and then do what He tells you. In doing so, great will your reward be in heaven! And great will be your eternal reward upon the kingdom of heaven that resides upon the earth!

When a gathering of people are united in common purpose, they will move mountains and give glory to God. However, when I see this same gathering of people divided by internal discord and civil strife, I see the hand of the enemy at work. Unity is one of the character qualities of the Godhead, while division is the trademark tool of the enemy. Whenever I see a community or a nation torn apart by division and civil unrest, I see the hand of the enemy manifested in those who do not comprehend spiritual matters, but Americans routinely elect people that are spiritually and rhetorically divisive in nature. This must stop! Some people are routinely offended by the mere mention of God's name, so if you lack the spiritual discernment to tell if someone is good or evil, then simply utter the name, Jesus Christ, to see what their reaction is. The enemy cannot withstand or tolerate the power that resides within the name of Jesus. This nation needs to convert quickly – and now you know one tool for doing so. However, hollering, fanatic ranting, boiled-up fervent foments and screaming the name of Jesus is totally unnecessary because demons and unclean spirits are not deaf, so remember… if Jesus has not told you to proclaim His name with a mighty royal shout, then proclaim Him in a dignified manner that gives Him glory without human-engineered drama and sensationalism. Just speak the truth in love – and the Holy Spirit will do the rest. God will use you to show Himself strong… not the other way around.

A New Word

On February 9, 2015, these words of understanding came to me by the Spirit:

The church age is over – the kingdom age has begun. We cannot fix the church model in time. It is broken and has become unwilling to listen to the guidance of the Holy Spirit. "For this reason, I am calling out to all those who will listen for the sound of My voice and follow Me." "A critical mass has happened, the acceleration has begun, the outpouring of My Spirit upon all flesh has now entered a new day. Faith is tested and refined in weeks rather than months, years and generations. A fresh wind has begun to blow, and those who hunger and thirst for My righteousness and truth will be called the redeemed. The spiritual laws that were established by this government, that was called according to My name, has lost its' way and is now walking in unbelief because you have listened to the many voices of the unredeemed. They tear you down and pull you apart – to their delight because their spiritual fathers have always refused to listen to My voice. They prefer the sound of their voice, not Mine. In a land of many voices, you embrace tolerance of things I am intolerant; you govern the rich and despise the needy with entitlements; you do not work for what you gain and then you spend it foolishly on governments that hate Me. You were called to change the world with the light I gave you, but you have adopted the sinful practices of the nations. Here I am, speaking once again, first to Israel, My chosen, and now to America, My called, and both of My elect have forsaken their ways and pursued many things which are not of Me. Since you want to be influenced by the nations, then I will let the nations sift you and judge you, but if you return to Me and walk according to My Spirit and listen obediently to the sound of My voice – and convert – I will heal your land. No more pious words. No more righteous thoughts. No more convocations. Do it – or don't. Don't make promises to Me that I know you will not honor! I know your thoughts. I can hear your thoughts. I can hear *all* your thoughts!"

"What way will you walk that honors Me and returns to Me My glory that I poured out among the nations. How can I stand back to watch as the nations tremble in the presence of My enemies. I called you to walk in righteousness and truth, but you walk in disobedience to gratify your own desires which are an offense to Me. What have I done to you that you despise Me so? Have I not held back your enemy time and time again? I gave you safe borders with broad waters to protect you from your enemies, but you invited them into your living rooms and universities and houses of governance. But – what house are you building for Me? Can My glory be found anywhere? What manner of men are you that you turn away from Me to imitate the nations? You follow false teachings and doctrines made by men. I gave you truth and doctrines of life, but you prefer death and legalism. How can I woo you any longer? You will not listen. You refuse to acknowledge Me. Your cisterns are full of death and disobedience, and you drink to the full. A measuring line has been placed upon you and scales have weighed the balance of your rebellion against Me."

"See, I am raising up one nation, even two, and many nations to shame you – before you become a reproach and they turn against you."

"Either you know Me or you don't. If you know Me, then walk in My ways. Your falsehood and your duplicitous words will no longer be tolerated. My light will shine upon all words to reveal truth – and lies. Do not allow the godless to rob you of your glory which I gave you to walk in. How can this be so? You remember Me only when it is convenient because you want what I have. You need many things of Mine, but you harden your hearts and refuse to acknowledge Me as the God "in whom you trust." Empty words are written on your currency and in your courts of law. My words mean nothing to you, but you pretend they do. Your words mean everything to you, but they mean nothing to Me."

"Give Me the glory that I deserve."

"If My glory is *not* in it, then I will get rid of it."

It's all about Jesus – and God gets the glory!

Closure

America was once referred to as paradise – and now the time has come for her to manifest this declaration. America is a mighty spiritual city that the Lord established to be set upon a hill for all to see, but her light has grown dim because her watchmen did not keep their eyes focused on her Redeemer – and they forgot *who* they are and *what* they are supposed to be doing.

Lord, America needs Your newness more than ever. Holy Spirit, awaken us from our spiritual slumber. Perhaps we will see the purpose You so patiently have waited for us to rediscover. America is the land of the free, a beacon for other nations desiring freedom, and a place for the ignition spark to start divine wildfires of revival all around the earth.

Before the shaking begins, Lord, give us one more chance…

…to give You glory in all we think and say and do.

The Lord has given us – His power, His authority, the keys of the kingdom, and the dominion to convert this world into one kingdom or the other; which kingdom are you going to start building?

Choose now, and determine in your heart to build either the kingdom of heaven or the kingdom of hell upon the earth. Will you continue to watch nightly news reports that discuss the tragedy of humanity – or will you listen to good reports that display the manifest glory of God?

"Abhor what is evil. Cling to what is good" (Rom. 12:8).

From now on, test everything according to this standard: **will God get the glory in it**? If God cannot receive glory from it, then stop doing it and stop promoting it.

"For as many as are led by the Spirit of God, these are sons of God" (Rom. 8:14).

The Lord is asking only one question: "Are you going to build My kingdom on Earth – or not?"

The kingdom of heaven is at hand… Here Now Is!

"No weapon formed against you will prosper" (Isa. 54:17).

"You are the light of the world." Be the light!

God's truth will set all men free!

It's all about Jesus – and God gets the glory!

12) Walking In Dominion Obedience

The Earthly Pattern verses the Spiritual Template

The New Earth doctrine will affect politics, governance, economics, business, commerce and trade, medicine, military protection, education, agriculture, arts, science and mathematics, mental health, natural resource management and resource distribution such that all worldly problems bow to heavenly solutions.

Governance and Dominion:

Why do we fearfully keep debating a "one world government" when we already have it… under the Lordship of Jesus Christ. "The government will be upon His shoulders" (Isa. 9:6, 7), "His kingdom is an everlasting kingdom," (Dan. 4:3; 7:27) "His dominion is an everlasting dominion, and His kingdom is from generation to generation" (Dan. 4:34; 7:14). All nations, under God, is not a united nations but a unity of ethnos nations under the dominion of one governing authority, Jesus Christ, that work in partnership with Him, in unity with Him, and in fellowship with one another through the Spirit whereby no man is hierarchically subjugated by another – having all things in common for the building up of the good of all.

Personal Guidance

As we have dominion, let us remember our five-fold "dominion" mandate:

1. Hear His voice – and live obediently
2. Host His presence – remember He dwells in you; abide in Divine relationship with Him
3. Believe all that He tells you, walk in all spiritual truth
4. Do those things you were commanded to do – being guided by the Holy Spirit

5. Occupy – remember who you are and why you are "put" in the place you're in

How do we know if we are living according to the truth?

How do we know if we are having dominion in the spiritual sense?

Can we take credit for our faithfulness even though it was done by the power of the Spirit?

Can we discern if other people's motives are genuinely "of God" or not?

How can we tell if we are giving God all the glory in what we do?

The simple answer for all these questions comes from a very simple question: does God get the glory from it – or not?

Glory and Grace

We are to no longer live with a spirit of fear… we live with the Spirit of life *in* Christ Jesus!

We live, no longer according to the flesh, but according to the Spirit; no longer building the kingdom of self, but the kingdom of heaven upon the earth.

We are no longer living life "in this world" but have now been made alive "*in* Christ." There are only two earthly paradigms to choose from: in this world – or in Christ Jesus. Which paradigm do you see getting your life from: that which the world gives or that which Christ gives?

In Christ, we are in the world but not of it, and if we are in Christ Jesus, then we are already in the New Jerusalem, that is in Christ that comes down "from out of" heaven.

Christ *In* Us

Jesus is Lord Almighty. We get our source of power from Jesus by His abiding *in* us. His power is released in us and, by His grace, He releases it through us because He is in us. Christ in us! Jesus is releasing His glory through us! Christ's power does not reside in any spiritual object, but Christ can manifest His power through any object He wants… even a donkey. Just as the law was effective for a season until Christ Himself fulfilled the law, likewise, many Christians have put the power of Christ in many things other than "Christ in you." Jesus Christ came mightily in word and deed, with power, filled with the Spirit, but we have associated Christ's power to religious sacraments, idols, the cross, the blood, communion wafers, word of faith "name it and claim it" teachings and a litany of other practices that places more emphasis on the doer and deed rather than the superiority of Lord Jesus and the Spirit who "empowers" us.

> "Not by might nor by power, but by My Spirit,' says the Lord of hosts" (Zech. 4:6).
>
> "For the kingdom of God is not in word but *in* power" (1 Cor. 4:20; and 2:4).
>
> "But we have this treasure in earthen vessels, that the excellence of the power may be of God and not of us" (2 Cor. 4:7).
>
> "For our gospel did not come to you in word only, but also *in* power, and *in* the Holy Spirit and in much assurance, as you know what kind of men we were among you for your sake" (1 Thess. 1:5).

The Gospel of Christ is not about us, nor is it about our words; it is about Christ (the living Word of truth) in us as He reveals Himself *in* power through our surrendered lives – to the praise of His marvelous glory!

Idols in our Hearts

If we are told to do something and we do it, we can still do it with wrong motives if there are idols in our heart, so learn from these examples:

- Ezek. 14:3-4
- Moses and Aaron established "the rod" as an idol in their mind because they saw how it seemed to wield the power of God – Ex. 7:17
- Balaam – Num. 22:15-35; 2 Pet. 2:15 (we look and see what we want to see)
- When we are mindful of earthly matters concerning the things of man, we can rebuke Jesus even moments after professing Him as Lord and Christ – Matt. 7:23

On one hand, the Lord will give us the desires of our heart, but our hearts must be pure and blameless before Him. We cannot have dominion as He intended if we are going to use it to advance our worldly cares, desires and agendas; we must maintain a dominion mindset and culture of heaven-mindedness whereby we are accomplishing God's will throughout the Earth, not our own will according to our purposes and plans.

We pray for many things but we do not pray aright because we often pray for our personal kingdom and not the dominion the Lord desires. There is nothing wrong with having a new house or a new car, especially when we justify it as a means to host church gatherings and shuttle people to church events, but if our initial desire is born out of materialism, abundant living, gaining attention to provoke jealousy or envy in others, self promotion, or justifying our righteousness through material blessings rather than a sincere and contrite heart as the sign of God dwelling within you – and His blessing upon you, then perhaps you should rethink the reason why you want what you want.

The Israelites were told by God to march around the city of Jericho for six days and then do it differently on the seventh day. The

Israelites did what they were commanded to do, and the Israelites got what God wanted them to have according the means and manner in which God wanted them to acquire it. If they did it in their own strength and courage, then the nations would fear the Jews, but when the Lord fought on behalf of the Israelites, the nations greatly feared the God of the Jews. Do you see the difference?

Look what happened during the Exodus through the Red Sea; a cloud of smoke and fire kept separation between the Israelites and Egyptians, and when the Egyptian chariots got bogged down in the ensuing chase after the Israelites, they said, "The Lord fights for them" (Ex. 14:25). If anyone fears "us" more than God Himself, then we have robbed God of His glory.

This is the kind of "living for Jesus" that He desires from us; Jesus gets all the praise and glory – when we deliver it into His hand. When we live with reckless love and unbridled passion for Him, when nothing in this life matters more than Jesus as the center of our life, when all our cares for this life are entrusted into His capable hands, when we trust Him regardless of the situations and circumstances that surround us, and when we give Him all the glory for every aspect of our victorious testimony, *then* the Lord will pour upon us a show-forth of His glory and grace as a demonstration to others to encourage them to live boldly for Jesus. God wants you to be a manifest declaration to others so that they may also live boldly, godly lives for Jesus.

Remember the promise – and remember the testimony of Jesus!

There are always two sides to the spiritual coin – and then a third as well. When we walk in faithful obedience, the Lord should bless us, but when we walk in a manner that does not glorify God, then the Lord should withhold His blessing and provision. The third side of the coin is Divine: God will do as He pleases. He is not under any obligation to bless us or withhold a blessing if we live with or without any understanding of Who He is or what He wants us to do; He is a merciful God and He reigns on the just and the unjust alike. He loves everyone equally and without partiality, but He is blessed by our faithful obedience… and He will honor it!

Why are you on earth? Are you an earth invader and world changer?

Your soul has two parts: mind and heart. The purpose of your mind is to think to produce thoughts. That's it! The mind thinks, contemplates, deliberates, quantifies and assembles numerous ideas to produce one thing: a thought. Then the mind plants these thoughts in the heart which are used to build a paradigm with understanding to produce one thing: building a kingdom in the heart.

What you plant and cultivate in your heart will mature and come out of you – and by these things you will be known by them. Were your thoughts based upon God's truth – or something else?

How your mind thinks and the thoughts it produces – is – the key to the kingdom!

What paradigm are you establishing in your mind?

What kingdom are "you" building in your heart?

The same promise God made to Abraham is the same promise He makes to everyone: listen to Me and walk by faith – and I will establish nations through you.

What kingdoms and nations are you releasing through your heart?

We need a paradigm shift of enormous magnitude!

13) The Eternal Paradigm

The door (portal or gateway) to Heaven is through your heart – and the Holy Spirit is the Doorkeeper, whom no man can deceive because He searches the thoughts and intents of the heart.

You cannot see what's on the other side of your heart because the spiritual reality is invisible and only the Holy Spirit can guide you to the Door – and only Jesus can lead you through it Himself – to the place that He has prepared for you, so you may live in oneness with the Father.

If you need help, or you need prayer for anything, or you desire the Divine relationship that only Jesus can provide, then look no further than deep within your heart. The King of the universe is waiting for you to enter into His presence. Let *nothing* come between you and Jesus; not parents, preachers, traditions, priests, sacraments, holy observances, doctrines, and most of all – fear or doubt that leads into unbelief – let nothing separate you from the love of Christ!

Of course… you cannot see this spiritual reality… which is why it's called faith. We know it's there because the scripture tells us it is, but there is only one way you will ever know for certain:

let go – and trust Jesus.

Your soul is a gateway for heavenly things to pass through your heart, so pray earnestly – in faith. Believe – and do not doubt! Earth becomes a manifestation of whatever flows through your heart as you build one kingdom or another.

You can think about the heavenly reality with your mind all day long, but until you believe it in your heart with confident certainty and the assurance that comes through faith, having been thoroughly persuaded and convinced by truth, you will never perceive this spiritual reality – until the working of the Holy Spirit is operating within you and partnering through you – as a new creation.

Your heart is the gateway for your soul and for this reason many have taught us that the soul is located in our heart. So, let me state this point clearly and emphatically: you are a soul. You are a spiritual being that is having a human experience and the gateway into eternity and all spiritual things is through your spiritual heart.

Your heart is the one and only gateway for your eternal soul – if you do not enter through the Door called Jesus Christ, who stands <u>as</u> the Door and bids you "come" – then your soul will remain upon the earth destined for the pit of eternal anguish. There is going to be a resurrection, as well as the judgment of all, so be mindful… you have an adversarial enemy that wants you to brush this off as religious hogwash so that you may agonize with him in eternal torment. The choice is yours – and your alone! Don't make the same unrepentant mistake Satan did.

Some people will begin to move through this spiritual dimension, like angels that are in heaven, because we are living in an open *'dianoigo'* heaven, and some will be manifest across great distances in various places – without the passing of any time, as if time stood still for eternity. This is to be anticipated for all spiritual beings under the lordship of Jesus Christ.

You cannot perceive this spiritual reality unless you have been converted, born anew and are being transformed into newness by the Holy Spirit. Understanding these spiritual matters does not come by the mere flicking of your wrist; conviction, conversion and sanctification to live according to righteousness *is a way of life.* It is a lifeway that you live according to every single moment of every day, not just during a fifty minute tribute on Sunday. Faith in Christ is a marathon, and it requires bold, courageous determination to endure all things until the end.

You are a gateway designed by God to live according to a lifeway known as "Christ in you – the hope of glory." There is no other way to avoid God's plan for judgment except to trust Jesus, live by faith and walk in the flow of the Holy Spirit who dwells within you.

- Heaven is God's throne.
- The kingdom of heaven is upon the earth. The kingdom of Christ is at hand! Here now is! Declare this good news to everyone.
- We are surrounded by a great cloud of witnesses, as well as adversaries, that are seated in heavenly places all around us – waiting to see what we are going to do for the sake of Christ and His kingdom. So, what are you going to do today that will last for all eternity?

Repent, believe, and enter into the Oneness of the heavenly reality that surrounds you.

Time has been shortened….

It's all about Jesus – and God gets the glory.

Jesus waited patiently 1,550 years for the children of Israel to accept His invitation to hear His voice, to know Him and understand His plan of redemption for all creation. At just the right time, Jesus came to teach them and remind all of us how to live right-side up in an upside-down world, and the Holy Spirit has been guiding Christians to live according to this right-side up reality for 2,000 years, but we have turned the Divine relationship into an inside-out performance of religious-based programs instead of an in-dwelt manifestation of His dunamis power and Spirit-anointed grace flowing through us. The kingdom of God is within us, the keys to the kingdom have been given to us and heaven itself resides within the hearts of regenerate men to release the kingdom of heaven into the earth. So now, what are you going to do about it?

The heavenly in-dwelt manifestation of His glory is being released *in* us and through us. The kingdom of heaven is neither up nor down, but in...

> ... and in Him all things consist.

The Father has given us the kingdom (Luke 12:32), Jesus has given us the keys of the kingdom (Matt. 16:19) and He has given us the authority to forgive sin (Matt. 6:14; Luke 24:47; John 20:23). All authority was delivered to Jesus (Matt. 11:27) and Jesus has delivered all authority back to us (Matt. 28:18); and to top it off, the glory that the Father gave Jesus (John 17:24) Jesus Himself has given to us (John 17:22) and He is glorified in us (John 17:10).

Can it get any better than this?

> "And now, O Father, glorify Me together with Yourself" (John 17:5) "that they may be one as We are" (John 17:11).

"We have been invited to enter into oneness with the Supreme Highest Commander of all things in Heaven and on Earth. And for what reason? Is it not to establish the kingdom of heaven in the midst of His enemies! The Lord removed Satan and His rebellious angels who made war in Heaven (Rev. 12), He cast them down to Earth, and then He sent the host of men to Earth to make war with Satan and overcome his dominion, clothed in mere human weakness, with nothing more than the truth, the power of their testimony, the fullness of the indwelling Holy Spirit – and the grace of God. And in this, the Lord will make known those who belong to Him according to the hearing of His voice and follow Him as His disciples, or those who live in rebellion by refusing to hear, believe and obey."[134]

> The kingdom of heaven is within you...
> ...and now it's time to let heaven out!
> Change this world from darkness to light.

---

[134] Excerpt from "Image" section titled "Friends and Brethren of Jesus."

"It seems we have been waiting for something to happen that has already happened, yet hoping to attain something we were never promised."

"The kingdom of heaven is neither up nor down – but in. And now it's time to let heaven out!"

Love one another, for such is the kingdom of God.

Two Scenario Finale

This summary was intentionally placed here because many people like to read the last pages of a book to see if it's worth reading. This one is worth reading – and contemplating very carefully!

The "men go to heaven" narrative is fraught with many inconsistencies which our doctrines bear out. How many different explanations and doctrines are there for end times, the great tribulation, the millennial reign and the regeneration? Only one... yet man's doctrines have produced dozens of intelligent scenarios... yet none of them are correct because they all teach the same goal of life: Heaven.

The goal for the host of earth (sons of men) is not Heaven; it's a relationship with Jesus. Our rightful place and domain in the cosmos is not Heaven either; it's a place called: Earth. Man was created for the earth – and earth was created for man. We know it well.

Why are you here – and what is your purpose in life? Well, the number of scenarios just increased dramatically. Why do bad things happen to good people? The number of scenarios just increased exponentially. Does any logic exist within these numerous scenarios to answer all the questions you have yet also remains consistent with biblical truth? I know of only one – and you're reading it: the Image Bearer series.

> "For God may speak in one way, or in another, yet man does not perceive it" (Job 33:14).

So now, let me propose two scenarios for why man is on earth and why bad things happen to him, one that is fraught with inconsistencies – and one with a uniquely different perspective:

1) We were born without any purpose except to glorify God, yet we struggle (like migratory trout) against various changes and elements and pitfalls and tribulations with great suffering and

affliction hoping somehow we find Jesus before we die so that we may go home to heaven and be with Him, yet billions never hear about Him, or

2) You were sent to earth by God on a mission to establish the kingdom of heaven on earth whereby God used two people to initiate your arrival onto earth to start this sojourn with the Spirit of God alongside you – as your Guide – to assist your efforts. You were sent behind enemy lines as an agent of Heaven to overthrow the kingdom of darkness on Earth – including all evil forces within the darkness that are in rebellion against Jesus and the kingdom of God. Our enemy is constantly coming against you to cause fear and doubt while they torment you with many woes to prevent you from accomplishing your mission as a co-redeemer sent in the likeness of your Redeemer, Jesus Christ.

Which sounds more logical now? At least now you know why bad things happen to good people!

In Option #1: you are aimlessly flailing and failing to make sense of why you are here on earth in the first place. You have a destiny, but you cannot figure it out. Some people have everything going their way, yet others struggle to find daily bread. There's no reason or purpose to who gets what and why… and then you die.

In Option #2: you are a soldier sent from heaven to re-establish the kingdom of heaven on earth by coming against an evil kingdom that took this earth captive after being exiled from heaven; you were sent behind enemy lines to come against an army that started a rebellion in heaven against God in which one/third was swept away. Your example to follow is: Jesus Christ, your Commander in Chief. Through faith, you are promised life eternal if you faithfully endure until the end… whereby death is merely an intermission between ages in the timeline of eternity.

Jesus is King of kings and Lord of lords. Jesus said: "The kingdom of heaven is at hand." That's because wherever the King of Heaven goes, He establishes His kingdom. So I ask: "Is Jesus abiding in your heart, through faith?" If you say yes (according to faith), then you must comprehend this: the kingdom of heaven in within you. Jesus Himself confirmed this to us:

"The kingdom of God is within you" (Luke 17:21).

We were not sent here to believe and attain heaven; we were sent to believe in Jesus as Lord God Almighty and establish the kingdom of heaven on earth... as it is in Heaven!

Life on this planet may seem mysterious and difficult to comprehend, as if we are trying to assemble a giant jigsaw puzzle without knowing what the original image looked like. Well, this is true in many respects and is even more complicated because we've made many terrible assumptions about why man is on earth in the first place... and it's not to get to heaven. We were sent to establish the kingdom of heaven on earth because... we are the host (army) of earth.

> "He has made everything beautiful in its time. Also He has put eternity in their hearts, except that no one can find out the work that God does from beginning to end" (Eccl. 3:11).

God put eternity in our heart. We don't have to die to attain life eternal... we are already living one season of eternity – right now (Psa. 49:9). The Image Bearer series explains virtually all the questions we've been seeking answers to for the past 6,000 years, which is very important for us to comprehend because... the kingdom age is upon us even now.

Trying to sort through the scriptures to find one consistent linear line of thinking has been an elusive Gordian knot for theologians and prophets alike, because the bible was revealed and recorded in a non-linear yet iterative manner with many, seemingly unsolvable mysteries. It would be like trying to reassemble a deck of playing cards after tossing it high into the air and then assembling it in perfect order when only half the cards are facing up. Impossible!

For example, "There is a way that seems right to a man, but its end is the way of death" (Prov. 14:12; 16:25). There are two basic fundamental ways upon the earth: a) the way of God or b) the path of rebellion against God (i.e. Christ vs. antichrist). There are numerous ways within antichrist that seem good and noble as much more attainable than God's way with much less suffering, however… that's not the point. Either you are walking in the way of God… or you're not. Apart from knowing God's perspective concerning man's purpose on earth under heaven, man's feeble attempts to resolve the mystery of life on earth remains completely veiled by a diabolical force called: sin. And all men have been corrupted by sin!

There are seven golden threads of truth woven throughout the scriptures to support one conclusion: put your trust and hope in Jesus as Lord God Almighty for eternal salvation – hear His voice and serve Him. All the rest are details that come by listening to His voice.

Now, go back and read this entire Spirit-inspired, biblically-based book – and be set free from the tyranny of manmade doctrines. You were sent here to have dominion over the works of the enemy… in the name of Jesus.

It's all about Jesus – and God get's the glory. Amen!

[page left blank for notes]

Read the entire Image Bearer series!

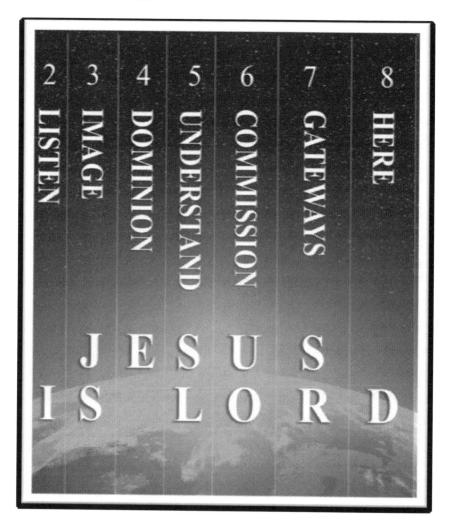

Grace and peace be yours in abundance, paul.

Made in the USA
Columbia, SC
11 November 2018